cookies

more than **200** recipes

Jill Snider

Robert
ROSE

For complete cataloguing information, see page 252.

Disclaimer
The recipes in this book have been carefully tested by our kitchen and our tasters. To the best of our knowledge, they are safe and nutritious for ordinary use and users. For those people with food or other allergies, or who have special food requirements or health issues, please read the suggested contents of each recipe carefully and determine whether or not they may create a problem for you. All recipes are used at the risk of the consumer.

    We cannot be responsible for any hazards, loss or damage which may occur as a result of any recipe use.

    For those with special needs, allergies, requirements or health problems, in the event of any doubt, please contact your medical adviser prior to the use of any recipe.

Editor: Judith Finlayson
Copy Editor: Eleanor Gasparik
Proofreader: Gillian Watts
Index: Belle Wong
Design & Production: Kevin Cockburn/PageWave Graphics Inc.
Photography: Colin Erricson
Food Stylist: Jill Snider
Prop Stylist: Charlene Erricson

Cover: Cranberry Almond Oatmeal Cookies (see recipe, page 16) and Seeds and Coconut Oatmeal Crisps (see recipe, page 17)

We acknowledge the financial support of the Government of Canada through the Book Publishing Industry Development Program (BPIDP) for our publishing activities.

Published by: Robert Rose Inc.
120 Eglinton Ave. E., Suite 800, Toronto, Ontario, Canada M4P 1E2
Tel: (416) 322-6552   Fax: (416) 322-6936

Printed in Canada

1 2 3 4 5 6 7 8 9   TCP   15 14 13 12 11 10 09 08 07

Contents

Acknowledgments

I'd like to thank the many talented people who helped make a cookbook on cookies a reality: my publisher, Bob Dees, who firmly believes that cookies are both delicious and easy to make; the team at PageWave Graphics — Andrew Smith, Joseph Gisini, Kevin Cockburn and Daniella Zanchetta — who work through editorial, design, layouts and production to put it all together; Laurie Andrechuk, who accurately input the recipes; Judith Finlayson and Eleanor Gasparik for their editorial support; Charlene Erricson for prop styling; and Colin Erricson for his outstanding photographs, which make everything jump off the page.

I'd also like to thank my wonderful mother, Teddy. Although she is no longer with me, I know she would have loved seeing some of her favorite recipes in my book. Her baking gave me a love and appreciation for "homemade."

Thanks also to my sister, Judie, and nieces, Jennie and Susie, for serving recipes from my previous books at every possible occasion and showing my books to everyone they know. And to all my friends and neighbors who tasted and commented on the recipes — and generously offered to take all those extra cookies off my hands after the testing was done.

Introduction

What beats the aroma of freshly baked cookies, still warm from the oven? Only eating them, perhaps. Cookies are the ultimate comfort food and they are hard to resist. Everyone loves cookies and they are welcome any time of the year. Bake these tasty treats for holiday cookie trays, for community bake sales or just for you to enjoy. Put them in lunch boxes, bring them to a potluck or savor them with a mug of steaming coffee or a glass of cold milk. Pack them in fancy wrapping for an always-valued gift.

Whether you are an experienced or novice baker, this book will help you to appreciate how easy and satisfying baking cookies can be. The fact that cookies don't take very long to bake — about 10 minutes for most — means you don't have to spend a long time in the kitchen to experience gratification. And you don't need any special equipment — just some good cookie sheets. Another advantage to cookies is they keep well when properly packed. They can be stored at room temperature, often for as long as a week. Many kinds of dough can be refrigerated or frozen and baked later, and most cookies freeze well, which makes them very convenient.

Baking cookies is a great way to get the whole family into the kitchen to enjoy time together. Whatever your tastes, whatever the occasion and whatever your timeframe, I'm sure you'll find recipes in this book that will inspire you to bake. Some recipes, perhaps those that qualify as family favorites, will bring back treasured memories. Others may seem new and — I hope — will inspire you to experiment. Whether you are baking for an everyday or a special occasion, I hope you have fun and enjoy the experience of baking cookies.

Happy baking and happy eating!

— *Jill Snider*

Baking for Success

Baking cookies is relatively quick and easy compared with other types of baking. To achieve success, you need only the basics: reliable, easy-to-follow recipes, good equipment, quality ingredients and attention to detail. The following information will help you achieve the best results every time you bake.

Know Your Oven

Oven temperature plays a critical role in baking. If your oven is too hot, your baked goods will be overly brown on the surface and may not be completely cooked through. If it is not hot enough, you'll end up overcooking the interior to achieve the desirable degree of browning.

Ideally, the temperature you set determines how hot the oven will be once it's finished preheating. The problem is that the actual temperature in most ovens is 25°F (10°C) hotter or cooler than the setting. Observing how quickly or slowly your oven cooks in relation to recipes you use will give you a general sense of whether it's hotter or cooler than the setting. A more accurate solution, which I recommend, is to purchase a reliable oven thermometer. This simple, inexpensive device will tell you the exact temperature in your oven, allowing you to adjust the setting accordingly.

Convection Ovens

If you're using a convection oven to bake the recipes in this book, check your manual and follow the instructions. Because convection ovens are more energy efficient than traditional models, you can either reduce the baking time by about 25% or lower the oven temperature by 25°F (10°C). As a rule of thumb, when baking anything for less than 15 minutes, reduce the oven temperature rather than the baking time. Convection ovens, like traditional ovens, need to be preheated to the desired temperature when baking.

Use the Right Equipment

Having good-quality equipment makes a big difference when baking. You don't need to invest a lot of money to produce great results. Often the most expensive pans and utensils aren't the best. But take time to ensure you have what you need and that it works best for you.

Baking Pans

In most cases, the only pan you will need to bake cookies is a cookie sheet. I like to have at least four without sides because the absence of sides allows the air to circulate properly.

I prefer regular metal pans over nonstick because nonstick surfaces are easy to ruin. Also, nonstick surfaces that are dark cause cookies to bake more quickly. If you're using these, decrease your oven temperature by 25°F (10°C).

Measuring Cups and Spoons

You will need glass or clear plastic measuring cups for liquid ingredients, a set of graduated dry ingredient measures and a set of measuring spoons.

Ice Cream Scoops

Using ice cream scoops with a wire release to drop the batter on your cookie sheet will give you uniform size and nicely shaped cookies. The small scoop holds about 1 tbsp (15 mL) of dough and is about $1\frac{1}{2}$ inches (4 cm) in diameter. For monster cookies, you can use a $\frac{1}{4}$-cup (50 mL) scoop, about $2\frac{1}{4}$ inches (5.5 cm) in diameter, or a dry measuring cup.

Bowls

Every kitchen needs a variety of bowls in different sizes for combining and mixing ingredients. Metal or glass bowls are preferable. Plastic does not work well for beating egg whites, as it retains oils, which can hamper results. Invest in a few bowls of each size: small, medium and large.

Wooden Spoons

These are great for mixing because the handles are sturdy and comfortable to hold.

Electric Mixer

An electric mixer is advantageous for creaming butter-and-sugar mixtures to a light and creamy texture, for beating in whole eggs and for beating egg whites to stiff peaks. You can use either an electric countertop (stand) mixer or a good-quality hand-held mixer. If you do a lot of baking, the countertop model is much more efficient and easier to use. It can also handle a stiffer dough.

TIP

Place cookies about 2 inches (5 cm) apart on the cookie sheet to allow for spreading. If the dough is one that doesn't spread too much, such as shortbread, 1 inch (2.5 cm) apart is usually enough. This placement will be indicated in the recipe.

Although many recipes call for an electric mixer when beating ingredients such as butter, sugar and eggs, you can also use a wooden spoon. It just takes more work. It is essential that the butter be soft when you start. By either method, beat until smoothly blended, about 3 minutes.

Food Processor

A food processor is a valuable kitchen tool that performs many tasks that can make cookie preparation faster and easier. It quickly chops, grinds and purées mixtures such as fruit and nuts. Some doughs, such as the Almond and Pine Nut Macaroons (see recipe, page 47), are prepared completely in a food processor.

Wire Whisks

Even if you use an electric mixer, you should have a couple of all-purpose wire whisks, in particular small and medium. These are useful for beating eggs before adding them to batters and for blending eggs and sugar and other mixtures that don't require much beating.

Rolling Pin

A rolling pin is essential for making cutout cookies as the dough must be rolled first.

Pastry Blender

For some cookies, such as those made with shortbread or pastry-like dough, I like to use a pastry blender to cut cold butter into the flour-sugar mixture. You can also use two knives, your fingers, a food processor or a mixer to achieve the desired crumble mixture. The butter should be cold and cubed, except when mixing by hand or using a mixer, in which case it should be soft. No matter the method, the crumbled mixture usually requires further mixing with your hands to achieve a smooth dough.

Cookie Press

Fancy pressed cookies are created when dough is pressed through a cookie press. A cookie press pushes dough down a cylinder and through decorative perforated plates. These devices are available in kitchen supply and cake decorating stores. A pastry bag and tip may be used instead if the dough is soft, such as that used to make meringues and macaroons. A press is needed for stiffer dough, such as that used for spritz cookies.

Spatulas

Rubber spatulas are useful for folding in ingredients and scraping down the sides of a mixing bowl. Silicone spatulas are a great asset when you're working with hot mixtures — for instance, the no-bake cookies that are made from ingredients melted on top of the stove. Offset spatulas, which have a bend in the metal spreader, are useful for flattening cookies and applying frosting. I like to have both small and medium ones in my kitchen. They are also handy for removing baked cookies from the cookie sheet.

Cookie Cutters

Have a set of round cutters in graduated sizes, as well as a selection of your favorite shapes and characters. Small aspic or canapé cutters are handy for sandwich cookies that have a small cutout on top through which the filling peeps. Cutters with a thin, sharp edge work best.

Racks

Wire racks are essential for cooling baked goods. Setting the cookie sheet on a wire rack allows circulating air to cool the bottom. It's a good idea to have a variety of sizes and shapes (square, rectangular) to suit whatever you're making. I recommend stainless-steel racks since they last a long time and won't rust.

Pan Preparation

To ensure that your cookies will be easy to remove from the sheets, invest in parchment paper. It is available in large sheets and rolls and is heatproof. Lining cookie sheets with parchment paper prevents cookies from sticking to and scratching the sheet. It's also convenient. If your cookie sheets have no sides, it's easy to slide the parchment paper on and off the sheet. While one batch of cookies is baking, you can be placing dough on another sheet of parchment paper so it's ready to be transferred to a cookie sheet that has come out of the oven and cooled. Washable silicone sheets also work well in place of parchment paper.

Cooling and Cutting Cookies

Most baked cookies are left on the sheet for about 5 minutes, then transferred to a rack to cool completely. If they seem fragile, they should be left on the sheet for another few minutes to firm up before moving. However, there are always exceptions. Some cookies, like meringues, are left on the sheet to cool completely. Specific cooling directions are indicated in each recipe.

TIP

When making rolled and cutout cookies, dip your cutter in flour to keep it from sticking to the dough. Cut the cookies as close together as you can. You can re-roll the scraps, but the less you handle the dough, the more tender your cookies will be.

TIP

If you choose to grease your cookie sheets rather than use parchment paper, use cooking spray or a light coating of shortening. Over-greasing causes cookies to spread excessively and brown too quickly around the edges. It isn't necessary to re-grease sheets between batches. Follow the instructions in your recipe as to whether or not the sheet should be left ungreased.

Storing and Freezing Cookies

Cool cookies completely before storing. Pack them in single layers in an airtight container with waxed paper between the layers to prevent sticking. Do not store crisp and soft cookies together in the same container. The moisture from the soft cookies will soften the crisp ones.

Most cookies can be frozen, even those with a glaze or frosting on top. (If the frosting is a bit soft, freeze the cookies unwrapped for about one hour to firm up the frosting.) Pack them in sealed plastic containers or freezer bags. They will keep frozen for up to 6 months. If your recipe calls for a dusting of confectioner's (icing) sugar or a chocolate dip, freeze the cookies while still plain, then decorate them before serving.

I prefer to freeze cookies after they are baked, but most cookie dough can be made ahead, stored in a tightly covered container and frozen for up to 6 months, or refrigerated for up to 1 week. When you want to use the frozen dough, thaw it overnight in the refrigerator or for 1 hour at room temperature before baking.

More Cookie Baking Tips

Although cookies are one of the simplest treats to bake, here are some helpful tips to make yours even better:

- If you prefer soft, chewy cookies, remove them from the oven about 2 minutes before they are done. If you like them crisp, bake 2 minutes longer.
- When baking, place your cookie sheet on the middle oven rack, making sure it doesn't touch the sides of the oven. This ensures the heat can circulate properly. For best results, bake only one sheet at a time. If you do bake two at a time, reverse the position of the sheets halfway through baking.
- Most cookies bake quickly, so pay attention to the timing. An extra minute can make a big difference. Always aim to under-bake rather than over-bake because cookies continue to bake after they come out of the oven. Since oven temperatures vary, check a few minutes before the recommended minimum baking time.
- Stick to the recipe or the variations. Do not use margarine identified as diet, liquid, soft or whipped. These contain added water and their soft texture will produce unsatisfactory results. Unsalted and salted butter are interchangeable. For the best results and flavor, I prefer butter, but margarine that is 80% fat will also work well in these recipes.
- Be sure to preheat your oven for at least 15 minutes before you're ready to bake so it is at the proper temperature before you put the cookies in.

- Have all your ingredients at room temperature before you start to bake. This makes for easy blending.
- Altering cookie recipes to make them healthier may sound like a great idea, but it often doesn't work out as planned. Any change in the proportion of ingredients also changes the result. In addition to adding flavor, sugar and fat make cookies crisp and tender. Reducing sugar and fat makes them softer and more cake-like. That said, here are some steps you can take to make cookies more nutritious:
  - Substitute whole wheat flour for half of the white flour to increase the range of nutrients and the amount of fiber.
  - Add dried fruits such as raisins, dates, apricots, figs and cranberries or some fresh chopped apple or grated carrot to up the nutrients and fiber.
  - Replace a whole egg with 2 egg whites if you're concerned about the cholesterol in food.
  - Use mini semi-sweet chocolate chips in place of the regular-size ones, but use half the amount. It gives the appearance that there is lots of chocolate and you'll still taste chocolate in every bite.

Fresh Fruit Yields

Often recipes call for a quantity of fruit such as 1 tsp (5 mL) lemon zest or 1 cup (250 mL) mashed banana. To make your baking easier, here are some measured yields for fresh fruits commonly used in making cookies.

Lemons: One medium lemon yields about 3 tbsp (45 mL) juice and 1 tbsp (15 mL) grated zest.

Limes: One lime yields about 3 tbsp (45 mL) juice and 1 tsp (5 mL) grated zest.

Oranges: One orange yields about $\frac{1}{3}$ cup (75 mL) juice and 4 tsp (20 mL) grated zest.

Apples: One pound (500 g), or 3 medium, yields about 2 cups (500 mL) sliced apples.

Bananas: One pound (500 g), or 2 or 3 large, yields about 1 cup (250 mL) mashed banana.

Strawberries: One pound (500 g) contains about $2\frac{2}{3}$ cups (650 mL) whole; 2 to $2\frac{1}{3}$ cups (500 to 575 mL) sliced; or $1\frac{2}{3}$ cups (400 mL) crushed.

Raspberries: One pound (500 g) contains about 4 cups (1 L) whole; or $1\frac{3}{4}$ to 2 cups (425 to 500 mL) crushed.

Ingredient Equivalents

INGREDIENT	WEIGHT OR QUANTITY	QUANTITY
Apricots (dried)	1 lb (500 g)	3 cups (750 mL)
Butter, margarine	1 lb (500 g)	2 cups (500 mL)
Cherries, maraschino	about 33	10-oz (300 mL) jar
Chocolate, baking	8-oz (225 g) pkg	8 squares
Chocolate chips	6-oz (175 g) bag	1 cup (250 mL)
Cocoa powder, unsweetened	8-oz (250 g) container	about 3 cups (750 mL)
Coconut, shredded or flaked	7-oz (225 g) bag	$2\frac{2}{3}$ cups (650 mL)
Cranberries, dried	8-oz (250 g) bag	about $2\frac{2}{3}$ cups (650 mL)
Cranberries, fresh or frozen	12-oz (340 g) bag	3 cups (750 mL)
Cream cheese	8-oz (250 g) pkg	1 cup (250 mL)
Dates (pitted), chopped	1 lb (500 g)	$2\frac{1}{2}$ cups (625 mL)
Egg product substitute	$\frac{1}{4}$ cup (50 mL)	1 whole large egg
Figs (dried), chopped	1 lb (500 g)	$2\frac{2}{3}$ cups (650 mL)
Flour, all-purpose	1 lb (500 g)	$3\frac{1}{3}$ cups (825 mL)
Flour, whole wheat	1 lb (500 g)	$3\frac{1}{2}$ cups (875 mL)
Honey	16-oz (500 g) jar	about $1\frac{1}{4}$ cups (300 mL)
Marshmallows, large	10-oz (300 g) bag	40 marshmallows
	5 marshmallows	$\frac{1}{2}$ cup (125 mL)
	1 large marshmallow	10 miniature
Marshmallows, miniature	$10\frac{1}{2}$-oz (320 g) bag	5 cups (1.25 L)
	$\frac{1}{2}$ cup (125 mL)	45 marshmallows
	10 miniature	1 large marshmallow
Milk, evaporated	14-oz (388 mL) can	$1\frac{1}{2}$ cups (375 mL)
Nuts, shelled		
Almonds (whole)	1 lb (500 g)	$3\frac{1}{2}$ cups (875 mL)
Peanuts (whole)	1 lb (500 g)	3 cups (750 mL)
Pecans (halves)	1 lb (500 g)	4 cups (1 L)
Walnuts (halves)	1 lb (500 g)	$6\frac{1}{4}$ cups (1.55 L)
Peanut butter	18-oz (550 g) jar	2 cups (500 mL)
Raisins	1 lb (500 g)	$2\frac{3}{4}$ cups (675 mL)
Sour cream	8-oz (250 g) container	1 cup (250 mL)
Sugar, brown	2 lb (1 kg)	about 5 cups (1.25 L) packed
Sugar, granulated	1 lb (500 g)	$2\frac{1}{4}$ cups (550 mL)
Sugar, confectioner's (icing)	2 lb (1 kg)	about $7\frac{1}{2}$ cups (1.875 L)

Emergency Substitutions

It's always best to use ingredients the recipe calls for as that reflects how they were tested. But in a pinch, here are some substitutions you can use to avoid a last-minute trip to the store.

Leavenings

1 tsp (5 mL) baking powder =
¼ tsp (1 mL) baking soda plus
½ tsp (2 mL) cream of tartar

Flour

1 cup (250 mL) all-purpose flour, unsifted =
1 cup (250 mL) plus 2 tbsp (25 mL) cake and pastry flour, unsifted

1 cup (250 mL) cake and pastry flour, unsifted =
1 cup (250 mL) minus 2 tbsp (25 mL) all-purpose flour, unsifted

1 cup (250 mL) whole wheat flour =
1 cup (250 mL) all-purpose flour

Unbleached all-purpose flour and all-purpose flour can be used interchangeably.

Sweeteners

1 cup (250 mL) granulated sugar =
1 cup (250 mL) packed brown sugar

1 cup (250 mL) packed brown sugar =
1 cup (250 mL) granulated sugar mixed with 2 tbsp (25 mL) molasses

Corn syrup =
Equal amount of maple syrup

1 cup (250 mL) honey =
1¼ cups (300 mL) granulated sugar plus ¼ cup (50 mL) liquid

Chocolate

1 square (1oz/28 g) unsweetened chocolate =
3 tbsp (45 mL) cocoa powder plus 1 tbsp (15 mL) shortening, butter or margarine

1 cup (250 mL) semi-sweet chocolate chips =
6 squares (1oz/28 g each) semi-sweet chocolate, chopped

Dairy Products

1 cup (250 mL) butter =
1 cup (250 mL) hard margarine
OR IN A PINCH
1 cup (250 mL) shortening plus 2 tbsp (25 mL) water

1 cup (250 mL) buttermilk or soured milk =
1 tbsp (15 mL) lemon juice or vinegar plus milk to make 1 cup (250 mL) (let stand for 5 minutes, then stir before using)

1 cup (250 mL) whole milk =
1 cup (250 mL) 2% milk
OR
½ cup (125 mL) evaporated milk plus ½ cup (125 mL) water
OR
1 cup (250 mL) skim milk plus 2 tbsp (25 mL) butter

1 cup (250 mL) sour cream =
⅞ cup (225 mL) buttermilk or plain yogurt plus 3 tbsp (45 mL) butter

1 cup (250 mL) whipping (35%) cream (for use in cooking, not for whipping) =
¾ cup (175 mL) whole milk plus ⅓ cup (75 mL) butter

Egg

1 whole egg =
2 egg whites
OR
2 egg yolks plus 1 tbsp (15 mL) water
OR
¼ cup (50 mL) egg substitute product

Spices

1 tsp (5 mL) ground cinnamon =
1 tsp (5 mL) pumpkin pie spice

1 tsp (5 mL) ground allspice =
½ tsp (2 mL) ground cinnamon plus pinch ground cloves

1 tbsp (15 mL) chopped gingerroot =
1 tsp (5 mL) ground dried ginger
OR
1 tbsp (15 mL) minced candied ginger with sugar washed off

Miscellaneous

½ cup (125 mL) raisins =
½ cup (125 mL) dried cranberries, dried cherries or dried blueberries or chopped pitted prunes, apricots or dates

Nuts (any amount)

Almonds, hazelnuts, pecans, walnuts and peanuts are interchangeable in any of the recipes in this book.

Drop Cookies

Drop cookies are the most common type of cookie, likely because they are the easiest to make. After you've prepared the dough, simply scoop out a spoonful and, using another spoon or a spatula, push the mound onto a cookie sheet. Or use a small ice cream scoop with a wire release, which ensures evenly sized and nicely rounded cookies. Keep the mounds of dough uniform in size to ensure even baking, and space them about 2 inches (5 cm) apart to allow for spreading.

Drop cookies are versatile. I've suggested plenty of variations to encourage you to have fun experimenting with your favorites.

◄ *Cranberry Almond Oatmeal Cookies and Seeds and Coconut Oatmeal Crisps*

Cranberry Almond Oatmeal Cookies

◆

The dried fruit makes this old-fashioned oatmeal cookie chewy, and the nuts provide pleasing crunch.

MAKES ABOUT 4 DOZEN COOKIES

- **Preparation: 25 minutes**
- **Baking: 14 minutes**
- **Freezing: excellent**

TIPS

I prefer combining the dry ingredients on a piece of waxed paper instead of dirtying a bowl. Then I use the paper as a funnel when adding them to the butter mixture.

I prefer to use parchment paper rather than just greasing the cookie sheet because it makes cleanup easy. It also solves the problem of cookies sticking to the pan.

Although recipes usually call for an electric mixer to blend ingredients, you can almost always use a wooden spoon when making cookies. It just takes more physical effort. With either method, it usually takes about 3 minutes to get a butter-and-sugar mixture light and creamy.

- **Preheat oven to 350°F (180°C)**
- **Cookie sheet, greased or lined with parchment paper**

1 ½ cups	all-purpose flour	375 mL
½ tsp	baking soda	2 mL
½ tsp	baking powder	2 mL
¼ tsp	salt	1 mL
½ tsp	ground cinnamon	2 mL
1 cup	butter, softened	250 mL
1 cup	packed brown sugar	250 mL
½ cup	granulated sugar	125 mL
2	eggs	2
½ tsp	almond extract	2 mL
2 cups	quick-cooking rolled oats	500 mL
1 ½ cups	dried cranberries	375 mL
1 cup	slivered almonds	250 mL

1. On a sheet of waxed paper or in a bowl, combine flour, baking soda, baking powder, salt and cinnamon. Set aside.

2. In a large bowl, using an electric mixer on medium speed, beat butter and brown and granulated sugars until blended. Add eggs and almond extract, beating until light and creamy, about 3 minutes. On low speed, gradually add flour mixture, beating until blended. With a wooden spoon, stir in oats, cranberries and almonds.

3. Drop dough by tablespoonfuls (15 mL) about 2 inches (5 cm) apart on prepared cookie sheet. Bake in preheated oven for 10 to 14 minutes or until golden. Cool for 5 minutes on sheet, then transfer to a rack and cool completely.

Variations

Replace cranberries with chopped dried cherries or apricots.
Replace almonds with pecans.

Seeds and Coconut Oatmeal Crisps

With three kinds of seeds, these cookies have lots of crunch and flavor.

MAKES ABOUT 2½ DOZEN COOKIES

- **Preparation: 25 minutes**
- **Standing: 2 hours**
- **Baking: 14 minutes**
- **Freezing: excellent**

TIPS

Don't be surprised — there is no flour in this recipe.

I like to use toasted wheat germ that is sold in bottles. It has a nice nutty flavor and crunchier texture than wheat germ that isn't toasted.

If you prefer chewy cookies, bake these for 10 minutes or until golden around the edges. For crisp cookies, bake for 14 minutes or until golden overall.

- **Preheat oven to 350°F (180°C)**
- **Cookie sheet, greased or lined with parchment paper**

2	eggs	2
1 cup	packed brown sugar	250 mL
½ cup	vegetable oil	125 mL
1 tsp	vanilla	5 mL
2 cups	quick-cooking rolled oats	500 mL
1 cup	sweetened flaked coconut	250 mL
½ cup	chopped pecans	125 mL
¼ cup	wheat germ	50 mL
¼ cup	sesame seeds	50 mL
¼ cup	sunflower seeds	50 mL
3 tbsp	flax seeds	45 mL

1. In a large bowl, using a wooden spoon, beat eggs, brown sugar, oil and vanilla until blended. Stir in oats, coconut, pecans, wheat germ, and sesame, sunflower and flax seeds. Cover bowl with plastic wrap and let stand at room temperature for 2 hours.

2. Drop dough by tablespoonfuls (15 mL) about 2 inches (5 cm) apart on prepared cookie sheet. Using an offset spatula or the back of a spoon, press until thin and flat. Bake in preheated oven for 10 to 14 minutes (see Tips). Cool for 10 minutes on sheet, then transfer to a rack and cool completely.

Variation

Vary the kinds of seeds you use. Try pumpkin seeds in place of the sunflower seeds or black sesame seeds in place of the white ones.

Cranberry Cashew Cookies

When you combine cashews with chocolate and cranberries, a mouthwatering cookie is guaranteed.

MAKES ABOUT 4½ DOZEN COOKIES

- **Preparation: 25 minutes**
- **Baking: 12 minutes**
- **Freezing: excellent**

TIPS

I prefer combining the dry ingredients on a piece of waxed paper instead of dirtying a bowl. Then I use the paper as a funnel when adding them to the butter mixture.

Store nuts in the freezer to retain their freshness.

Although recipes usually call for an electric mixer to blend ingredients, you can almost always use a wooden spoon when making cookies. It just takes more physical effort. With either method, it usually takes about 3 minutes to get a butter-and-sugar mixture light and creamy.

- **Preheat oven to 375°F (190°C)**
- **Cookie sheet, ungreased**

2¼ cups	all-purpose flour	550 mL
1 tsp	baking soda	5 mL
¼ tsp	salt	1 mL
1 cup	butter, softened	250 mL
¾ cup	granulated sugar	175 mL
¾ cup	packed brown sugar	175 mL
2	eggs	2
1 tsp	vanilla	5 mL
1¾ cups	white chocolate chips	425 mL
1 cup	dried cranberries	250 mL
1 cup	coarsely chopped cashews	250 mL

1. On a sheet of waxed paper or in a bowl, combine flour, baking soda and salt. Set aside.

2. In a large bowl, using an electric mixer on medium speed, beat butter, granulated and brown sugars, eggs and vanilla until light and creamy, about 3 minutes. On low speed, gradually add flour mixture, beating until blended. With a wooden spoon, stir in chocolate chips, cranberries and cashews.

3. Drop dough by tablespoonfuls (15 mL) about 2 inches (5 cm) apart on cookie sheet. Bake in preheated oven for 8 to 12 minutes or until golden. Cool for 5 minutes on sheet, then transfer to a rack and cool completely.

Variation

Substitute an equal quantity of chopped dried cherries or apricots for the cranberries.

White Chocolate Nut Crisps

Lots of crunchy nuts and creamy white chocolate make these cookies irresistible.

MAKES ABOUT 4 DOZEN COOKIES

- **Preparation: 25 minutes**
- **Baking: 18 minutes**
- **Freezing: excellent**

TIPS

I prefer combining the dry ingredients on a piece of waxed paper instead of dirtying a bowl. Then I use the paper as a funnel when adding them to the butter mixture.

Parchment paper makes cleanup easy. It also solves the problem of cookies sticking to the pan. Washable silicone sheets also work well.

For chewy cookies, bake about 14 minutes or until golden around the edges. For crisp cookies, bake about 18 minutes or until top of cookie is also light golden.

- **Preheat oven to 300°F (150°C)**
- **Cookie sheet, greased or lined with parchment paper**

2 cups	all-purpose flour	500 mL
1 tsp	baking soda	5 mL
1/4 tsp	salt	1 mL
3/4 cup	butter, softened	175 mL
1 cup	packed brown sugar	250 mL
3/4 cup	granulated sugar	175 mL
2	eggs	2
1 tsp	vanilla	5 mL
10	squares (1 oz/28 g each) white chocolate, cut in chunks	10
1 cup	coarsely chopped macadamia nuts	250 mL
1/2 cup	coarsely chopped pecans	125 mL

1. On a sheet of waxed paper or in a bowl, combine flour, baking soda and salt. Set aside.

2. In a large bowl, using an electric mixer on medium speed, beat butter and brown and granulated sugars until blended. Add eggs, one at a time, beating well after each addition. Add vanilla. On low speed, gradually add flour mixture, beating until blended. With a wooden spoon, stir in chocolate, macadamia nuts and pecans.

3. Drop dough by heaping tablespoonfuls (20 mL) about 2 inches (5 cm) apart on prepared cookie sheet. Bake in preheated oven for 14 to 18 minutes (see Tips). Cool for 5 minutes on sheet, then transfer to a rack and cool completely.

Variation

Replace macadamia nuts with slivered almonds.

Frosted Carrot Cake Cookies

These cookies taste like bite-size morsels of carrot cake. Better still, you don't need a plate and fork to eat them.

MAKES ABOUT 4 DOZEN COOKIES

- **Preparation: 35 minutes**
- **Baking: 14 minutes**
- **Freezing: excellent**

TIPS

When making these cookies, I prefer to combine the flour, baking soda, salt, cinnamon, nutmeg and cloves on a piece of waxed paper instead of dirtying a bowl. Then I use the paper as a funnel when adding it to the egg mixture.

Be sure to peel the carrots. If peel is left on, sometimes it will show up as green flecks in baked cookies.

Parchment paper makes cleanup easy. It also solves the problem of cookies sticking to the pan. Washable silicone sheets also work well.

- **Preheat oven to 350°F (180°C)**
- **Cookie sheet, greased or lined with parchment paper**

COOKIE

2½ cups	all-purpose flour	625 mL
½ tsp	baking soda	2 mL
¼ tsp	salt	1 mL
1 tsp	ground cinnamon	5 mL
¼ tsp	ground nutmeg	1 mL
¼ tsp	ground cloves	1 mL
1 cup	butter, softened	250 mL
¾ cup	granulated sugar	175 mL
¾ cup	packed brown sugar	175 mL
2	eggs	2
2 cups	shredded peeled carrots	500 mL
1 cup	chopped pecans	250 mL

FROSTING

4 oz	cream cheese, softened	125 g
¼ cup	butter, softened	50 mL
2 cups	confectioner's (icing) sugar, sifted	500 mL
	Chopped pecans, optional	

1. *Cookie:* Combine flour, baking soda, salt, cinnamon, nutmeg and cloves. Set aside.

2. In a bowl, using an electric mixer on medium speed, beat butter and granulated and brown sugars until blended. Add eggs, beating until light and creamy. On low speed, gradually add flour mixture, beating until blended. Stir in carrots and pecans.

3. Drop dough by tablespoonfuls (15 mL) about 2 inches (5 cm) apart on prepared cookie sheet. Bake in preheated oven for 10 to 14 minutes or until golden. Cool for 5 minutes on sheet, then transfer to a rack and cool completely.

4. *Frosting:* In a bowl, using an electric mixer on medium speed, beat cream cheese and butter until smooth. On low speed, gradually add confectioner's sugar, beating until blended. Spread over tops of cookies and sprinkle with nuts, if using.

Variation

Substitute walnuts, raisins or dried cranberries for the pecans.

Chocolate Caramel Oat Cookies

These taste like a mound of soft chocolate caramels in cookie form.

MAKES ABOUT 4 DOZEN COOKIES

- **Preparation: 25 minutes**
- **Baking: 12 minutes**
- **Freezing: excellent**

TIPS

Be sure to use parchment paper when baking with caramels as, once melted, they stick to the pan, making cleanup difficult.

You can use four 1.8 oz (52 g) chocolate-covered caramel bars in place of the rolls.

I use Rolo rolls. You can also buy bags of chocolate-covered caramels. Chill chocolate caramel candy for easier cutting.

A reliable oven thermometer is a good investment. It will tell you whether your oven heat is aligned with the setting. If not, you can adjust it accordingly.

- **Preheat oven to 375°F (190°C)**
- **Cookie sheet, lined with parchment paper**

2 cups	all-purpose flour	500 mL
1 cup	quick-cooking rolled oats	250 mL
1 tsp	baking soda	5 mL
¼ tsp	salt	1 mL
1 cup	butter, softened	250 mL
¾ cup	packed brown sugar	175 mL
½ cup	granulated sugar	125 mL
1	egg	1
1 tsp	vanilla	5 mL
4	rolls (1.8 oz/52 g each) chocolate-covered caramels, quartered	4
¾ cup	coarsely chopped cashews	175 mL

1. On a sheet of waxed paper or in a bowl, combine flour, oats, baking soda and salt. Set aside.

2. In a large bowl, using an electric mixer on medium speed, beat butter, brown and granulated sugars, egg and vanilla until smooth and creamy, about 3 minutes. On low speed, gradually add flour mixture, beating until blended. With a wooden spoon, stir in chocolate caramels and cashews.

3. Drop dough by tablespoonfuls (15 mL) about 2 inches (5 cm) apart on prepared cookie sheet. Bake in preheated oven for 8 to 12 minutes or until golden around edges. Cool for 5 minutes on sheet, then transfer to a rack and cool completely.

Variation

Replace cashews with pecans.

Chocolate Apricot Pecan Cookies

If you're a fan of apricots, you'll love these cookies.

**MAKES ABOUT
5 DOZEN COOKIES**

- **Preparation: 25 minutes**
- **Baking: 12 minutes**
- **Freezing: excellent**

TIP

If you like your cookies chewy, bake for the minimum time, about 8 minutes. Bake longer if you like crisp cookies.

- **Preheat oven to 375°F (190°C)**
- **Cookie sheet, ungreased**

2¼ cups	all-purpose flour	550 mL
1 tsp	baking soda	5 mL
¼ tsp	salt	1 mL
1 cup	butter, softened	250 mL
¾ cup	granulated sugar	175 mL
¾ cup	packed brown sugar	175 mL
2	eggs	2
1 tsp	vanilla	5 mL
2 cups	milk chocolate chips	500 mL
1 cup	chopped dried apricots	250 mL
1 cup	chopped pecans	250 mL

1. On a sheet of waxed paper or in a bowl, combine flour, baking soda and salt. Set aside.

2. In a large bowl, using an electric mixer on medium speed, beat butter and granulated and brown sugars until blended. Add eggs and vanilla, beating until light and creamy, about 3 minutes. On low speed, gradually add flour mixture, beating until blended. With a wooden spoon, stir in chocolate chips, apricots and pecans.

3. Drop dough by tablespoonfuls (15 mL) about 2 inches (5 cm) apart on cookie sheet. Bake in preheated oven for 8 to 12 minutes or until golden around edges. Cool for 5 minutes on sheet, then transfer to a rack and cool completely.

Variations

Replace apricots with dried cranberries.

Use white chocolate chips or a combination of white and milk chocolate chips.

Crunchy Cereal Cookies

Breakfast couldn't taste better. These cookies are delicious any time of the day.

MAKES ABOUT 4 DOZEN COOKIES

- **Preparation: 25 minutes**
- **Baking: 13 minutes**
- **Freezing: excellent**

TIPS

I like to use toasted wheat germ, which is sold in bottles. It has a nice nutty flavor and pleasing texture.

Store wheat germ in the freezer to keep it fresh.

Although recipes usually call for an electric mixer to blend ingredients, you can almost always use a wooden spoon when making cookies. It just takes more physical effort. With either method, it usually takes about 3 minutes to get a butter-and-sugar mixture light and creamy.

- **Preheat oven to 350°F (180°C)**
- **Cookie sheet, ungreased**

1 ½ cups	all-purpose flour	375 mL
½ tsp	baking soda	2 mL
½ tsp	cream of tartar	2 mL
¼ tsp	salt	1 mL
½ cup	butter, softened	125 mL
1 cup	packed brown sugar	250 mL
½ cup	vegetable oil	125 mL
1	egg	1
1 tsp	vanilla	5 mL
1 cup	crisp rice cereal	250 mL
½ cup	quick-cooking rolled oats	125 mL
½ cup	sliced almonds	125 mL
⅓ cup	unsweetened flaked coconut	75 mL
⅓ cup	sunflower seeds	75 mL
¼ cup	wheat germ	50 mL

1. On a sheet of waxed paper or in a bowl, combine flour, baking soda, cream of tartar and salt. Set aside.

2. In a large bowl, using an electric mixer on medium speed, beat butter, brown sugar, oil, egg and vanilla until smooth and creamy, about 3 minutes. On low speed, gradually add flour mixture, beating until blended. With a wooden spoon, stir in rice cereal, oats, almonds, coconut, sunflower seeds and wheat germ.

3. Drop dough by tablespoonfuls (15 mL) about 2 inches (5 cm) apart on cookie sheet. Bake in preheated oven for 9 to 13 minutes or until light golden. Cool for 5 minutes on sheet, then transfer to a rack and cool completely.

Variations

Other crisp cereals, such as crushed corn flakes, work well in place of the rice cereal.

Replace almonds with pecans or walnuts.

Ragged Robins

I'm not sure where the name originated, but the basic recipe for these cookies qualifies as "heritage." Obviously, they endured because they taste so good.

MAKES ABOUT 2½ DOZEN COOKIES

- **Preparation: 20 minutes**
- **Baking: 23 minutes**
- **Freezing: excellent**

TIPS

Measure the cereal, then crush it slightly.

These cookies will hold together when baked, although they may not seem like they will in the dough state.

- **Preheat oven to 325°F (160°C)**
- **Cookie sheet, greased or lined with parchment paper**

1¾ cups	corn flakes cereal, slightly crushed	425 mL
1½ cups	chopped dates	375 mL
1 cup	chopped walnuts	250 mL
½ cup	chopped red candied cherries	125 mL
3	egg whites	3
Pinch	salt	Pinch
½ tsp	vanilla	2 mL
½ cup	granulated sugar	125 mL

1. In a large bowl, combine cereal, dates, walnuts and cherries. Set aside.
2. In a small bowl, using an electric mixer on high speed, beat egg whites, salt and vanilla until stiff. With a wooden spoon, stir in sugar. Add to cereal mixture, mixing until well coated.
3. Drop dough by tablespoonfuls (15 mL) about 2 inches (5 cm) apart on prepared cookie sheet. Bake in preheated oven for 18 to 23 minutes or until set and light golden. Cool for 5 minutes on sheet, then transfer to a rack and cool completely.

Variations

Replace cherries with flaked coconut.
Replace corn flakes cereal with crisp rice cereal.

Raspberry Coconut Pinwheels

Here's an easy way to make an attractive swirl on top of a cookie.

MAKES ABOUT 5 DOZEN COOKIES

- **Preparation: 30 minutes**
- **Baking: 14 minutes**
- **Freezing: excellent**

TIPS

Use sweetened or unsweetened coconut — the choice is yours.

Although recipes usually call for an electric mixer to blend ingredients, you can almost always use a wooden spoon when making cookies. It just takes more physical effort. With either method, it usually takes about 3 minutes to get a butter-and-sugar mixture light and creamy.

- **Preheat oven to 375°F (190°C)**
- **Cookie sheet, ungreased**

3 cups	all-purpose flour	750 mL
½ cup	quick-cooking rolled oats	125 mL
1 tsp	baking soda	5 mL
¼ tsp	salt	1 mL
1 cup	butter, softened	250 mL
1 cup	packed brown sugar	250 mL
⅔ cup	granulated sugar	150 mL
2	eggs	2
½ cup	water	125 mL
1 tsp	almond extract	5 mL
2 cups	sweetened flaked coconut	500 mL
⅓ cup	raspberry jam	75 mL

1. On a sheet of waxed paper or in a bowl, combine flour, oats, baking soda and salt. Set aside.

2. In a large bowl, using an electric mixer on medium speed, beat butter and brown and granulated sugars until blended. Add eggs, water and almond extract, beating until light and creamy, about 3 minutes. On low speed, gradually add flour mixture and coconut, beating until blended.

3. Set aside about ¾ cup (175 mL) of the dough. Drop remaining dough by tablespoonfuls (15 mL) about 2 inches (5 cm) apart on cookie sheet. Make a small cavity in each cookie using a floured finger. Place ¼ tsp (1 mL) jam in cavity. Put ½ tsp (2 mL) of reserved dough on top of jam, not quite covering it. Bake in preheated oven for 10 to 14 minutes or until golden. Cool for 5 minutes on sheet, then transfer to a rack and cool completely.

Variation

Try other jams, such as blackberry, strawberry or apricot.

Tropical Fruit Macaroons

The combination of crushed pineapple and coconut gives these cookies a taste of the tropics.

MAKES ABOUT 4 DOZEN COOKIES

- **Preparation: 20 minutes**
- **Baking: 20 minutes**
- **Freezing: excellent**

TIPS

Both flaked and shredded coconut work well in macaroons.

If you prefer, use unsweetened coconut. The sweetened variety is usually easier to find in regular grocery stores, but unsweetened is always available in stores that sell bulk products.

- **Preheat oven to 350°F (180°C)**
- **Cookie sheet, lined with parchment paper**

1 cup	all-purpose flour	250 mL
1 tsp	baking powder	5 mL
2/3 cup	drained crushed pineapple	150 mL
1	can (14 oz/396 g OR 300 mL) sweetened condensed milk	1
1/2 cup	butter, melted	125 mL
2 1/2 cups	sweetened flaked coconut	625 mL
1 cup	chopped almonds	250 mL
2 tsp	grated lemon zest	10 mL

1. On a sheet of waxed paper or in a bowl, combine flour and baking powder. Set aside.
2. In a large bowl, using a wooden spoon, combine pineapple, sweetened condensed milk, melted butter, coconut, almonds and lemon zest, stirring until thoroughly blended. Add flour mixture, mixing until blended.
3. Drop dough by tablespoonfuls (15 mL) about 1 inch (2.5 cm) apart on prepared cookie sheet. Bake in preheated oven for 15 to 20 minutes or until golden around edges. Cool for 5 minutes on sheet, then transfer to a rack and cool completely.

Variations

Replace lemon zest with lime, orange or grapefruit zest.

Omit lemon zest and stir in 1/2 tsp (2 mL) almond extract.

Hermits

I'm not sure where the name originated, but these heritage cookies, which usually contain raisins and walnuts, have been around for a long time. They were my grandmother's favorite.

**MAKES ABOUT
4 DOZEN COOKIES**

- **Preparation: 25 minutes**
- **Baking: 13 minutes**
- **Freezing: excellent**

TIPS

I like the flavor of Medjool dates or honey dates, especially when they are soft and fresh. They're wonderful for snacking on as well, so be sure to buy more than your recipe calls for.

Buy dates already pitted. It makes preparation quicker and easier.

- **Preheat oven to 375° (190°C)**
- **Cookie sheet, greased or lined with parchment paper**

1¾ cups	all-purpose flour	425 mL
½ tsp	baking soda	2 mL
¼ tsp	salt	1 mL
1 tsp	ground cinnamon	5 mL
½ tsp	ground nutmeg	2 mL
¼ tsp	ground cloves	1 mL
⅔ cup	butter, softened	150 mL
¾ cup	packed brown sugar	175 mL
½ cup	granulated sugar	125 mL
1	egg	1
¼ cup	cold strong coffee	50 mL
1 cup	raisins	250 mL
1 cup	chopped dates	250 mL
¾ cup	coarsely chopped walnuts	175 mL

1. On a sheet of waxed paper or in a bowl, combine flour, baking soda, salt, cinnamon, nutmeg and cloves. Set aside.

2. In a large bowl, using an electric mixer on medium speed, beat butter, brown and granulated sugars, egg and coffee until light and creamy, about 3 minutes. On low speed, gradually add flour mixture, beating until blended. With a wooden spoon, stir in raisins, dates and walnuts.

3. Drop dough by tablespoonfuls (15 mL) about 2 inches (5 cm) apart on prepared cookie sheet. Bake in preheated oven for 9 to 13 minutes or until lightly browned. Cool for 5 minutes on sheet, then transfer to a rack and cool completely.

Variations

Use all dates or all raisins to suit your preference.
Omit nuts.

Fruit and Nut Overload

These cookies are so full of fruit and nuts they are almost like a power bar.

**MAKES ABOUT
5 DOZEN COOKIES**

- **Preparation: 30 minutes**
- **Baking: 13 minutes**
- **Freezing: excellent**

TIPS

The amount of dough may seem inadequate for all the fruit and nuts, but it works. If you're having trouble keeping the dough together, squeeze each mound with moistened fingertips after you drop it on the sheet. It will meld during baking.

These cookies keep well and are nice to ship as they are not fragile.

- **Preheat oven to 350°F (180°C)**
- **Cookie sheet, greased or lined with parchment paper**

1 1/2 cups	coarsely chopped Brazil nuts	375 mL
3/4 cup	coarsely chopped hazelnuts	175 mL
1/2 cup	chopped pecans	125 mL
1 1/4 cups	chopped dried apricots	300 mL
3/4 cup	chopped dried cranberries	175 mL
1/2 cup	chopped dates	125 mL
2 slices	dried pineapple, chopped	2 slices
1 1/4 cups	all-purpose flour, divided	300 mL
1/2 tsp	baking powder	2 mL
1/2 tsp	baking soda	2 mL
1/4 tsp	salt	1 mL
1/2 tsp	ground cinnamon	2 mL
1/2 cup	butter, softened	125 mL
3/4 cup	packed brown sugar	175 mL
1	egg	1

1. In a large bowl, combine Brazil nuts, hazelnuts, pecans, apricots, cranberries, dates and pineapple. Add 1/4 cup (50 mL) of the flour and mix until fruit and nuts are coated with flour. Set aside.

2. On a sheet of waxed paper or in a bowl, combine remaining 1 cup (250 mL) flour, baking powder, baking soda, salt and cinnamon. Set aside.

3. In a bowl, using an electric mixer on medium speed, beat butter, sugar and egg until light and creamy, about 3 minutes. On low speed, gradually add flour mixture, beating until blended. With a wooden spoon, stir in fruit mixture.

4. Drop dough by tablespoonfuls (15 mL) about 2 inches (5 cm) apart on prepared cookie sheet. Bake in preheated oven for 9 to 13 minutes or until light golden. Cool for 5 minutes on sheet, then transfer to a rack and cool completely.

Variations

Omit pineapple. The dough will hold together better.

Try other combinations of nuts and fruit, keeping the quantities the same as in the original recipe.

Sour Cream Cashew Cookies

This soft, moist cookie has chunks of luscious cashews in every bite. Not only does the frosting look attractive, it adds a unique sweet and salty flavor.

MAKES ABOUT 4 DOZEN COOKIES

- **Preparation: 35 minutes**
- **Baking: 14 minutes**
- **Cooking (Frosting): 4 minutes**
- **Freezing: excellent**

TIPS

If you're adding chopped cashews to a recipe, buy small cashews or cashew pieces. They are much more economical and make sense when size doesn't matter.

Use salted or unsalted cashews in the cookie, depending on your preference.

Although recipes usually call for an electric mixer to blend ingredients, you can almost always use a wooden spoon when making cookies. It just takes more physical effort. With either method, it usually takes about 3 minutes to get a butter-and-sugar mixture light and creamy.

- **Preheat oven to 350°F (180°C)**
- **Cookie sheet, greased or lined with parchment paper**

COOKIE

2 cups	all-purpose flour	500 mL
¾ tsp	baking powder	3 mL
¾ tsp	baking soda	3 mL
¼ tsp	salt	1 mL
½ cup	butter, softened	125 mL
1 cup	packed brown sugar	250 mL
1	egg	1
⅓ cup	sour cream	75 mL
1 tsp	vanilla	5 mL
2 cups	cashew halves	500 mL

FROSTING, OPTIONAL

½ cup	butter	125 mL
3 cups	confectioner's (icing) sugar, sifted	750 mL
3 tbsp	milk	45 mL
¾ cup	finely chopped salted cashews	75 mL

1. *Cookie:* On a sheet of waxed paper or in a bowl, combine flour, baking powder, baking soda and salt. Set aside.

2. In a large bowl, using an electric mixer on medium speed, beat butter, brown sugar, egg, sour cream and vanilla until light and creamy, about 3 minutes. On low speed, gradually add flour mixture, beating until blended. With a wooden spoon, stir in cashews.

3. Drop dough by tablespoonfuls (15 mL) about 2 inches (5 cm) apart on prepared cookie sheet. Bake in preheated oven for 10 to 14 minutes or until golden. Cool for 5 minutes on sheet, then transfer to a rack and cool completely.

4. *Frosting, optional:* In a small saucepan, melt butter over medium-high heat, cooking until it becomes foamy and starts to turn golden, about 4 minutes. Remove from heat. Transfer to a bowl and let cool for 10 minutes. Using an electric mixer on low speed, gradually add confectioner's sugar and milk, beating until blended. If necessary add a little more milk to make a spreadable consistency.

5. Spread frosting on top of cookies. Sprinkle chopped cashews on top. Press lightly into frosting. Let frosting set about 1 hour.

Key Lime Coconut Macaroons

These easy-to-make cookies will be particularly appealing to coconut-lovers.

MAKES ABOUT 2½ DOZEN COOKIES

- **Preparation: 15 minutes**
- **Baking: 25 minutes**
- **Freezing: excellent**

TIPS

When zesting and juicing a lime, remove lime zest first, then warm the fruit in a microwave oven for 5 seconds to obtain the most juice.

Drizzle melted chocolate over top of cookies for an attractive finish.

- **Preheat oven to 350°F (180°C)**
- **Cookie sheet, lined with parchment paper**

1	can (14 oz/396 g OR 300 mL) sweetened condensed milk	1
⅓ cup	freshly squeezed Key lime juice	75 mL
⅓ cup	all-purpose flour	75 mL
2⅔ cups	sweetened shredded coconut	650 mL
1 tbsp	grated Key lime zest	15 mL

1. In a large bowl, combine sweetened condensed milk and lime juice, whisking until blended. With a wooden spoon, stir in flour, mixing until thoroughly blended. Stir in coconut and zest.

2. Drop dough by tablespoonfuls (15 mL) about 1 inch (2.5 cm) apart on prepared cookie sheet. Bake in preheated oven for 20 to 25 minutes or until golden around edges. Cool for 15 minutes on sheet, then transfer to a rack and cool completely.

Variations
Substitute Persian limes for the Key limes.

Chocolate Toffee Cranberry Crunchies

These cookies are crisp on the outside, chewy on the inside and have a great butter and caramel flavor throughout.

**MAKES ABOUT
5 DOZEN COOKIES**

- **Preparation: 20 minutes**
- **Baking: 15 minutes**
- **Freezing: excellent**

TIPS

Parchment paper always makes cleanup easy, but it's practically mandatory when baking with sticky ingredients such as toffee. It solves the problem of cookies sticking to the pan.

I usually use Skor bars, but Heath bars also make great cookies with a similar taste.

Although recipes usually call for an electric mixer to blend ingredients, you can almost always use a wooden spoon when making cookies. It just takes more physical effort. With either method, it usually takes about 3 minutes to get a butter-and-sugar mixture light and creamy.

- **Preheat oven to 350°F (180°C)**
- **Cookie sheet, lined with parchment paper**

2 cups	all-purpose flour	500 mL
1 ½ cups	quick-cooking rolled oats	375 mL
1 tsp	baking soda	5 mL
¼ tsp	salt	1 mL
1 cup	butter, softened	250 mL
¾ cup	granulated sugar	175 mL
¾ cup	packed brown sugar	175 mL
2	eggs	2
1 ½ cups	dried cranberries	375 mL
5	(1.4 oz/39 g each) crunchy chocolate-covered toffee bars, chopped	5

1. On a sheet of waxed paper or in a bowl, combine flour, oats, baking soda and salt. Set aside.

2. In a large bowl, using an electric mixer on medium speed, beat butter and granulated and brown sugars until smooth and creamy, about 3 minutes. Add eggs, one at a time, beating well after each addition. On low speed, gradually add flour mixture, beating until blended. With a wooden spoon, stir in cranberries and chopped chocolate bars.

3. Drop dough by tablespoonfuls (15 mL) about 2 inches (5 cm) apart on prepared cookie sheet. Bake in preheated oven for 11 to 15 minutes or until light golden. Cool for 5 minutes on sheet, then transfer to a rack and cool completely.

Variation

Replace chopped chocolate bars with ¾ cup (175 mL) toffee bits and 1 cup (250 mL) miniature semi-sweet chocolate chips.

Toffee Crisp Oatmeal Cookies

Surprisingly for an oatmeal cookie, these have a candy bar-like taste.

MAKES ABOUT 5 DOZEN COOKIES

- **Preparation: 25 minutes**
- **Baking: 13 minutes**
- **Freezing: excellent**

TIPS

I prefer combining the dry ingredients on a piece of waxed paper instead of dirtying a bowl. Then I use the paper as a funnel when adding them to the butter mixture.

Make large cookies using a ⅓ cup (75 mL) dry measure or ice cream scoop to form balls of dough. Place about 4 inches (10 cm) apart on cookie sheet. Bake for 10 to 14 minutes or until golden around edges.

- **Preheat oven to 350°F (180°)**
- **Cookie sheet, lined with parchment paper**

1 cup	all-purpose flour	250 mL
¾ cup	wheat germ	175 mL
1 tsp	baking powder	5 mL
1 tsp	baking soda	5 mL
¼ tsp	salt	1 mL
2 cups	butter, softened	500 mL
1 cup	granulated sugar	250 mL
1 cup	packed brown sugar	250 mL
2	eggs	2
1 tsp	vanilla	5 mL
3¼ cups	quick-cooking rolled oats	800 mL
1 cup	toffee bits	250 mL
1 cup	semi-sweet chocolate chips	250 mL

1. On a sheet of waxed paper or in a bowl, combine flour, wheat germ, baking powder, baking soda and salt. Set aside.

2. In a large bowl, using an electric mixer on medium speed, beat butter and granulated and brown sugars until smooth and creamy, about 3 minutes. Add eggs, one at a time, beating well after each addition. Add vanilla. On low speed, gradually add flour mixture, beating until blended. With a wooden spoon, stir in oats, toffee bits and chocolate chips.

3. Drop dough by tablespoonfuls (15 mL) about 2 inches (5 cm) apart on prepared cookie sheet. Bake in preheated oven for 9 to 13 minutes or until golden. Cool for 5 minutes on sheet, then transfer to a rack and cool completely.

Variations

Replace toffee bits with raisins or dried cranberries.

For an all-chocolate cookie, omit toffee bits and use 1½ cups (375 mL) semi-sweet or milk chocolate chips.

Butterscotch Coconut Oatmeal Cookies

Whenever my niece's husband goes on a fishing trip, she bakes a batch of these for him to take along.

MAKES ABOUT 5 DOZEN COOKIES

- **Preparation: 25 minutes**
- **Baking: 11 minutes**
- **Freezing: excellent**

TIPS

I prefer combining the dry ingredients on a piece of waxed paper instead of dirtying a bowl. Then I use the paper as a funnel when adding them to the butter mixture.

For chewy cookies, bake 7 to 9 minutes or just until lightly browned around edges. If you prefer a crispier cookie, bake 9 to 11 minutes or until lightly browned overall.

There are no nuts in these, so they're perfect to send to school with your children.

- **Preheat oven to 375°F (190°C)**
- **Cookie sheet, ungreased**

1 ¼ cups	all-purpose flour	300 mL
1 tsp	baking soda	5 mL
¼ tsp	salt	1 mL
½ tsp	ground cinnamon	2 mL
1 cup	butter, softened	250 mL
¾ cup	granulated sugar	175 mL
¾ cup	packed brown sugar	175 mL
2	eggs	2
1 tsp	vanilla	5 mL
3 cups	quick-cooking rolled oats	750 mL
2 cups	butterscotch chips	500 mL
½ cup	sweetened flaked coconut	125 mL

1. On a sheet of waxed paper or in a bowl, combine flour, baking soda, salt and cinnamon. Set aside.

2. In a large bowl, using an electric mixer on medium speed, beat butter and granulated and brown sugars until blended. Add eggs, one a time, beating well after each addition. Add vanilla. On low speed, gradually add flour mixture, beating until blended. With a wooden spoon, stir in oats, butterscotch chips and coconut.

3. Drop dough by tablespoonfuls (15 mL) about 2 inches (5 cm) apart on cookie sheet. Bake in preheated oven for 7 to 11 minutes or until lightly browned around edges. Cool for 5 minutes on sheet, then transfer to a rack and cool completely.

Variation
Omit coconut.

Honey Cranberry Oat Cookies

Here's a healthy, tasty cookie the whole family will enjoy.

MAKES ABOUT 5 DOZEN COOKIES

- **Preparation: 25 minutes**
- **Baking: 12 minutes**
- **Freezing: excellent**

TIPS

For a more "oaty" taste and slightly drier texture, use large-flake old-fashioned rolled oats.

Cookies made with honey usually have a dense, moist, slightly chewy texture and a unique flavor. They usually keep well, too.

Although recipes usually call for an electric mixer to blend ingredients, you can almost always use a wooden spoon when making cookies. It just takes more physical effort. With either method, it usually takes about 3 minutes to get a butter-and-sugar mixture light and creamy.

- **Preheat oven to 375°F (190°C)**
- **Cookie sheet, greased or lined with parchment paper**

2 cups	all-purpose flour	500 mL
1 tsp	baking soda	5 mL
1/4 tsp	salt	1 mL
1 cup	butter, softened	250 mL
1 cup	packed brown sugar	250 mL
1 cup	liquid honey	250 mL
2	eggs	2
1 1/2 cups	quick-cooking rolled oats	375 mL
1 1/2 cups	dried cranberries	375 mL
1 cup	slivered almonds	250 mL
1 cup	sunflower seeds	250 mL

1. On a sheet of waxed paper or in a bowl, combine flour, baking soda and salt. Set aside.

2. In a large bowl, using an electric mixer on medium speed, beat butter, brown sugar, honey and eggs until smooth and creamy, about 3 minutes. On low speed, gradually add flour mixture, beating until blended. With a wooden spoon, stir in oats, cranberries, almonds and sunflower seeds.

3. Drop dough by tablespoonfuls (15 mL) about 2 inches (5 cm) apart on prepared cookie sheet. Bake in preheated oven for 8 to 12 minutes or until golden. Cool for 5 minutes on sheet, then transfer to a rack and cool completely.

Variation
Add 1 tbsp (15 mL) grated orange zest along with the honey.

Black Forest Cookies

These scrumptious cookies have all the flavors of Black Forest cake, but in bite-size form.

MAKES ABOUT 5 DOZEN COOKIES

- **Preparation: 25 minutes**
- **Baking: 13 minutes**
- **Freezing: excellent**

TIPS

Dried fruits such as apricots, raisins, cranberries and cherries should be soft when they are fresh. Store them in the freezer to retain their freshness. If they seem hard, pour boiling water over them and let stand for 5 minutes to soften. Drain well and pat dry with paper towel.

The tartness of the dried cherries nicely complements the creamy sweetness of white chocolate, with just a touch of semi-sweet chocolate. But if you prefer, use all semi-sweet chocolate chips.

- **Preheat oven to 350°F (180°C)**
- **Cookie sheet, ungreased**

1²⁄₃ cups	all-purpose flour	400 mL
1 tsp	baking powder	5 mL
1 tsp	baking soda	5 mL
¼ tsp	salt	1 mL
1 cup	butter, softened	250 mL
¾ cup	packed brown sugar	175 mL
½ cup	granulated sugar	125 mL
2	eggs	2
1 tsp	vanilla	5 mL
2 cups	quick-cooking rolled oats	500 mL
1¼ cups	white chocolate chips	300 mL
1 cup	semi-sweet chocolate chips	250 mL
1 cup	dried cherries, coarsely chopped	250 mL
¾ cup	slivered almonds	175 mL

1. On a sheet of waxed paper or in a bowl, combine flour, baking powder, baking soda and salt. Set aside.

2. In a large bowl, using an electric mixer on medium speed, beat butter and brown and granulated sugars until light and creamy, about 3 minutes. Add eggs, one at a time, beating well after each addition. Add vanilla. On low speed, gradually add flour mixture, beating until blended. With a wooden spoon, stir in oats, white and semi-sweet chocolate chips, cherries and almonds.

3. Drop dough by tablespoonfuls (15 mL) about 2 inches (5 cm) apart on cookie sheet. Bake in preheated oven for 9 to 13 minutes or until golden. Cool for 5 minutes on sheet, then transfer to a rack and cool completely.

Variations

Substitute dried cranberries for the cherries. There is no need to chop the cranberries as they are smaller.

For a very different taste, use maraschino cherries, chopped and patted dry with paper towel.

Cranberry Pecan Oatmeal Cookies

Depending upon how you bake them, these cookies can be soft and chewy or crispy. They are delicious either way, so the choice is yours.

MAKES ABOUT 4 DOZEN COOKIES

- **Preparation: 25 minutes**
- **Baking: 15 minutes**
- **Freezing: excellent**

TIP

Bake the minimum time for chewy cookies. They will look like they are not quite done when you take them out of the oven, but they will continue to cook on the sheet. Bake longer, until golden, if you prefer crisp cookies.

- **Preheat oven to 350°F (180°C)**
- **Cookie sheet, greased or lined with parchment paper**

¾ cup	all-purpose flour	175 mL
¾ tsp	baking soda	3 mL
¼ tsp	salt	1 mL
1 tsp	ground cinnamon	5 mL
¾ cup	butter, softened	175 mL
¾ cup	packed brown sugar	175 mL
½ cup	granulated sugar	125 mL
1	egg	1
2 tbsp	milk	25 mL
3 cups	quick-cooking rolled oats	750 mL
1 cup	dried cranberries	250 mL
¾ cup	chopped pecans	175 mL
⅓ cup	sunflower seeds	75 mL

1. On a sheet of waxed paper or in a bowl, combine flour, baking soda, salt and cinnamon. Set aside.

2. In a large bowl, using an electric mixer on medium speed, beat butter, brown and granulated sugars, egg and milk until light and creamy, about 3 minutes. On low speed, gradually add flour mixture, beating until blended. With a wooden spoon, stir in oats, cranberries, pecans and sunflower seeds.

3. Drop dough by tablespoonfuls (15 mL) about 2 inches (5 cm) apart on prepared cookie sheet. Press flat with a fork dipped in flour. Bake in preheated oven for 11 to 15 minutes (see Tips). Cool for 5 minutes on sheet, then transfer to a rack and cool completely.

Variation

Omit cinnamon. Replace milk with orange juice and 1 tbsp (15 mL) grated orange zest.

Frosted Cashew Drops

An optional browned butter frosting transforms these simple cashew cookies into a special treat.

MAKES ABOUT 3 DOZEN COOKIES

- **Preparation: 35 minutes**
- **Baking: 14 minutes**
- **Cooking (Frosting): 4 minutes**
- **Freezing: excellent**

TIPS

I prefer combining the dry ingredients on a piece of waxed paper instead of dirtying a bowl. Then I use the paper as a funnel when adding them to the butter mixture.

Confectioner's sugar clumps during storage. Measure, then sift before using. If you don't have a sifter, a fine sieve works well.

- **Preheat oven to 350°F (180°C)**
- **Cookie sheet, ungreased**

COOKIE

2¼ cups	all-purpose flour	550 mL
1 tsp	baking soda	5 mL
¼ tsp	salt	1 mL
1 cup	butter, softened	250 mL
1 cup	packed brown sugar	250 mL
½ cup	granulated sugar	125 mL
1	egg	1
1 tsp	vanilla	5 mL
1½ cups	coarsely chopped cashews	375 mL

FROSTING, OPTIONAL

½ cup	butter	125 mL
3 cups	confectioner's (icing) sugar, sifted	750 mL
3 tbsp	milk	45 mL
1 tsp	vanilla	5 mL
½ cup	finely chopped cashews	125 mL

1. *Cookie:* On a sheet of waxed paper or in a bowl, combine flour, baking soda and salt. Set aside.

2. In a large bowl, using an electric mixer on medium speed, beat butter, brown and granulated sugars, egg and vanilla until light and creamy, about 3 minutes. On low speed, gradually add flour mixture, beating until blended. With a wooden spoon, stir in cashews.

3. Drop dough by tablespoonfuls (15 mL) about 2 inches (5 cm) apart on cookie sheet. Bake in preheated oven for 10 to 14 minutes or until golden. Cool for 5 minutes on sheet, then transfer to rack and cool completely.

4. *Frosting, optional:* In a small saucepan, on medium heat, cook butter until it foams and starts to turn golden, about 4 minutes. Remove from heat. Pour into a bowl and let cool for 10 minutes. Using an electric mixer on low speed, gradually add confectioner's sugar, milk and vanilla, beating until blended. If necessary, add a little more milk to make a spreadable consistency.

5. Spread frosting on top of cooled cookies. Sprinkle with chopped cashews, pressing lightly into frosting. Let frosting set, about 1 hour.

Maple Pecan Drops

Maple and pecan is always a great combination, particularly in this old-fashioned oatmeal cookie.

MAKES ABOUT 5 DOZEN COOKIES

- **Preparation: 25 minutes**
- **Baking: 13 minutes**
- **Freezing: excellent**

TIPS

Use quick-cooking oats if you prefer. Your cookies will be slightly moister and won't have as pronounced an "oaty" taste.

These cookies freeze well, as do most cookies. See instructions, page 10.

- **Preheat oven to 350°F (180°C)**
- **Cookie sheet, ungreased**

2 cups	all-purpose flour	500 mL
1½ cups	large-flake old-fashioned rolled oats	375 mL
1 tsp	baking soda	5 mL
¼ tsp	salt	1 mL
1 cup	butter, softened	250 mL
1⅓ cups	packed brown sugar	325 mL
2	eggs	2
2½ tsp	maple extract	12 mL
2 cups	coarsely chopped pecans	500 mL
60	small pecan halves	60

1. On a sheet of waxed paper or in a bowl, combine flour, oats, baking soda and salt. Set aside.

2. In a large bowl, using an electric mixer on medium speed, beat butter, brown sugar, eggs and maple extract until light and creamy, about 3 minutes. On low speed, gradually add flour mixture, beating until blended. With a wooden spoon, stir in chopped pecans.

3. Drop dough by tablespoonfuls (15 mL) about 2 inches (5 cm) apart on cookie sheet. Press a pecan half on top of each cookie. Bake in preheated oven for 9 to 13 minutes or until lightly browned around edges. Cool for 5 minutes on sheet, then transfer to a rack and cool completely.

Variation
Replace pecans with walnuts.

Chocolate Peanut Butter Oatmeal Cookies

◆

The three most popular cookies — chocolate chip, oatmeal and peanut butter — combine in one sumptuous cookie.

MAKES ABOUT 4 DOZEN COOKIES

- **Preparation: 25 minutes**
- **Baking: 13 minutes**
- **Freezing: excellent**

TIPS

Buy light-colored cookie sheets with low or no sides for even baking. The darker nonstick ones absorb more heat, causing cookies to brown on the bottoms before the tops are cooked.

These cookies are perfect for a lunch box or as an after-school snack with a glass of cold milk or a mug of hot chocolate.

- **Preheat oven to 375°F (190°C)**
- **Cookie sheet, ungreased**

1¼ cups	all-purpose flour	300 mL
1 tsp	baking powder	5 mL
½ tsp	baking soda	2 mL
¼ tsp	salt	1 mL
¾ cup	butter, softened	175 mL
½ cup	creamy peanut butter	125 mL
¾ cup	granulated sugar	175 mL
¾ cup	packed brown sugar	175 mL
2	eggs	2
1 tsp	vanilla	5 mL
2 cups	quick-cooking rolled oats	500 mL
1½ cups	chocolate-covered peanuts, chopped	375 mL
½ cup	crisp rice cereal	125 mL

1. On a sheet of waxed paper or in a bowl, combine flour, baking powder, baking soda and salt. Set aside.

2. In a large bowl, using an electric mixer on medium speed, beat butter, peanut butter and granulated and brown sugars until smooth and creamy, about 3 minutes. Add eggs, one at a time, beating well after each addition. Add vanilla. On low speed, gradually add flour mixture, beating until blended. With a wooden spoon, stir in oats, chocolate peanuts and cereal.

3. Drop dough by tablespoonfuls (15 mL) about 2 inches (5 cm) apart on cookie sheet. Press flat with a fork dipped in flour. Bake in preheated oven for 9 to 13 minutes or until crisp and golden. Cool for 5 minutes on sheet, then transfer to a rack and cool completely.

Variation

Replace chocolate-covered peanuts with 1 cup (250 mL) semi-sweet or milk chocolate chips and ½ cup (125 mL) chopped peanuts.

White Chocolate Fruit and Nut Cookies

Crisp around the edges and chewy inside, these cookies taste every bit as good as they look.

MAKES ABOUT 6 DOZEN COOKIES

- **Preparation: 30 minutes**
- **Baking: 12 minutes**
- **Freezing: excellent**

TIPS

Most baked cookies freeze well. Store them frozen in airtight containers or freezer bags for up to 6 months.

To grate citrus zest, use a fine-hole, sharp-toothed grater or Microplane made for zesting. Use only the colored outer portion of the rind, not the white inner portion, which is quite bitter.

You should get about 4 tsp (20 mL) zest from 1 orange.

- **Preheat oven to 375°F (190°C)**
- **Cookie sheet, greased or lined with parchment paper**

2¼ cups	all-purpose flour	550 mL
1 tsp	baking soda	5 mL
½ tsp	salt	2 mL
1 cup	butter, softened	250 mL
¾ cup	packed brown sugar	175 mL
½ cup	granulated sugar	125 mL
2	eggs	2
1 tbsp	grated orange zest	15 mL
8	squares (1 oz/28 g each) white chocolate, cut in chunks	8
1¼ cups	coarsely chopped cashews	300 mL
¾ cup	dried cranberries	175 mL
½ cup	chopped dried mango	125 mL

1. On a sheet of waxed paper or in a bowl, combine flour, baking soda and salt. Set aside.

2. In a large bowl, using an electric mixer on medium speed, beat butter and brown and granulated sugars until light and creamy, about 3 minutes. Add eggs, one at a time, beating well after each addition. Add orange zest. On low speed, gradually add flour mixture, beating until blended. With a wooden spoon, stir in white chocolate, cashews, cranberries and mango.

3. Drop dough by heaping tablespoonfuls (20 mL) about 2 inches (5 cm) apart on prepared cookie sheet. Bake in preheated oven for 8 to 12 minutes or until golden around edges. Cool for 5 minutes on sheet, then transfer to a rack and cool completely.

Variations

Add ½ cup (125 mL) flaked coconut along with the mango.

Replace cashews with macadamia nuts or almonds.

Replace mango with chopped dried apricot.

Date 'n' Nut Meringues

This is a nice light cookie, perfect for those times when you need a little "lift."

**MAKES ABOUT
3 DOZEN COOKIES**

- **Preparation: 20 minutes**
- **Baking: 12 minutes**
- **Freezing: not recommended**

TIP

Unlike most meringues, these contain flour, which gives a more cookie-like texture.

- **Preheat oven to 350°F (180°C)**
- **Cookie sheet, greased or lined with parchment paper**

3	egg whites	3
1/4 tsp	salt	1 mL
1 tsp	vanilla	5 mL
1 cup	granulated sugar	250 mL
1 cup	all-purpose flour	250 mL
1 cup	chopped dates	250 mL
1 cup	chopped pecans	250 mL

1. In a bowl, using an electric mixer on medium speed, beat egg whites, salt and vanilla to soft peaks. Gradually add sugar, 2 tbsp (25 mL) at a time, beating until stiff peaks form. With a wooden spoon, stir in flour, dates and pecans. Mix well.

2. Drop by scant tablespoonfuls (10 mL) about 2 inches (5 cm) apart on prepared cookie sheet. Bake in preheated oven for 8 to 12 minutes or until lightly browned around edges. Cool for 5 minutes on sheet, then transfer to a rack and cool completely.

Lacy Pecan Thins

These cookies are like candy "brittle" in texture and taste. For a special treat, serve them with ice cream or fresh berries.

**MAKES ABOUT
3 1/2 DOZEN COOKIES**

- **Preparation: 15 minutes**
- **Cooking: 4 minutes**
- **Baking: 13 minutes**
- **Freezing: not recommended**

- **Preheat oven to 325°F (160°C)**
- **Cookie sheet, lined with parchment paper**

2/3 cup	packed brown sugar	150 mL
1/2 cup	butter	125 mL
1/2 cup	corn syrup	125 mL
1 cup	all-purpose flour	250 mL
1/2 cup	finely chopped pecans	125 mL
1/2 cup	unsweetened flaked coconut	125 mL

1. In a large saucepan, over medium-high heat, combine brown sugar, butter and corn syrup, stirring until melted and smooth. Remove from heat. Stir in flour, pecans and coconut.

2. Drop mixture by slightly rounded teaspoonfuls (7 mL) about 2 inches (5 cm) apart on prepared cookie sheet. Bake in preheated oven for 9 to 13 minutes or until golden. Cool for 5 minutes on sheet, then transfer to a rack and cool completely.

Almond and Pine Nut Macaroons

These cookies may not have many ingredients, but they sure have a lot of flavor.

**MAKES ABOUT
2 DOZEN COOKIES**

- **Preparation: 15 minutes**
- **Baking: 25 minutes**
- **Freezing: not recommended**

- **Preheat oven to 350°F (180°C)**
- **Cookie sheet, lined with parchment paper**

8 oz	almond paste, broken into pieces	250 g
1/2 cup	granulated sugar	125 mL
1/4 cup	confectioner's (icing) sugar, sifted	50 mL
1/4 tsp	salt	1 mL
3	egg whites	3
2/3 cup	pine nuts	150 mL

1. In a food processor, process almond paste into fine pieces. Add granulated and confectioner's sugars and salt and process until blended. Add egg whites and process until smoothly blended. Transfer to a bowl. Stir in pine nuts.
2. Drop dough by scant tablespoonfuls (10 mL) about 2 inches (5 cm) apart on prepared cookie sheet. Bake in preheated oven for 20 to 25 minutes or until golden. Cool completely on sheet.

Mixed Nut Macaroons

Not only are these cookies easy to make, but the blend of sweet and salty flavors is particularly delicious.

**MAKES ABOUT
3 1/2 DOZEN COOKIES**

- **Preparation: 20 minutes**
- **Baking: 25 minutes**
- **Freezing: not recommended**

TIP
Have egg whites at room temperature to obtain the best volume.

- **Preheat oven to 325°F (160°C)**
- **Cookie sheet, lined with parchment paper**

2 cups	sweetened flaked coconut	500 mL
2/3 cup	granulated sugar	150 mL
1/4 cup	all-purpose flour	50 mL
4	egg whites	4
1/2 tsp	almond extract	2 mL
1 1/2 cups	chopped deluxe salted mixed nuts (no peanuts)	375 mL

1. In a small bowl, combine coconut, sugar and flour. Mix well. Set aside.
2. In a large bowl, whisk egg whites and almond extract until foamy. With a wooden spoon, stir in coconut mixture and nuts, mixing until all ingredients are moistened.
3. Drop mixture by tablespoonfuls (15 mL) about 2 inches (5 cm) apart on prepared cookie sheet. Bake in preheated oven for 20 to 25 minutes or until golden. Cool completely on sheet.

White Chocolate Cashew Cookies

Crunchy cereal adds a pleasant texture to these and other cookies. It stays crisp during baking.

MAKES ABOUT 3½ DOZEN COOKIES

- **Preparation: 25 minutes**
- **Baking: 14 minutes**
- **Freezing: excellent**

TIPS

Cookies don't seem to be baked when they actually are. They firm up on cooling.

When storing cookies, be sure they are completely cool before packing. Otherwise, they will become soft.

- **Preheat oven to 375°F (190°C)**
- **Cookie sheet, ungreased**

½ cup	semi-sweet chocolate chips	125 mL
1⅓ cups	all-purpose flour	325 mL
1 tsp	baking soda	5 mL
¼ tsp	salt	1 mL
½ cup	butter, softened	125 mL
⅓ cup	granulated sugar	75 mL
⅓ cup	packed brown sugar	75 mL
1	egg	1
1½ cups	slightly crushed corn flakes cereal	375 mL
1 cup	white chocolate chips	250 mL
¾ cup	coarsely chopped cashews	175 mL

1. In a small saucepan over low heat, melt semi-sweet chocolate chips, stirring constantly, until smooth. Set aside to cool.

2. Meanwhile, on a sheet of waxed paper or in a bowl, combine flour, baking soda and salt. Set aside.

3. In a large bowl, using an electric mixer on medium speed, beat butter, granulated and brown sugars and egg until light and creamy, about 3 minutes. Add melted chocolate, mixing until blended. On low speed, gradually add flour mixture, beating until blended. With a wooden spoon, stir in cereal, white chocolate chips and cashews.

4. Drop dough by tablespoonfuls (15 mL) about 2 inches (5 cm) apart on cookie sheet. Flatten slightly with a fork dipped in granulated sugar. Bake in preheated oven for 10 to 14 minutes or until just set but still soft in the center. Cool for 5 minutes on sheet, then transfer to a rack and cool completely.

Variations

Replace corn flakes cereal with crisp rice cereal.

Replace cashews with dried cranberries.

Hawaiian Chews

Crispy outside and chewy inside, these cookies have great flavor and texture. I love the combination of crunchy nuts and chewy coconut and pineapple.

MAKES ABOUT 4½ DOZEN COOKIES

- **Preparation: 25 minutes**
- **Baking: 12 minutes**
- **Freezing: excellent**

TIPS

Brazil nuts have an earthy flavor and unique texture similar to macadamia nuts. They are one of my favorites.

Don't over-bake these cookies, as they'll get too crunchy.

- **Preheat oven to 350°F (180°C)**
- **Cookie sheet, greased or lined with parchment paper**

2 cups	all-purpose flour	500 mL
1 tsp	baking powder	5 mL
½ tsp	baking soda	2 mL
¼ tsp	salt	1 mL
1 tsp	ground cinnamon	5 mL
½ tsp	ground nutmeg	2 mL
½ cup	butter, softened	125 mL
1½ cups	packed brown sugar	375 mL
2	eggs	2
1 tsp	vanilla	5 mL
1½ cups	sweetened flaked coconut	375 mL
1 cup	coarsely chopped Brazil nuts	250 mL
¾ cup	chopped dried pineapple	175 mL

1. On a sheet of waxed paper or in a bowl, combine flour, baking powder, baking soda, salt, cinnamon and nutmeg. Set aside.

2. In a large bowl, using an electric mixer on medium speed, beat butter, brown sugar, eggs and vanilla until light and creamy, about 3 minutes. On low speed, gradually add flour mixture, beating until blended. With a wooden spoon, stir in coconut, nuts and pineapple.

3. Drop dough by tablespoonfuls (15 mL) about 2 inches (5 cm) apart on prepared cookie sheet. Flatten slightly with floured offset spatula or the palm of your hand. Bake in preheated oven for 8 to 12 minutes or until lightly browned around edges. Cool for 5 minutes on sheet, then transfer to a rack and cool completely.

Variation

Replace pineapple with dried mango.

Refrigerator Cookies

Refrigerator cookies, sometimes called icebox cookies or slice-and-bake cookies, are perfect for busy people. They offer old-fashioned homemade goodness and the convenience of ready-made dough. Here's the secret: you make your own dough in advance, shape it into a roll, wrap and refrigerate or freeze. The dough is ready to slice and bake as required. I've noted the minimum chilling time required in all the recipes, but usually it's most convenient for people to prepare dough a day ahead of baking and refrigerate overnight.

Cookie dough, wrapped in plastic wrap, can be refrigerated for up to 2 weeks or frozen for up to 3 months. When freezing, freeze until firm, then wrap the dough again in heavy foil or place it in freezer bags. When you're getting ready to bake, thaw the dough at room temperature for about an hour, or in the refrigerator overnight, until it can be sliced easily.

The most common shape for refrigerator cookies is 2-inch (5 cm) rounds, cut from simple rolls that width in diameter. However, you can also make square cookies by packing the dough into square boxes such as those containing waxed paper or aluminum foil. Whatever their eventual shape, with just one afternoon of preparation, you can make enough cookie dough to last for months. And, if you're prone to over-indulging in freshly baked cookies, refrigerator cookies can help you keep your Cookie Monster appetite in check. You can portion the dough into several smaller rolls, then bake a few cookies at a time rather than a large batch, and savor every little bite.

◄ *Butterscotch Cashew Cookies*

Butterscotch Cashew Cookies

◆

These chewy cookies are a great choice for school lunches. You can bake them as you need them, so they're always fresh.

MAKES ABOUT 4½ DOZEN COOKIES

- **Preparation: 25 minutes**
- **Chilling: 4 hours**
- **Baking: 14 minutes**
- **Freezing: excellent**

TIPS

I prefer combining the dry ingredients on a piece of waxed paper instead of dirtying a bowl. Then I use the paper as a funnel when adding them to the butter mixture.

Chips harden during chilling, which makes it difficult to slice the rolls. That's why these slices are thicker than usual, but they flatten and spread during baking.

For a chewy texture, bake cookies just until golden around the edges. For crisp cookies, bake for the maximum time or until golden overall.

- **Cookie sheet, greased or lined with parchment paper**

2½ cups	all-purpose flour	625 mL
1 tsp	baking soda	5 mL
¼ tsp	salt	1 mL
1 cup	butter, softened	250 mL
1½ cups	packed brown sugar	375 mL
2	eggs	2
1 tsp	vanilla	5 mL
2 cups	butterscotch chips	500 mL
1 cup	chopped cashews	250 mL

1. On a sheet of waxed paper or in a bowl, combine flour, baking soda and salt. Set aside.

2. In a large bowl, using an electric mixer on medium speed, beat butter and brown sugar until light and creamy, about 3 minutes. Add eggs, one at a time, beating well after each addition. Add vanilla. On low speed, gradually add flour mixture, beating until blended. With a wooden spoon, stir in butterscotch chips and cashews. Divide dough into halves. Shape each into a roll 13 inches (32.5 cm) long. Wrap and chill until firm, at least 4 hours.

3. Fifteen minutes before you're ready to bake, preheat oven to 350°F (180°C). Cut rolls into ½-inch (1 cm) slices. Place about 2 inches (5 cm) apart on prepared cookie sheet. Bake in preheated oven for 10 to 14 minutes or until edges are golden and tops are just starting to brown. Cool for 5 minutes on sheet, then transfer to a rack and cool completely.

Variations

Add ½ cup (125 mL) unsweetened flaked coconut along with the chips and nuts.

Substitute peanuts for the cashews.

Peanut Butter Icebox Cookies

Keep a roll of this dough in your refrigerator so you can serve freshly made warm cookies and milk at the drop of a hat. When making refrigerator cookies, I usually chill the dough overnight and bake the following day.

MAKES ABOUT 8 DOZEN COOKIES

- **Preparation: 25 minutes**
- **Chilling: 4 hours**
- **Baking: 11 minutes**
- **Freezing: excellent**

TIPS

If you prefer, use a wooden spoon instead of a mixer.

When cutting dough, ensure that your knife is sharp. I prefer to use a serrated knife for this dough as it contains nuts.

Be sure your peanut butter is fresh. Its high fat content makes it susceptible to rancidity.

When wrapping dough for freezing or storage, wrap tightly in plastic wrap. If you plan to use the dough in the immediate future, waxed paper will do. See page 10 for instructions on freezing dough.

- **Cookie sheet, ungreased**

2 1/4 cups	all-purpose flour	550 mL
3/4 tsp	baking powder	3 mL
3/4 tsp	baking soda	3 mL
1/4 tsp	salt	1 mL
1/2 cup	butter, softened	125 mL
1/2 cup	creamy peanut butter	125 mL
3/4 cup	packed brown sugar	175 mL
2	eggs	2
1 tsp	vanilla	5 mL
1 cup	finely chopped peanuts	250 mL

1. On a sheet of waxed paper or in a bowl, combine flour, baking powder, baking soda and salt. Set aside.

2. In a large bowl, using an electric mixer on medium speed, beat butter, peanut butter, brown sugar, eggs and vanilla until light and creamy, about 3 minutes. On low speed, gradually add flour mixture, beating until blended. With a wooden spoon, stir in peanuts. Divide dough into halves. Shape each into a roll 12 inches (30 cm) long. Wrap and chill until firm, at least 4 hours.

3. Fifteen minutes before you're ready to bake, preheat oven to 375°F (190°C). Cut rolls into 1/4-inch (0.5 cm) slices. Place about 2 inches (5 cm) apart on cookie sheet. Bake in preheated oven for 7 to 11 minutes or until golden. Cool for 5 minutes on sheet, then transfer to a rack and cool completely.

Variations

Add 1/2 cup (125 mL) miniature chocolate chips and reduce peanuts to 1/2 cup (125 mL). The chips are a bit harder to cut, but the taste is great.

Instead of adding the peanuts to the dough, spread them on a sheet of waxed paper and roll the logs in them, pressing lightly into the dough. This gives the cookies a different look.

Seeds and Coconut Refrigerator Cookies

◆

Crunchy with nuts and seeds, the wonderful taste of coconut and, of course, butter — these cookies are simply delightful. This is a big batch recipe — you may want to freeze one or two of the rolls for longer storage.

MAKES ABOUT 13 DOZEN COOKIES

- **Preparation: 25 minutes**
- **Chilling: 3 hours**
- **Baking: 24 minutes**
- **Freezing: excellent**

TIPS

For a different look, roll the logs of dough in finely chopped nuts, colored sugar or chocolate sprinkles before chilling.

When cutting dough, always ensure that your knife is sharp. I prefer to use a serrated knife for this dough as it contains seeds and nuts.

If you like crispy cookies, bake them a little longer, until golden overall. Or try cutting the slices a little thinner. The thinner the cookie, the crispier the texture.

- **Cookie sheet, greased or lined with parchment paper**

2 cups	butter, softened	500 mL
1½ cups	granulated sugar	375 mL
½ tsp	salt	2 mL
3 cups	all-purpose flour	750 mL
2 cups	sweetened shredded coconut	500 mL
½ cup	finely chopped pecans	125 mL
½ cup	sesame seeds	125 mL
¼ cup	flax seeds	50 mL
¼ cup	sunflower seeds	50 mL

1. In a large bowl, using an electric mixer on medium speed, beat butter and sugar until light and creamy, about 3 minutes. On low speed, add salt, then gradually add flour, beating until dough becomes too stiff for the mixer, then finish mixing with a wooden spoon. Stir in coconut, pecans, sesame seeds, flax seeds and sunflower seeds. Using your hands, knead to form a smooth dough. Divide dough into thirds. Shape each into a roll 13 inches (32.5 cm) long. Wrap and chill until firm, at least 3 hours.

2. Fifteen minutes before you're ready to bake, preheat oven to 300°F (150°C). Cut rolls into ¼-inch (0.5 cm) slices. Place about 1 inch (2.5 cm) apart on prepared cookie sheet. Bake in preheated oven for 19 to 24 minutes or until golden. Cool for 5 minutes on sheet, then transfer to a rack and cool completely.

Variations

Vary the seeds to suit your taste. Pumpkin seeds are a nice addition, or use only two kinds of seeds — just make sure the quantity of seeds totals 1 cup (250 mL).

Omit pecans.

Lemon Cranberry Pistachio Wafers

This cookie has a tender, buttery, shortbread-like texture and colorful red and green flecks scattered throughout.

MAKES ABOUT 4 DOZEN COOKIES

- **Preparation: 25 minutes**
- **Chilling: 3 hours**
- **Baking: 12 minutes**
- **Freezing: excellent**

TIPS

In refrigerator rolls, ingredients like nuts and fruit are much easier to slice if they are chopped fairly fine.

When cutting dough, always ensure that your knife is sharp. I prefer to use a serrated knife for this dough as it contains nuts.

- **Cookie sheet, ungreased**

1¾ cups	all-purpose flour	425 mL
¼ tsp	baking powder	1 mL
¼ tsp	salt	1 mL
¾ cup	butter, softened	175 mL
½ cup	confectioner's (icing) sugar, sifted	125 mL
1	egg	1
1 tbsp	grated lemon zest	15 mL
⅓ cup	finely chopped pistachios	75 mL
¼ cup	chopped dried cranberries	50 mL

1. On a sheet of waxed paper or in a bowl, combine flour, baking powder and salt. Set aside.

2. In a large bowl, using an electric mixer on medium speed, beat butter, confectioner's sugar, egg and lemon zest until light and creamy, about 3 minutes. On low speed, gradually add flour mixture, beating until blended. With a wooden spoon, stir in pistachios and cranberries. Shape into a roll 12 inches (30 cm) long. Wrap and chill until firm, at least 3 hours.

3. Fifteen minutes before you're ready to bake, preheat oven to 375°F (190°C). Cut roll into ¼-inch (0.5 cm) slices. Place about 1 inch (2.5 cm) apart on cookie sheet. Bake in preheated oven for 8 to 12 minutes or until golden. Cool for 5 minutes on sheet, then transfer to a rack and cool completely.

Variations

Replace lemon zest with orange zest.

Replace dried cranberries with dried cherries.

Dip half of each cookie in melted white or dark chocolate.

Lemon Lime Slices

These small delicate cookies are incredibly tender and have a wonderful burst of citrus flavor. They're nice with a cup of tea or dish of sherbet.

MAKES ABOUT 6 DOZEN COOKIES

- Preparation: 25 minutes
- Chilling: 3 hours
- Baking: 12 minutes
- Freezing: excellent

TIPS

I recommend using a sharp serrated knife to slice these cookies. When slicing, rotate the roll frequently to avoid flattening one side and to ensure evenly shaped cookies that are round.

A reliable oven thermometer is a good investment. It will tell you whether your oven heat is aligned with the setting. If not, you can adjust it accordingly.

- **Cookie sheet, greased or lined with parchment paper**

1¾ cups	all-purpose flour	425 mL
¼ cup	cornstarch	50 mL
¼ tsp	salt	1 mL
¾ cup	butter, softened	175 mL
⅓ cup	confectioner's (icing) sugar, sifted	75 mL
1 tbsp	grated lemon zest	15 mL
1 tbsp	grated lime zest	15 mL
2 tbsp	freshly squeezed lemon juice	25 mL
2 tbsp	freshly squeezed lime juice	25 mL
⅔ cup	colored coarse sugar	150 mL

1. On a sheet of waxed paper or in a bowl, combine flour, cornstarch and salt. Set aside.

2. In a large bowl, using an electric mixer on medium speed, beat butter, confectioner's sugar, lemon and lime zests, and lemon and lime juices until light and creamy. On low speed, gradually add flour mixture until dough becomes too stiff for the mixer, then finish mixing with a wooden spoon until smooth. Divide dough into halves. Shape each into a roll 9 inches (22.5 cm) long. Spread colored sugar on a sheet of waxed paper and roll logs in it until nicely coated. Wrap and chill until firm, at least 3 hours.

3. Fifteen minutes before you're ready to bake, preheat oven to 350°F (180°C). Cut rolls into ¼-inch (0.5 cm) slices. Place about 1 inch (2.5 cm) apart on prepared cookie sheet. Bake in preheated oven for 8 to 12 minutes or until golden around edges. Cool for 10 minutes on sheet.

Variations

If you like lemon, substitute additional lemon zest and juice for the lime. Or omit lime zest and juice and add, if desired, ¼ cup (50 mL) poppy seeds with the dry ingredients.

For a different finish, place ⅔ cup (150 mL) confectioner's sugar in a plastic bag. Add warm cookies in batches and toss until coated. Transfer to a rack and cool completely, then place in bag with remaining sugar and shake again.

These make nice sandwich cookies. Spread a little lemon curd between two cookies.

Chocolate-Dipped Cinnamon Hazelnut Rounds

Keep dough for these cookies on hand if your family or friends love eating nuts. You'll be able to bake them as an unexpected treat in a matter of minutes.

MAKES ABOUT 3½ DOZEN COOKIES

- **Preparation: 35 minutes**
- **Chilling: 3 hours**
- **Baking: 22 minutes**
- **Cooking (Glaze): 4 minutes**
- **Freezing: excellent**

TIPS

This dough can be mixed in a food processor. Cut cold butter into chunks before using.

To toast hazelnuts, place them in a shallow pan and bake, stirring occasionally, at 350°F (180°C) for 8 to 10 minutes or until fragrant and starting to turn golden. Cool completely before using.

When grinding nuts in a food processor, add a bit of the flour or sugar from the recipe to prevent clumping.

- **Cookie sheet, greased or lined with parchment paper**

COOKIE

1 cup	all-purpose flour	250 mL
½ cup	hazelnuts, toasted and ground (see Tips)	125 mL
½ tsp	ground cinnamon	2 mL
¼ tsp	salt	1 mL
½ cup	butter, softened	125 mL
½ cup	confectioner's (icing) sugar, sifted	125 mL
1	egg white	1
½ tsp	vanilla	2 mL

GLAZE

5	squares (1 oz/28 g each) semi-sweet chocolate, chopped	5
1 tsp	vegetable oil	5 mL

1. *Cookie:* On a sheet of waxed paper or in a bowl, combine flour, hazelnuts, cinnamon and salt. Set aside.

2. In a large bowl, using an electric mixer on medium speed, beat butter, confectioner's sugar, egg white and vanilla until light and creamy, about 3 minutes. On low speed, gradually add flour mixture, mixing until blended. Shape dough into a roll 11 inches (27.5 cm) long. Wrap and chill until firm, at least 3 hours.

3. Fifteen minutes before you're ready to bake, preheat oven to 325°F (160°C). Cut roll into ¼-inch (0.5 cm) slices. Place about 1 inch (2.5 cm) apart on prepared cookie sheet. Bake in preheated oven for 18 to 22 minutes or until golden around edges. Let cool for 5 minutes on sheet, then transfer to a rack and cool completely.

4. *Glaze:* In small saucepan over low heat, heat chocolate and oil, stirring until chocolate is melted and mixture is smooth. Dip half of each cookie in chocolate mixture. Place on rack over a piece of waxed paper. Set aside until chocolate hardens, about 1 hour.

Variations

Replace hazelnuts with unblanched almonds or pecans.

Add a pinch each of ground nutmeg and ground cloves.

Maple Walnut
Slice-and-Bake Cookies

◆

To double the maple impact, serve these cookies with a dish of maple walnut ice cream or use them to make ice cream sandwiches.

**MAKES ABOUT
8 DOZEN COOKIES**

- **Preparation: 25 minutes**
- **Chilling: 4 hours**
- **Baking: 12 minutes**
- **Freezing: excellent**

TIPS

Although it's not as common as some other extracts, maple extract is an excellent product with a true maple flavor. It's sold in grocery stores where you find vanilla.

To get perfectly round cookies, pack the dough into an appropriate-size used roll from waxed paper, plastic wrap or aluminum foil. Once chilled, simply cut the tube open. When using frozen rolls of dough, let them thaw in the refrigerator overnight or for about 1 hour at room temperature, until they can be sliced easily.

- **Cookie sheet, ungreased**

2²⁄₃ cups	all-purpose flour	650 mL
1 tsp	baking powder	5 mL
½ tsp	baking soda	2 mL
¼ tsp	salt	1 mL
1 cup	butter, softened	250 mL
½ cup	granulated sugar	125 mL
½ cup	packed brown sugar	125 mL
2	eggs	2
1½ tsp	maple extract	7 mL
1½ cups	chopped walnuts	375 mL

1. On a sheet of waxed paper or in a bowl, combine flour, baking powder, baking soda and salt. Set aside.

2. In a large bowl, using an electric mixer on medium speed, beat butter, granulated and brown sugars, eggs and maple extract until light and creamy, about 3 minutes. On low speed, gradually add flour mixture, beating until blended. With a wooden spoon, stir in walnuts. Divide dough into halves. Shape each into a roll 12 inches (30 cm) long. Wrap and chill until firm, at least 4 hours.

3. Fifteen minutes before you're ready to bake, preheat oven to 375°F (190°C). Cut rolls into ¼-inch (0.5 cm) slices. Place about 1 inch (2.5 cm) apart on cookie sheet. Bake in preheated oven for 8 to 12 minutes or until lightly browned. Cool for 5 minutes on sheet, then transfer to a rack and cool completely.

Variation
Replace maple extract with vanilla and walnuts with pecans.

Brazil Nut Squares

These squares work on the same principle as refrigerator rolls, but they are a different shape.

**MAKES ABOUT
4 DOZEN COOKIES**

- **Preparation: 25 minutes**
- **Chilling: 4 hours**
- **Baking: 12 minutes**
- **Freezing: excellent**

TIPS

Use a small, empty waxed paper, plastic wrap or aluminum foil box.

For fancier presentation, dip half of each cookie, on the diagonal, in melted chocolate.

For a crispier cookie, bake a little longer until golden overall, not just around the edges.

Brazil nuts have a buttery flavor that is quite different from other nuts. With their golden color and traces of dark skin, they give a nice rustic look to the cookies, too.

- **Cookie sheet, ungreased**

1¾ cups	all-purpose flour	425 mL
¼ tsp	baking powder	1 mL
¼ tsp	baking soda	1 mL
¼ tsp	salt	1 mL
¾ cup	butter, softened	175 mL
½ cup	packed brown sugar	125 mL
1	egg	1
1 tsp	vanilla	5 mL
1 cup	finely chopped Brazil nuts	250 mL

1. On a sheet of waxed paper or in a bowl, combine flour, baking powder, baking soda and salt. Set aside.

2. In a large bowl, using an electric mixer on medium speed, beat butter, brown sugar, egg and vanilla until light and creamy, about 3 minutes. On low speed, gradually add flour mixture, beating until blended. With a wooden spoon, stir in nuts.

3. Line a 12- by 2- by 2-inch (30 cm by 5 cm by 5 cm) box with plastic wrap (see Tips). Pack dough into box firmly and evenly. Cover and chill until firm, at least 4 hours.

4. Fifteen minutes before you're ready to bake, preheat oven to 375°F (190°C). Cut bar into ¼-inch (0.5 cm) slices. Place 1 inch (2.5 cm) apart on cookie sheet. Bake in preheated oven for 8 to 12 minutes or until golden around edges. Cool for 5 minutes on sheet, then transfer to a rack and cool completely.

Variations

Replace Brazil nuts with cashews, pecans or hazelnuts.
Shape the dough into a roll for round cookies.

Oatmeal Raisin Rounds

Here's an old-fashioned favorite in an easy-to-bake form.

MAKES ABOUT 5 DOZEN COOKIES

- **Preparation: 25 minutes**
- **Chilling: 4 hours**
- **Baking: 12 minutes**
- **Freezing: excellent**

TIPS

There are a lot of raisins in this dough, which gives the cookies a nice flavor and appearance. Chop them very finely to make slicing easy.

If your dough doesn't cut nicely, simply reshape the cookies as you put them on the cookie sheet, using your fingers to stick the dough together.

A reliable oven thermometer is a good investment. It will tell you whether your oven heat is aligned with the setting. If not, you can adjust it accordingly.

- **Cookie sheet, ungreased**

1 cup	all-purpose flour	250 mL
½ tsp	baking soda	2 mL
¼ tsp	salt	1 mL
1 tsp	ground cinnamon	5 mL
½ cup	butter, softened	125 mL
½ cup	granulated sugar	125 mL
½ cup	packed brown sugar	125 mL
1	egg	1
2 tbsp	molasses	25 mL
1½ cups	quick-cooking rolled oats	375 mL
1 cup	raisins, finely chopped	250 mL

1. On a sheet of waxed paper or in a small bowl, combine flour, baking soda, salt and cinnamon. Set aside.

2. In a large bowl, using an electric mixer on medium speed, beat butter, granulated and brown sugars, egg and molasses until light and creamy, about 3 minutes. On low speed, gradually add flour mixture, beating until blended. With a wooden spoon, stir in oats and raisins. Divide dough into halves. Shape each into a roll 8 inches (20 cm) long. Wrap and chill until firm, at least 4 hours.

3. Fifteen minutes before you're ready to bake, preheat oven to 375°F (190°C). Cut rolls into ¼-inch (0.5 cm) slices. Place about 2 inches (5 cm) apart on cookie sheet. Bake in preheated oven for 8 to 12 minutes or until golden. Cool for 5 minutes on sheet, then transfer to a rack and cool completely.

Variations

Replace raisins with dates or dried cranberries.

The hint of molasses is nice, but it can be omitted if you prefer.

Add 1 tbsp (15 mL) grated orange or lemon zest along with the egg.

Roll logs in finely chopped walnuts before chilling.

Orange Fig Pinwheels

I speak from experience when I say that even people who claim they don't like figs, love these cookies.

MAKES ABOUT 4 DOZEN COOKIES

- **Preparation: 40 minutes**
- **Chilling: 4 hours**
- **Baking: 16 minutes**
- **Freezing: excellent**

TIPS

Use whatever variety of fig you prefer. Golden Calimyrna figs look the best with apricot jam. If you're using Black Mission figs, substitute an equal quantity of raspberry jam for the apricot.

Be sure to cut the woody stems off the figs before chopping.

Use thick jam, not light, sugar-reduced spread, which is too soft to work in these cookies.

- **Cookie sheet, greased or lined with parchment paper**

1¾ cups	all-purpose flour	425 mL
2 tsp	baking powder	10 mL
¼ tsp	salt	1 mL
½ cup	butter, softened	125 mL
1 cup	granulated sugar	250 mL
1	egg	1
1 tsp	vanilla	5 mL
¾ cup	finely chopped dried figs	175 mL
⅓ cup	sweetened flaked coconut	75 mL
½ cup	apricot jam	125 mL

1. On a sheet of waxed paper or in a bowl, combine flour, baking powder and salt. Set aside.

2. In a large bowl, using an electric mixer on medium speed, beat butter, sugar, egg and vanilla until light and creamy, about 3 minutes. On low speed, gradually add flour mixture, beating until dough becomes too stiff for the mixer, then finish mixing with a wooden spoon. Using your hands, knead to form a smooth dough. Between two sheets of waxed paper, roll out dough into a 12- by 9-inch (30 cm by 23 cm) rectangle.

3. In a small bowl, combine figs, coconut and jam. Mix well. Remove top sheet of waxed paper from dough. Spread jam mixture evenly over dough leaving a ½-inch (1 cm) border along one long side. Starting with the opposite long side and using the bottom sheet of waxed paper to help you, roll up the dough tightly jelly-roll fashion. Press edge to seal and, using your hands, mold roll into nicely rounded shape. Wrap and chill until firm, at least 4 hours.

4. Fifteen minutes before you're ready to bake, preheat oven to 375°F (190°C). Cut roll into ¼-inch (0.5 cm) slices. Place about 2 inches (5 cm) apart on prepared cookie sheet. Bake in preheated oven for 12 to 16 minutes or until golden around edges. Cool for 5 minutes on sheet, then transfer to a rack and cool completely.

Variations

Replace figs with dried apricots or chopped nuts.

Use marmalade or peach jam and golden Calimyrna figs.

Thin Oatmeal Crisps

◆

These cookies are great on their own and, with a date or raspberry jam filling, they also make delicious sandwich cookies.

**MAKES ABOUT
14 DOZEN COOKIES**

- **Preparation: 20 minutes**
- **Chilling: 4 hours**
- **Baking: 12 minutes**
- **Freezing: excellent**

TIPS

This is a big-batch recipe — you may want to freeze one or two of the rolls for longer storage.

Although recipes usually call for an electric mixer to blend ingredients, you can almost always use a wooden spoon when making cookies. It just takes more physical effort. With either method, it usually takes about 3 minutes to get a butter-and-sugar mixture light and creamy.

A thin, sharp serrated knife, like a bread knife, works well for cutting this dough into thin slices.

- **Cookie sheet, greased or lined with parchment paper**

2 cups	all-purpose flour	500 mL
1 tsp	baking soda	5 mL
½ tsp	salt	2 mL
1 cup	butter, softened	250 mL
1 cup	packed brown sugar	250 mL
½ cup	water	125 mL
3 cups	quick-cooking rolled oats	750 mL

1. On a sheet of waxed paper or in a bowl, combine flour, baking soda and salt. Set aside.

2. In a large bowl, using an electric mixer on medium speed, beat butter and brown sugar until smooth and creamy, about 3 minutes. On low speed, add water and oats. Gradually add flour mixture, beating until blended. Divide dough into halves. Shape each into a roll 11 inches (27.5 cm) long. Wrap and chill until firm, at least 4 hours.

3. Fifteen minutes before you're ready to bake, preheat oven to 375°F (190°C). Cut rolls into ⅛-inch (0.25 cm) slices. Place about 1 inch (2.5 cm) apart on prepared cookie sheet. Bake in preheated oven for 8 to 12 minutes or until golden. Cool for 5 minutes on sheet, then transfer to a rack and cool completely.

Variations
Add 1½ tsp (7 mL) ground cinnamon to the dry ingredients.

Add 1 tbsp (15 mL) grated orange zest to the butter mixture.

Fruit and Spice Rounds

◆

These cookies have a crispy texture and the blend of spices nicely complements the abundance of fruit and nuts. This is a big-batch recipe — you may want to freeze one or two of the rolls for longer storage.

MAKES ABOUT 13 DOZEN COOKIES

- **Preparation: 25 minutes**
- **Chilling: 4 hours**
- **Baking: 12 minutes**
- **Freezing: excellent**

TIPS

Use a food processor to easily chop the dates, raisins and nuts.

When wrapping dough for freezing or storage, wrap tightly in plastic wrap. If you're using the dough in the immediate future, waxed paper will do.

• **Cookie sheet, greased or lined with parchment paper**

3¼ cups	all-purpose flour	800 mL
1 tsp	baking soda	5 mL
2 tsp	ground cinnamon	10 mL
½ tsp	ground cloves	2 mL
½ tsp	ground nutmeg	2 mL
1 cup	butter, softened	250 mL
1½ cups	granulated sugar	375 mL
3	eggs	3
1 cup	chopped dates	250 mL
1 cup	chopped raisins	250 mL
1 cup	finely chopped walnuts	250 mL

1. On a sheet of waxed paper or in a bowl, combine flour, baking soda, cinnamon, cloves and nutmeg. Set aside.

2. In a large bowl, using an electric mixer on medium speed, beat butter and sugar until light and creamy, about 3 minutes. Add eggs, one at a time, beating well after each addition. On low speed, gradually add flour mixture, beating until blended. With a wooden spoon, stir in dates, raisins and walnuts. Divide dough into thirds. Shape each into a roll 13 inches (32.5 cm) long. Wrap and chill until firm, at least 4 hours.

3. Fifteen minutes before you're ready to bake, preheat oven to 375°F (190°C). Cut rolls into ¼-inch (0.5 cm) slices. Place about 2 inches (5 cm) apart on prepared cookie sheet. Bake in preheated oven for 8 to 12 minutes or until lightly browned. Cool for 5 minutes on sheet, then transfer to a rack and cool completely.

Variations

Replace raisins with dried cranberries or apricots.

Omit walnuts or use your favorite nut.

To dress up these cookies, add a lemon glaze. Mix 2 cups (500 mL) confectioner's (icing) sugar, sifted, with ¼ cup (50 mL) lemon juice. Spread evenly over tops.

Apricot Almond Refrigerator Cookies

You can't go wrong with a few rolls of these tasty cookies tucked away in your freezer.

MAKES ABOUT 9 DOZEN COOKIES

- **Preparation: 25 minutes**
- **Chilling: 4 hours**
- **Baking: 12 minutes**
- **Freezing: excellent**

TIPS

The dough for refrigerator cookies is often soft when you shape it, but it firms up with chilling. I prefer to leave it overnight to make sure it is firm enough for easy cutting.

I prefer combining the dry ingredients on a piece of waxed paper instead of dirtying a bowl. Then I use the paper as a funnel when adding them to the butter mixture.

Check your cookie sheets. Dark, nonstick ones bake cookies faster, so it's wise to set your timer for the minimum time. You can always bake longer, but you can't change over-baked cookies.

◆

- **Cookie sheet, ungreased**

2¾ cups	all-purpose flour	675 mL
1 tsp	baking powder	5 mL
½ tsp	baking soda	2 mL
¼ tsp	salt	1 mL
1 cup	butter, softened	250 mL
1 cup	granulated sugar	250 mL
2	eggs	2
1 tsp	vanilla	5 mL
¾ cup	finely chopped almonds	175 mL
¾ cup	finely chopped dried apricots	175 mL

1. On a sheet of waxed paper or in a bowl, combine flour, baking powder, baking soda and salt. Set aside.

2. In a large bowl, using an electric mixer on medium speed, beat butter, sugar, eggs and vanilla until light and creamy, about 3 minutes. On low speed, gradually add flour mixture, beating until blended. With a wooden spoon, stir in almonds and apricots. Divide dough into halves. Shape each into a roll 14 inches (35 cm) long. Wrap and chill until firm, at least 4 hours.

3. Fifteen minutes before you're ready to bake, preheat oven to 375°F (190°C). Cut rolls into ¼-inch (0.5 cm) slices. Place about 2 inches (5 cm) apart on cookie sheet. Bake in preheated oven for 8 to 12 minutes or until golden. Cool for 5 minutes on sheet, then transfer to a rack and cool completely.

Chocolate Orange Almond Slices

◆

Although these cookies look like they would be difficult to make, they are actually quite easy. The checkerboard appearance is achieved by cutting the dough in half, flavoring it differently, then assembling it before baking.

MAKES ABOUT 8 DOZEN COOKIES

- **Preparation: 40 minutes**
- **Chilling: 6 hours, divided**
- **Baking: 12 minutes**
- **Freezing: excellent**

TIPS

The same 2 doughs can be used to make several different looks. You can simply make 2 layers or 4 layers for striped cookies in a square bar.

Dough for refrigerator cookies is often soft when you shape it, but it firms up with chilling. I prefer to leave it overnight to make sure it is firm enough for easy cutting.

When cutting dough, always ensure that your knife is sharp.

- **Cookie sheet, ungreased**

2½ cups	all-purpose flour	625 mL
1½ tsp	baking powder	7 mL
¼ tsp	salt	1 mL
1 cup	butter, softened	250 mL
1 cup	granulated sugar	250 mL
½ cup	packed brown sugar	125 mL
1	egg	1
1 tbsp	grated orange zest	15 mL
⅓ cup	ground almonds	75 mL
2	squares (1 oz/28 g each) semi-sweet chocolate, melted and cooled	2

1. On a sheet of waxed paper or in a bowl, combine flour, baking powder and salt. Set aside.

2. In a large bowl, using an electric mixer on medium speed, beat butter, granulated and brown sugars and egg until light and creamy, about 3 minutes. On low speed, gradually add flour mixture, beating until blended. Divide dough into halves. With a wooden spoon, stir orange zest and almonds into 1 portion. Stir melted chocolate into the other portion. Shape each into a roll 12 inches (30 cm) long. Chill until firm, about 2 hours.

3. Cut each roll lengthwise into quarters. Reassemble 2 rolls, alternating chocolate and orange sections. Wrap and chill until firm, at least 4 hours.

4. Fifteen minutes before you're ready to bake, preheat oven to 375°F (190°C). Cut rolls into ¼-inch (0.5 cm) slices. Place about 1 inch (2.5 cm) apart on cookie sheet. Bake in preheated oven for 8 to 12 minutes or until golden around the edges. Cool for 5 minutes on sheet, then transfer to a rack and cool completely.

Spumoni Slices

These cookies have the appearance and flavor of the popular Italian ice cream. Their colorful layers are sure to be a hit.

MAKES ABOUT 4 DOZEN COOKIES

- **Preparation: 35 minutes**
- **Chilling: 3 hours**
- **Baking: 11 minutes**
- **Freezing: excellent**

TIPS

The amount of food coloring you'll need depends upon the kind you're using. Paste colors are much stronger than liquid ones, so judge accordingly. Add just enough to make a pleasant color.

To distribute food coloring evenly, knead it into the dough using the palm of your hand. Add a little at a time until the right shade is reached. Keep in mind that color lightens slightly during baking.

- **Cookie sheet, ungreased**

2¼ cups	all-purpose flour	550 mL
¼ tsp	baking soda	1 mL
¼ tsp	salt	1 mL
1 cup	butter, softened	250 mL
⅔ cup	granulated sugar	150 mL
1	egg	1
1	square (1 oz/28 g) semi-sweet chocolate, melted and cooled	1
⅓ cup	finely chopped pistachios	75 mL
	Green food coloring	
⅓ cup	finely chopped red candied cherries	75 mL
¼ tsp	almond extract	1 mL
	Red food coloring	

1. On a sheet of waxed paper or in a bowl, combine flour, baking soda and salt. Set aside.

2. In a large bowl, using an electric mixer on medium speed, beat butter, sugar and egg until light and creamy, about 3 minutes. On low speed, gradually add flour mixture, mixing until smooth. Divide dough into thirds. With a wooden spoon, stir melted chocolate into 1 portion. Stir pistachios and enough green food coloring to make a pastel dough into the second portion (see Tips). Stir cherries, almond extract and enough red coloring to make a pink dough into the third portion. Line an empty 12- by 2- by 2-inch (30 cm by 5 cm by 5 cm) waxed paper box with waxed paper or plastic wrap. Press pink dough evenly into box. Cover with chocolate dough, then green dough. Press down firmly to make even layers. Cover and chill until firm, at least 3 hours.

3. Fifteen minutes before you're ready to bake, preheat oven to 375°F (190°C). Cut roll into ¼-inch (0.5 cm) slices. Place about 2 inches (5 cm) apart on cookie sheet. Bake in preheated oven for 7 to 11 minutes or until set and lightly browned around edges. Cool for 5 minutes on sheet, then transfer to a rack and cool completely.

Chocolate Chip Refrigerator Cookies

Once you've tried these, you'll never buy another roll of slice 'n' bake chocolate chip cookies. They are delicious and very easy to make.

MAKES ABOUT 8 DOZEN COOKIES

- **Preparation: 30 minutes**
- **Chilling: 4 hours**
- **Baking: 12 minutes**
- **Freezing: excellent**

TIPS

When chilling, wrap dough in waxed paper or plastic wrap.

The chocolate chips make cutting a bit difficult, but not to worry. If the rounds aren't even, reshape them on the cookie sheet with your fingers. The cookies will look great when baked and taste even better.

Rolls of cookie dough can also be frozen. Thaw for about an hour at room temperature or in the refrigerator overnight, until the dough can be sliced easily.

- **Cookie sheet, ungreased**

2¾ cups	all-purpose flour	675 mL
1 tsp	baking soda	5 mL
¼ tsp	baking powder	1 mL
¼ tsp	salt	1 mL
1 cup	butter, softened	250 mL
1 cup	packed brown sugar	250 mL
½ cup	granulated sugar	125 mL
2	eggs	2
1 tsp	vanilla	5 mL
1 cup	semi-sweet chocolate chips	250 mL
½ cup	finely chopped pecans	125 mL

1. On a sheet of waxed paper or in a bowl, combine flour, baking soda, baking powder and salt. Set aside.

2. In a large bowl, using an electric mixer on medium speed, beat butter and brown and granulated sugars until light and creamy, about 3 minutes. Add eggs, one at a time, beating well after each addition. Add vanilla. On low speed, gradually add flour mixture, beating until blended. With a wooden spoon, stir in chocolate chips and pecans. Divide dough into halves. Shape each into a roll 12 inches (30 cm) long. Wrap and chill until firm, at least 4 hours.

3. Fifteen minutes before you're ready to bake, preheat oven to 350°F (180°C). Cut rolls into ¼-inch (0.5 cm) slices. Place about 2 inches (5 cm) apart on cookie sheet. Bake in preheated oven for 8 to 12 minutes or until light golden. Cool for 5 minutes on sheet, then transfer to a rack and cool completely.

Variations

Use milk chocolate chips or miniature semi-sweet chocolate chips.

Omit nuts or replace pecans with your favorite nut.

Slice 'n' Bake Brownie Cookies

◆

These yummy cookies remind me of bite-size brownies.

**MAKES ABOUT
5½ DOZEN COOKIES**

- **Preparation: 30 minutes**
- **Chilling: 2 hours**
- **Baking: 12 minutes**
- **Freezing: excellent**

TIPS

I prefer combining the dry ingredients on a piece of waxed paper instead of dirtying a bowl. Then I use the paper as a funnel when adding them to the butter mixture.

As you cut the roll, rotate it frequently to avoid flattening one side.

If a recipe makes more than one roll, remove only one at a time from the refrigerator for slicing.

- **Cookie sheet, ungreased**

2½ cups	all-purpose flour	625 mL
1 tsp	baking powder	5 mL
½ tsp	baking soda	2 mL
¼ tsp	salt	1 mL
1 cup	butter, softened	250 mL
1½ cups	granulated sugar	375 mL
1	egg	1
1 cup	milk chocolate chips, melted and cooled	250 mL
¾ cup	miniature semi-sweet chocolate chips	175 mL
¾ cup	finely chopped pecans	175 mL
⅓ cup	coarse granulated sugar	75 mL

1. On a sheet of waxed paper or in a bowl, combine flour, baking powder, baking soda and salt. Set aside.

2. In a large bowl, using an electric mixer on medium speed, beat butter, granulated sugar and egg until light and creamy, about 3 minutes. On low speed, beat in melted chocolate. Gradually add flour mixture, beating until blended. With a wooden spoon, stir in chocolate chips and pecans. Divide dough into halves. Shape each into a roll 13 inches (32.5 cm) long. Wrap and chill until firm, at least 2 hours.

3. Fifteen minutes before you're ready to bake, preheat oven to 375°F (190°C). Cut rolls into ⅜-inch (0.95 cm) slices. Place about 2 inches (5 cm) apart on cookie sheet. Sprinkle coarse sugar evenly over tops. Bake in preheated oven for 8 to 12 minutes or until golden around edges. Cool for 5 minutes on sheet, then transfer to a rack and cool completely.

Variations

For a stronger chocolate flavor, replace milk chocolate chips with semi-sweet chocolate chips.

The coarse sugar on top adds a nice finishing touch, but it can be omitted. Look for it in bulk or cake decorating stores.

Orange Coffee Pecan Slices

These refrigerator cookies are a good choice if you have people with egg allergies in the house. Keep a roll handy in your refrigerator. They're ready when you need them.

MAKES ABOUT 8 DOZEN COOKIES

- **Preparation: 30 minutes**
- **Chilling: 2 hours**
- **Baking: 11 minutes**
- **Freezing: excellent**

TIPS

Be sure to remove the zest from oranges and lemons before you cut them to squeeze out the juice. Oranges with a thick, rough skin will give you more zest, but less juice.

One orange should give you about $1/3$ cup (75 mL) juice and 4 tsp (20 mL) grated zest.

A thin knife is usually the best choice for cutting dough, but if it contains chunky ingredients, you may find a serrated knife works better. Just make sure your knife is sharp.

- **Cookie sheet, greased or lined with parchment paper**

2¾ cups	all-purpose flour	675 mL
1 tbsp	instant espresso coffee powder	15 mL
2 tsp	baking powder	10 mL
¼ tsp	salt	1 mL
¾ cup	butter, softened	175 mL
1 cup	packed brown sugar	250 mL
1 tbsp	grated orange zest	15 mL
¼ cup	orange juice	50 mL
1 cup	chopped pecans	250 mL

1. On a sheet of waxed paper or in a bowl, combine flour, coffee powder, baking powder and salt. Set aside.

2. In a large bowl, using an electric mixer on medium speed, beat butter, brown sugar, and orange zest and juice until smooth. On low speed, gradually add flour mixture, beating until blended. With a wooden spoon, stir in pecans. Divide dough into halves. Shape each into a roll 12 inches (30 cm) long. Wrap and chill until firm, at least 2 hours.

3. Fifteen minutes before you're ready to bake, preheat oven to 375°F (190°C). Cut rolls into ¼-inch (0.5 cm) slices. Place about 1 inch (2.5 cm) apart on prepared cookie sheet. Bake in preheated oven for 7 to 11 minutes or until golden around edges. Cool for 5 minutes on sheet, then transfer to a rack and cool completely.

Variation
Omit the coffee powder if you prefer a plain orange flavor.

Ginger Orange Pecan Crisps

◆

These cookies are a good choice for ginger fans. This is a big-batch recipe. You may want to freeze one of the rolls for future use.

MAKES ABOUT 14½ DOZEN COOKIES

- **Preparation: 25 minutes**
- **Chilling: 4 hours**
- **Baking: 12 minutes**
- **Freezing: excellent**

TIPS

Turbinado is a raw sugar that is golden in color. It is available in most large grocery stores, bulk stores and natural foods stores. Demerara, muscovado or other raw sugars work equally well on these cookies. You can also use coarse or regular granulated sugar.

Instead of sprinkling sugar on top of the cookies, you can roll the logs in sugar to coat the edges. You'll need about ¾ cup (175 mL) sugar for 2 rolls.

Crystallized ginger is sold in small rounds and chunks. I find the rounds easier to cut.

- **Cookie sheet, ungreased**

1 cup	butter, softened	250 mL
1 cup	confectioner's (icing) sugar, sifted	250 mL
1	egg	1
1 tbsp	grated orange zest	15 mL
¼ tsp	salt	1 mL
2¼ cups	all-purpose flour	550 mL
¾ cup	coarsely chopped almonds	175 mL
¾ cup	finely chopped crystallized ginger	175 mL
⅓ cup	turbinado or other raw cane sugar (see Tips)	75 mL

1. In a large bowl, using an electric mixer on medium speed, beat butter and confectioner's sugar until light and creamy, about 3 minutes. Add egg and orange zest, mixing until smooth. On low speed, add salt, then gradually add flour, beating until dough becomes too stiff for the mixer, then finish mixing with a wooden spoon. Stir in almonds and ginger. Divide dough into halves. Shape each into a roll 11 inches (27.5 cm) long. Wrap and chill until firm, at least 4 hours.

2. Fifteen minutes before you're ready to bake, preheat oven to 375°F (190°C). Cut rolls into ⅛-inch (0.25 cm) slices. Place about 1 inch (2.5 cm) apart on cookie sheet. Sprinkle sugar over tops. Bake in preheated oven for 8 to 12 minutes or until golden around edges. Cool for 5 minutes on sheet, then transfer to a rack and cool completely.

Variation
Omit orange zest.

Pressed, Cutout and Sandwich Cookies

Pressed cookies result when relatively soft dough is pushed through a pastry bag or a cookie press. A cookie press is a device that comes with a variety of design plates. It is easy to operate — all you do is choose your design, pack the dough into the tube and press it through onto the cookie sheet. Using this device, anyone can produce perfectly shaped cookies with relatively intricate designs. When using a cookie press, follow the manufacturer's instructions. Be sure to pack the dough tightly to ensure there are no air holes, otherwise you won't get smooth shapes.

Cutout or rolled cookies are another example of cookie artistry at work. Sometimes the cookies are sprinkled with plain or colored sugar, frosted or embellished with decorations, such as chocolate sprinkles or candies. There are so many interesting cookie cutters available that making cutout cookies can be a terrific project that's fun for all family members. I've suggested specific cutters in my recipes, but you can substitute the shapes you prefer.

Sandwich cookies, as the name implies, are two cookies sandwiched together with filling in the middle. They come in a variety of shapes, sizes and flavors. Virtually any kind of cookie can be used and the filling can be very simple or more elaborate. The combination of cookies and filling really expands the possibilities for making something unique, with unusual flavors and textures.

Sugar Cookies

There are many variations of sugar cookies, each slightly different in flavor and texture. This is my favorite recipe. Not only does it taste great, but the dough is easy to work with.

MAKES ABOUT 5 DOZEN COOKIES

- **Preparation: 30 minutes**
- **Baking: 15 minutes**
- **Freezing: excellent**

TIPS

Use different-sized cookie cutters if you prefer. The size noted refers to the longest measurement. Bake larger shapes for a longer time than smaller ones.

Dip your cookie cutters in flour between each cut to prevent them from sticking to the dough.

Roll dough $1/4$-inch (0.5 cm) thick if you prefer a softer cookie. Bake for 13 to 18 minutes. Baking time will depend on size and thickness of cookies. They should just be starting to brown around the edges.

- **Preheat oven to 325°F (160°C)**
- **2½-inch (6 cm) cookie cutters (see Tips)**
- **Cookie sheet, ungreased**

4 cups	all-purpose flour	1 L
1 tsp	baking powder	5 mL
$1/4$ tsp	salt	1 mL
1 cup	butter, softened	250 mL
2 cups	granulated sugar	500 mL
2	eggs	2
2 tbsp	grated lemon zest	25 mL
2 tbsp	freshly squeezed lemon juice	25 mL
	Coarse or granulated sugar	

1. On a sheet of waxed paper or in a bowl, combine flour, baking powder and salt. Set aside.

2. In a large bowl, using an electric mixer on medium speed, beat butter and sugar until light and creamy, about 3 minutes. Add eggs, one at a time, beating well after each addition. Add lemon zest and juice. On low speed, gradually add flour mixture, beating until dough becomes too stiff for the mixer, then finish mixing with a wooden spoon to form a smooth dough.

3. On a floured surface, roll out dough to $1/4$-inch (0.5 cm) thickness. Cut into desired shapes using floured cookie cutters. Place about 1 inch (2.5 cm) apart on cookie sheet. Bake in preheated oven for 10 to 15 minutes or until light golden around edges. Cool for 5 minutes on sheet, then transfer to a rack and cool completely.

Variations

Change the cookie shape to match the occasion. Cut out bunnies and eggs for Easter, hearts for Valentine's Day, and trees, stars and bells for Christmas.

Sprinkle regular or colored sugar on cookies before baking, or leave them plain and decorate with icing and sprinkles later. Royal Icing (see page 250) looks particularly nice on these cookies.

Spritz Cookies

Spritz cookies are a bit like shortbread because they contain a large amount of butter. A Scandinavian specialty, they are tender, crisp and buttery-tasting. Pushed through a press into pretty designs, they add a festive note to any occasion.

MAKES ABOUT 5 DOZEN COOKIES

- **Preparation: 25 minutes**
- **Baking: 10 minutes**
- **Freezing: excellent**

TIPS

Baking time will depend upon the size and shape of your cookies.

The dough should be soft enough so it can be pushed through a press easily. If it is too soft, add a little flour. If it's too stiff, mix in a little more softened butter.

- **Preheat oven to 375°F (190°C)**
- **Cookie press, fitted with design plate of your choice**
- **Cookie sheet, ungreased**

1 cup	butter, softened	250 mL
1 cup	confectioner's (icing) sugar, sifted	250 mL
2	egg yolks	2
1/2 tsp	vanilla	2 mL
1/4 tsp	almond extract	1 mL
1/4 tsp	salt	1 mL
2 cups	all-purpose flour	500 mL
	Colored sugar, optional	

1. In a large bowl, using an electric mixer on medium speed, beat butter and confectioner's sugar until light and creamy, about 3 minutes. Add egg yolks, beating until well blended. Add vanilla and almond extract. On low speed, add salt, then gradually add flour, beating until dough becomes too stiff for the mixer, then finish mixing with a wooden spoon until smooth.

2. Pack dough into fitted cookie press and press onto cookie sheet, about 1 inch (2.5 cm) apart. Sprinkle with colored sugar, if using. Bake in preheated oven for 6 to 10 minutes or until just starting to brown around edges. Cool for 5 minutes on sheet, then transfer to a rack and cool completely.

Variation

Spritz dough can be colored with food coloring. For instance, if you're using a wreath design, color the dough green. Try yellow if you are making flowers, and place a small piece of candied cherry in the center before baking.

Almond Paste Macaroons

Most people associate macaroons with coconut, but ground almonds are actually the key ingredient. These cookies have amazing taste and are easy to make.

**MAKES ABOUT
4 DOZEN COOKIES**

- **Preparation: 15 minutes**
- **Baking: 20 minutes**
- **Freezing: excellent**

- **Pastry bag, fitted with ½-inch (1 cm) star tube**
- **Cookie sheet, lined with parchment paper**

8 oz	almond paste	250 g
¾ cup	confectioner's (icing) sugar, sifted	175 mL
¼ cup	granulated sugar	50 mL
2	egg whites	2
48	slivered almond pieces	48

1. In a food processor, combine almond paste and confectioner's and granulated sugars. Process until blended. Add egg whites and process until smooth, scraping down the sides of the bowl.

2. Pack dough into fitted pastry bag. Pipe 1-inch (2.5 cm) rosettes about 1 inch (2.5 cm) apart on prepared cookie sheet. Press an almond sliver on top of each. Bake in preheated oven for 15 to 20 minutes or until firm and golden. Cool for 10 minutes on sheet, then transfer to a rack and cool completely.

Red Raspberry Meringues

These tasty cookies are a colorful addition to a cookie box or tray. They also make a nice accompaniment for raspberry sherbet or a bowl of fresh berries.

**MAKES ABOUT
4½ DOZEN COOKIES**

- **Preparation: 15 minutes**
- **Baking: 2 hours**
- **Freezing: not recommended**

- **Preheat oven to 225°F (110°C)**
- **Pastry bag fitted with a ½-inch (1 cm) star tube**
- **Cookie sheet, lined with parchment paper**

3	egg whites	3
¼ tsp	cream of tartar	1 mL
Pinch	salt	Pinch
¾ cup	granulated sugar	175 mL
¼ cup	raspberry jam	50 mL
6 to 10	drops red food coloring	6 to 10

1. Using an electric mixer on high speed, beat egg whites, cream of tartar and salt until soft peaks form. Add sugar, 2 tbsp (25 mL) at a time, beating until stiff peaks form, about 10 minutes. Add jam and food coloring. Beat 1 minute.

2. Spoon meringue into fitted pastry bag. Pipe 1-inch (2.5 cm) rosettes about 1 inch (2.5 cm) apart on prepared cookie sheet. Bake in preheated oven for 1¾ to 2 hours or until crisp and dry. Cool completely on sheet.

Empire Cookies

I'm not sure where the name originated, but these have always been a favorite in my family, as well as with anyone else who has tasted this recipe.

MAKES ABOUT 2 DOZEN SANDWICH COOKIES

- **Preparation: 45 minutes**
- **Baking: 12 minutes**
- **Freezing: excellent**

TIPS

It takes about 3 minutes of beating to get a butter, sugar and egg mixture light and creamy.

The frosting will be soft and spreadable. It will spread out smoothly and dry nicely.

Use a small offset spatula for the frosting, spreading it as close to the edges as you can.

- **Preheat oven to 350°F (180°C)**
- **2-inch (5 cm) round cookie cutter**
- **Cookie sheet, greased or lined with parchment paper**

COOKIE

1²⁄₃ cups	all-purpose flour	400 mL
½ tsp	baking powder	2 mL
Pinch	salt	Pinch
½ cup	butter, softened	125 mL
½ cup	granulated sugar	125 mL
1	egg	1
1 tsp	vanilla	5 mL

FROSTING

1½ cups	confectioner's (icing) sugar, sifted	375 mL
6 to 7 tsp	boiling water	30 to 35 mL
2 tsp	corn syrup	10 mL
¼ tsp	almond extract	2 mL

GARNISH AND FILLING

7	red candied cherries, quartered	7
⅓ cup	raspberry jam	75 mL

1. *Cookie:* Combine flour, baking powder and salt. Set aside.
2. In a large bowl, using an electric mixer on medium speed, beat butter, sugar, egg and vanilla until light and creamy. On low speed, gradually add flour mixture, beating until blended. Using your hands, knead to form a smooth dough.
3. Divide dough into halves. On a floured surface, roll out 1 portion at a time to ⅛-inch (0.25 cm) thickness. Dip cutter in flour and cut into rounds. Place about 1 inch (2.5 cm) apart on prepared cookie sheet. Bake in preheated oven for 8 to 12 minutes or until golden around the edges. Cool for 5 minutes on sheet, then transfer to a rack and cool completely.
4. *Frosting:* Beat confectioner's sugar, boiling water, corn syrup and almond extract until smooth. If necessary, add more water, ½ tsp (2 mL) at a time, to make a spreadable consistency.
5. Divide cookies into 2 batches. Spread frosting over top side of 1 batch. Place a piece of cherry in center of each frosted cookie. Let stand until frosting hardens, about 1 hour.
6. *Assembly:* Spread about ½ tsp (2 mL) jam on flat side of unfrosted cookies. Top with frosted cookies.

Viennese Fingers

These luscious treats are a sandwich cookie, shaped like fingers and filled with a coffee filling. When my niece got married, she requested a huge box of these cookies for a wedding present. When I bake my Christmas cookies, they are a staple.

**MAKES ABOUT
3½ DOZEN SANDWICH
COOKIES**

- **Preparation: 30 minutes**
- **Baking: 7 minutes**
- **Freezing: excellent**

TIPS

The dough should be slightly soft so it can be pushed through a cookie press easily. If it is too stiff to press easily, mix in another tablespoon (15 mL) of softened butter. If it is too soft, add a little flour.

These cookies will have slightly different lengths. Pair them up during assembly.

You can make these any length you like. Short ones are nice for a cookie tray but longer ones (about 3 inches/7.5 cm) make a nice hostess gift.

- **Preheat oven to 375°F (190°C)**
- **Cookie press with ½-inch (1 cm) star-shaped nozzle**
- **Cookie sheet, ungreased**

COOKIE

2 cups	all-purpose flour	500 mL
¼ tsp	baking powder	1 mL
1 cup	butter, softened	250 mL
½ cup	confectioner's (icing) sugar, sifted	125 mL
½ tsp	vanilla	2 mL

FILLING

3 tbsp	butter, softened	45 mL
1 cup	confectioner's (icing) sugar, sifted	250 mL
1½ tsp	instant coffee powder, dissolved in	7 mL
1½ tsp	hot water	7 mL

1. *Cookie:* On a sheet of waxed paper or in a bowl, combine flour and baking powder. Set aside.

2. In a large bowl, using an electric mixer on medium speed, beat butter, confectioner's sugar and vanilla until light and creamy, about 3 minutes. On low speed, gradually add flour mixture, beating until smooth (see Tips). Pack dough into fitted cookie press and press into strips about 1½ inches (4 cm) long, about 1 inch (2.5 cm) apart on cookie sheet. Bake in preheated oven for 5 to 7 minutes or until starting to brown around edges. Cool for 5 minutes on sheet, then transfer to a rack and cool completely.

3. *Filling:* In a small bowl, using a wooden spoon, combine butter and confectioner's sugar. Stir in coffee solution, mixing until smooth. If necessary, add a little milk or water to make a spreadable consistency.

4. *Assembly:* Divide cookies into 2 batches. Spread about 2 tsp (10 mL) filling over flat side of 1 batch. Place remainder on top, flat side down. Press lightly together.

Variation

Dip ends in melted chocolate for a fancier presentation.

Apricot Date Oatmeal Turnovers

◆

Here's an old-fashioned favorite — a date square in cookie form.

MAKES ABOUT 3½ DOZEN COOKIES

- **Preparation: 45 minutes**
- **Chilling: 2 hours**
- **Cooking (Filling): 5 minutes**
- **Baking: 17 minutes**
- **Freezing: excellent**

TIPS

For convenience, use a food processor to chop the dates and apricots.

Try not to use too much flour when rolling. It will toughen any dough. You need just enough on the surface of the dough, your hands and the rolling pin to prevent sticking. If you use a pastry cloth and rolling pin cover, you'll have no problems with the dough sticking.

- **2½-inch (6 cm) round cookie cutter**
- **Cookie sheet, greased or lined with parchment paper**

DOUGH

2 cups	all-purpose flour	500 mL
½ tsp	baking soda	2 mL
¼ tsp	salt	1 mL
¾ tsp	ground cinnamon	3 mL
1 cup	butter, softened	250 mL
1 cup	granulated sugar	250 mL
1	egg	1
¼ cup	milk	50 mL
2½ cups	quick-cooking rolled oats	625 mL
½ cup	sweetened flaked coconut	125 mL

FILLING

1½ cups	chopped dates	375 mL
½ cup	chopped dried apricots	125 mL
½ cup	granulated sugar	125 mL
⅔ cup	hot water	150 mL
1 tbsp	butter	15 mL

1. *Cookie:* Combine flour, baking soda, salt and cinnamon. Set aside.

2. Using an electric mixer on medium speed, beat butter and sugar until light and creamy. Add egg and milk, beating until smooth. On low speed, gradually add flour mixture, beating until blended. With a wooden spoon, stir in oats and coconut. Divide dough into thirds. Cover and chill for at least 2 hours.

3. *Filling:* In a saucepan, over medium heat, bring dates, apricots, sugar, water and butter to a boil. Reduce heat and simmer until thick, stirring frequently. Set aside to cool.

4. Fifteen minutes before you are ready to bake, preheat oven to 350°F (180°C). On a floured surface, roll out 1 portion of dough to ⅛-inch (0.25 cm) thickness. Dip cutter in flour and cut into rounds. Spread 1 tsp (5 mL) filling in center, leaving edges clean. Top with a second round. Using a fork dipped in flour, lightly press edges together to seal. Prick top with fork to let steam escape. Repeat with remaining dough. Place on prepared cookie sheet, about 1 inch (2.5 cm) apart. Bake in preheated oven for 13 to 17 minutes or until golden. Cool for 5 minutes on sheet, then transfer to a rack and cool completely.

Raspberry Jam Tarts

◆

These cookies are full of possibilities. Change the flavor with different jams. Change the look by using different cutters for the tops.

MAKES ABOUT 2 DOZEN COOKIES

- **Preparation: 35 minutes**
- **Baking: 15 minutes**
- **Freezing: excellent**

TIPS

Aspic cutters are great for making the small cutouts or you can use the tip of a sharp knife.

Dip your cookie cutters in flour between each cut to prevent them from sticking to the dough.

You can re-roll the scraps that are left over when you cut out the rounds. Cut shapes as closely together as possible to minimize the scraps.

- **Preheat oven to 350°F (180°C)**
- **2½-inch (6 cm) round cookie cutter**
- **¾-inch (1.5 cm) round cookie cutter (see Tips)**
- **Cookie sheet, ungreased**

2½ cups	all-purpose flour	625 mL
1 tsp	baking powder	5 mL
¼ tsp	salt	1 mL
1 cup	butter, softened	250 mL
1 cup	granulated sugar	250 mL
1	egg	1
2 tbsp	freshly squeezed lemon juice	25 mL
¾ cup	raspberry jam	175 mL

1. On a sheet of waxed paper or in a bowl, combine flour, baking powder and salt. Set aside.

2. In a large bowl, using an electric mixer on medium speed, beat butter and sugar until blended, about 1 minute. Add egg and lemon juice, beating until smooth. On low speed, gradually add flour mixture, beating until blended.

3. Divide dough into halves. On a floured surface, roll out 1 portion to ⅛-inch (0.25 cm) thickness. Dip 2½-inch (6 cm) cutter in flour and cut into rounds. Place about 1 inch (2.5 cm) apart on cookie sheet and place 1 tsp (5 mL) jam in center of each. Roll out remaining dough and cut into 2½-inch (6 cm) rounds then, using the small cutter, make a cutout in center. Place over filled cookies. Press around edges with floured fork to seal. Bake in preheated oven for 11 to 15 minutes or until golden around edges. Cool for 5 minutes on sheet, then transfer to a rack and cool completely.

Variations

Replace the raspberry jam with apricot, peach or pineapple.

Sprinkle coarse or granulated sugar on top of cookies before baking.

Glazed Lemon Poppy Seed Flowers

◆

These cookies are very tender and practically melt in your mouth. The tart lemon glaze with the crunchy poppy seeds is irresistible.

MAKES ABOUT 5 DOZEN COOKIES

- **Preparation: 30 minutes**
- **Chilling: 1 hour**
- **Baking: 14 minutes**
- **Freezing: excellent**

TIPS

Cut other shapes, such as hearts, circles and bells — just be sure your cutters are the same size at their longest measurement or adjust the baking time accordingly.

Dip your cookie cutters in flour between each cut to prevent them from sticking to the dough.

This dough can be prepared and refrigerated for up to 3 days. Let stand at room temperature just long enough to make rolling easy.

- **2$\frac{1}{2}$-inch (6 cm) daisy-shaped cookie cutter (see Tips)**
- **Cookie sheet, greased or lined with parchment paper**

COOKIE

2 cups	all-purpose flour	500 mL
$\frac{1}{4}$ cup	poppy seeds	50 mL
$\frac{1}{4}$ tsp	salt	1 mL
1 cup	butter, softened	250 mL
$\frac{1}{2}$ cup	granulated sugar	125 mL
1	egg yolk	1
1 tbsp	grated lemon zest	15 mL
1 tsp	lemon extract	5 mL

GLAZE

1 cup	confectioner's (icing) sugar, sifted	250 mL
1 tbsp	butter, softened	15 mL
3 tbsp	whipping (35%) cream	45 mL
1 tsp	freshly squeezed lemon juice	5 mL

1. *Cookie:* On a sheet of waxed paper or in a bowl, combine flour, poppy seeds and salt. Set aside.

2. In a large bowl, using an electric mixer on medium speed, beat butter, sugar, egg yolk, lemon zest and lemon extract until light and creamy, about 3 minutes. On low speed, gradually add flour mixture, beating until blended. Cover and chill dough for at least 1 hour for easy rolling.

3. Fifteen minutes before you're ready to bake, preheat oven to 350°F (180°C). On a floured surface, roll out dough to $\frac{1}{4}$-inch (0.5 cm) thickness. Dip cutter in flour and cut out daisies. Place about 1 inch (2.5 cm) apart on prepared cookie sheet. Bake in preheated oven for 10 to 14 minutes or until golden around edges. Cool for 5 minutes on sheet, then transfer to a rack and cool for 15 minutes before glazing.

4. *Glaze:* In a small bowl, using an electric mixer on low speed, beat confectioner's sugar, butter, cream and lemon juice until smooth. If necessary, add a little more lemon juice to make a spreadable consistency. Using a small offset spatula, spread glaze over top of cookies. Cool completely on rack.

Lemon Lime Cookies

A strong hit of lemon makes these tender, crisp cookies particularly delicious.

MAKES ABOUT 6 DOZEN COOKIES

- **Preparation: 25 minutes**
- **Baking: 11 minutes**
- **Freezing: excellent**

TIPS

I prefer combining the dry ingredients on a piece of waxed paper instead of dirtying a bowl. Then I use the paper as a funnel when adding them to the butter mixture.

For a softer cookie, roll out dough to ¼-inch (0.5 cm) thickness.

Try not to use too much flour when rolling. It will toughen any dough. You need just enough on the surface of the dough, your hands and the rolling pin to prevent sticking. If you use a pastry cloth and rolling pin cover, you'll have no problems with the dough sticking.

- **Preheat oven to 350°F (180°C)**
- **2-inch (5 cm) round cookie cutter**
- **Cookie sheet, ungreased**

3½ cups	all-purpose flour	875 mL
2 tsp	baking powder	10 mL
½ tsp	salt	2 mL
1 cup	butter, softened	250 mL
1¼ cups	granulated sugar	300 mL
2	eggs	2
2 tbsp	grated lemon zest	25 mL
2 tbsp	grated lime zest	25 mL
½ tsp	lemon extract	2 mL

1. On a sheet of waxed paper or in a bowl, combine flour, baking powder and salt. Set aside.

2. In a large bowl, using an electric mixer on medium speed, beat butter and sugar until light and creamy, about 3 minutes. Add eggs, one at a time, beating well after each addition. Add lemon zest, lime zest and lemon extract. On low speed, gradually add flour mixture, beating until dough becomes too stiff for the mixer, then finish mixing with a wooden spoon. Using your hands, knead to form a smooth dough.

3. On a floured surface, roll out dough to ⅛-inch (0.25 cm) thickness. Using cutter dipped in flour, cut into rounds. Place about 1 inch (2.5 cm) apart on cookie sheet. Bake in preheated oven for 7 to 11 minutes or until lightly browned around edges. Cool for 5 minutes on sheet, then transfer to a rack and cool completely.

Variations

Lemon Glaze: In a bowl, combine 1½ cups (375 mL) confectioner's (icing) sugar and 4 to 5 tbsp (60 to 75 mL) freshly squeezed lemon juice. Mix until smooth. Brush over cooled cookies.

Reduce lemon and lime zests to 1 tbsp (15 mL) each and add 1 tbsp (15 mL) orange zest.

Filled with lime or rainbow sherbet or vanilla ice cream, these make wonderful ice cream sandwiches.

Chocolate Caramel Pecan Rounds

These will remind you of the famous Turtle chocolates.

MAKES ABOUT 2½ DOZEN COOKIES

- Preparation: 35 minutes
- Baking: 14 minutes
- Cooking (Topping): 8 minutes
- Standing: 1 hour
- Freezing: not recommended

TIPS

Dip your cookie cutters in flour between each cut to prevent them from sticking to the dough.

You can re-roll the scraps that are left over when you cut out the rounds. Cut shapes as closely together as possible to minimize scraps.

- **Preheat oven to 350°F (180°C)**
- **2-inch (5 cm) round cookie cutter**
- **Cookie sheet, ungreased**

COOKIE

1 cups	butter, softened	250 mL
⅓ cup	granulated sugar	75 mL
½ tsp	vanilla	2 mL
¼ tsp	salt	1 mL
2 cups	all-purpose flour	500 mL

TOPPING

12	vanilla caramels	12
1½ tsp	half-and-half (10%) cream	7 mL
½ cup	chopped pecans	125 mL
1	square (1 oz/28 g) semi-sweet chocolate, chopped and melted	1

1. *Cookie:* In a large bowl, using a wooden spoon, beat butter, sugar and vanilla until blended, about 3 minutes. Gradually add salt and flour. Mix well. Using your hands, knead to form a smooth dough.

2. On a lightly floured surface, roll out dough to ¼-inch (0.5 cm) thickness. Using a cookie cutter dipped in flour, cut into rounds. Place on cookie sheet about 1 inch (2.5 cm) apart. Bake in preheated oven for 10 to 14 minutes or until golden around edges. Cool for 10 minutes on sheet, then transfer to a rack and cool completely.

3. *Topping:* In a small saucepan, over low heat, combine caramels and cream, stirring until melted and smooth. Dip one side of each cookie (about ⅓ of the surface) in caramel mixture, then into pecans. Place on a sheet of waxed paper and drizzle melted chocolate over top. Set aside until set, about 1 hour.

Variations

Place a pecan half on top of cookie before drizzling with chocolate.

Substitute peanuts or cashews for the pecans.

Chocolate Peppermint Patties

These cookies remind me of those classic chocolate mint candies, but in a softer form. They don't seem quite as decadent, meaning you can probably eat more.

MAKES ABOUT 2 DOZEN SANDWICH COOKIES

- **Preparation: 35 minutes**
- **Baking: 12 minutes**
- **Freezing: excellent (filled)**

TIPS

If you're not a big mint fan, decrease the peppermint extract to $\frac{1}{8}$ tsp (0.5 mL).

If any cookie dough that requires shaping or rolling seems soft, chill it for about 30 minutes for easier handling. This is better than adding more flour, which can toughen a cookie.

- **Preheat oven to 350°F (180°C)**
- **Cookie sheet, greased or lined with parchment paper**

COOKIE

1 $\frac{1}{4}$ cups	all-purpose flour	300 mL
$\frac{1}{2}$ tsp	baking powder	2 mL
$\frac{1}{4}$ tsp	salt	1 mL
$\frac{1}{4}$ cup	unsweetened cocoa powder, sifted	50 mL
$\frac{1}{2}$ cup	butter, softened	125 mL
1 cup	packed brown sugar	250 mL
1	egg	1
1 tsp	vanilla	5 mL

FILLING

2 tbsp	butter, softened	25 mL
1 $\frac{2}{3}$ cups	confectioner's (icing) sugar, sifted	400 mL
2 to 3 tbsp	half-and-half (10%) cream	30 to 45 mL
$\frac{1}{4}$ tsp	peppermint extract	1 mL

1. *Cookie:* On a sheet of waxed paper or in a bowl, combine flour, baking powder, salt and cocoa. Set aside.

2. In a bowl, using an electric mixer on medium speed, beat butter, brown sugar, egg and vanilla until light and creamy. On low speed, gradually add flour mixture, beating until blended.

3. Shape dough into $\frac{3}{4}$-inch (2 cm) balls. Place about 2 inches (5 cm) apart on prepared cookie sheet. Flatten with the palm of your hand to a 1$\frac{1}{4}$-inch (3 cm) circle. Bake in preheated oven for 8 to 12 minutes or until set. Cool for 5 minutes on sheet, then transfer to a rack and cool completely.

4. *Filling:* In a small bowl, using an electric mixer on medium speed (or a wooden spoon, if you prefer), beat butter until creamy. On low speed, add confectioner's sugar, cream and peppermint extract, using just enough cream to make a spreadable consistency.

5. *Assembly:* Divide cookies into 2 batches. Spread about 1 tbsp (15 mL) filling on flat side of 1 batch. Place remaining cookies on top, flat side down. Press gently together.

Variation
Add green food coloring to the filling.

Oatmeal Date Sandwich Cookies

These are like old-fashioned date turnovers in cookie form. I prefer the cookie version since you get a lot more filling.

MAKES ABOUT 2½ DOZEN SANDWICH COOKIES

- **Preparation: 35 minutes**
- **Cooking (Filling): 5 minutes**
- **Cooling (Filling): 2 hours**
- **Baking: 14 minutes**
- **Freezing: excellent (filled)**

TIPS

Prepare the filling up to two days ahead.

A food processor makes chopping dates an easy chore.

Make bite-size cookies if you prefer. Drop by scant tablespoonfuls (10 mL) and bake for 8 to 12 minutes.

Once filled, these cookies quickly become soft and chewy. I actually like them this way, but if you prefer a crisp cookie, make the parts beforehand but assemble no earlier than a day ahead.

- **Preheat oven to 350°F (180°C)**
- **Cookie sheet, greased or lined with parchment paper**

COOKIE

⅔ cup	all-purpose flour	150 mL
¼ tsp	baking soda	1 mL
¼ tsp	salt	1 mL
¾ cup	butter, softened	175 mL
1 cup	packed brown sugar	250 mL
½ cup	granulated sugar	125 mL
1	egg	1
1 tbsp	grated orange zest	15 mL
2 tbsp	freshly squeezed orange juice	25 mL
3 cups	quick-cooking rolled oats	750 mL

FILLING

1 lb	chopped pitted dates	500 g
1 cup	granulated sugar	250 mL
1 cup	water	250 mL
2 tbsp	freshly squeezed lemon juice	25 mL

1. *Cookie:* On a sheet of waxed paper or in a bowl, combine flour, baking soda and salt. Set aside.

2. In a large bowl, using an electric mixer on medium speed, beat butter, brown and granulated sugars, egg, and orange zest and juice until light and creamy, about 3 minutes. On low speed, gradually add flour mixture, beating until blended. With a wooden spoon, stir in oats.

3. Drop dough by heaping tablespoonfuls (20 mL) about 2 inches (5 cm) apart on prepared cookie sheet. Using a fork dipped in flour, press down lightly to flatten. Bake in preheated oven for 10 to 14 minutes or until light golden. Cool for 5 minutes on sheet, then transfer to a rack and cool completely.

4. *Filling:* In a large saucepan over medium heat, combine dates, sugar, water and lemon juice. Bring to a boil, reduce heat and simmer, stirring occasionally, until thickened, about 5 minutes. Remove from heat. Cool.

5. *Assembly:* Divide cookies into 2 batches. Spread about 1 tbsp (15 mL) filling over flat side of 1 batch. Place remaining cookies on top, flat side down. Press gently together.

Chocolate Ginger Sandwiches

◆

A crisp oatmeal cookie with a hint of ginger is twice as good when two of them are joined with melted chocolate.

MAKES ABOUT 2½ DOZEN SANDWICH COOKIES

- **Preparation: 35 minutes**
- **Baking: 12 minutes**
- **Cooking (Filling): 4 minutes**
- **Chilling: 30 minutes**
- **Freezing: not recommended**

TIPS

Parchment paper always makes cleanup easy, but it's practically mandatory when baking with sticky ingredients such as corn syrup or honey. It solves the problem of cookies sticking to the pan. Washable silicone sheets also work well.

Serve these with a dish of ice cream or a latte.

Use a level teaspoonful (5 mL) of dough for each cookie. These cookies will really spread and flatten during baking, which gives them a nice lacy look, brittle texture and caramel flavor.

- **Preheat oven to 375°F (190°C)**
- **Cookie sheet, lined with parchment paper**

COOKIE

2 cups	quick-cooking rolled oats	500 mL
1 cup	granulated sugar	250 mL
⅔ cup	all-purpose flour	150 mL
½ tsp	ground ginger	2 mL
⅔ cup	butter, melted	150 mL
¼ cup	corn syrup	50 mL
¼ cup	milk	50 mL

FILLING

6	squares (1 oz/28 g each) semi-sweet chocolate, chopped	6
6	squares (1 oz/28 g each) white chocolate, chopped	6

1. *Cookie:* On a sheet of waxed paper or in a bowl, combine oats, sugar, flour and ginger. Set aside.

2. In a large bowl, combine melted butter, corn syrup and milk. With a wooden spoon, stir until smooth. Add flour mixture, mixing until blended.

3. Drop dough by teaspoonfuls (5 mL) about 3 inches (7.5 cm) apart on prepared cookie sheet. With a wet offset spatula or your finger, press flat. Bake in preheated oven for 8 to 12 minutes or until light golden. Cool completely on sheet.

4. *Filling:* In separate small saucepans over low heat, melt semi-sweet and white chocolate, stirring until smooth. Remove from heat and set aside to cool slightly, until chocolate is a soft spreading consistency.

5. *Assembly:* Divide cookies into 4 batches. Spread semi-sweet chocolate over flat side of 1 batch. Top with second batch, flat side down. Repeat with remainder using white chocolate. Set on a sheet of waxed paper on a cookie sheet. Chill to harden chocolate, about 30 minutes.

Variation

These cookies are also great plain or with a chocolate drizzle on top.

Chocolate Oat Sandwich Bites

Chocolate and peanut butter make a great filling for small oatmeal cookies. They taste like a chocolate-covered granola bar, only better.

MAKES ABOUT 16 SANDWICH COOKIES

- **Preparation: 35 minutes**
- **Baking: 10 minutes**
- **Cooking (Filling): 4 minutes**
- **Chilling: 30 minutes**
- **Freezing: excellent (filled)**

TIPS

Your peanut butter should be soft and creamy. Some peanut butters settle, leaving an oil layer on top. If this happens, stir well before using.

Quick-cooking oats are the most common variety used for cookies. Old-fashioned or large-flake are specified when a more "oaty" taste and appearance is desired.

- **Preheat oven to 350°F (180°C)**
- **Cookie sheet, greased or lined with parchment paper**

COOKIE

$^2/_3$ cup	butter	150 mL
1 cup	all-purpose flour	250 mL
1 cup	quick-cooking rolled oats	250 mL
$^1/_2$ cup	packed brown sugar	125 mL
1 tbsp	liquid honey	15 mL
$^1/_2$ tsp	baking soda	2 mL
1	egg	1
$^1/_4$ cup	finely chopped peanuts	50 mL

FILLING

$^3/_4$ cup	semi-sweet chocolate chips	175 mL
3 tbsp	creamy peanut butter	45 mL

1. *Cookie:* In a large saucepan over medium heat, melt butter. Remove from heat. With a wooden spoon, stir in flour, oats, brown sugar, honey, baking soda, egg and peanuts, mixing until smooth.

2. Shape dough into $^3/_4$-inch (2 cm) balls. Place about 2 inches (5 cm) apart on prepared cookie sheet. Using an offset spatula or your fingers, press flat to $1^1/_4$-inch (3 cm) rounds. Bake in preheated oven for 6 to 10 minutes or until golden. Cool for 5 minutes on sheet, then transfer to a rack and cool completely.

3. *Filling:* In a small saucepan over low heat, melt chocolate, stirring until smooth. Remove from heat. With a wooden spoon, stir in peanut butter until smooth. Cool slightly, about 2 minutes.

4. *Assembly:* Divide cookies into 2 batches. Spread a scant tablespoonful (10 mL) filling over flat side of 1 batch. Place remaining cookies on top, flat side down. Chill to set filling, about 30 minutes.

Variations

Omit peanut butter in filling.

Replace semi-sweet chocolate chips with milk chocolate chips.

Cinnamon Raspberry Stacks

The extra time it takes to make these cookies is well spent as they are very attractive and the combination of differently flavored dough is quite delectable.

MAKES ABOUT 22 SANDWICH COOKIES

- **Preparation: 45 minutes**
- **Cooking: 12 minutes**
- **Chilling: 1 hour**
- **Baking: 12 minutes**
- **Freezing: excellent (unfilled)**

TIPS

Aspic or canapé cutters, which come in a variety of shapes (such as triangle, star, circle or heart), are perfect for making the center cutouts. They are available at kitchen stores.

A small offset spatula works well for spreading small amounts of filling on cookies.

If you're planning to freeze these cookies, do so before you fill them. You can thaw as many as you want when you're ready to fill.

After cutting, re-roll scraps of dough to make more cookies.

- **Preheat oven to 375°F (190°C)**
- **2½-inch (6 cm) and ½-inch (1 cm) cookie cutter (see Tips)**
- **Cookie sheet, ungreased**

CINNAMON DOUGH

½ cup	butter	125 mL
½ cup	confectioner's (icing) sugar, sifted	125 mL
1	egg yolk	1
1½ tsp	ground cinnamon	7 mL
1 cup	all-purpose flour	250 mL

PLAIN DOUGH

½ cup	butter, softened	125 mL
½ cup	confectioner's (icing) sugar sifted	125 mL
1	egg yolk	1
1 tsp	vanilla	5 mL
1¼ cups	all-purpose flour	300 mL

FILLING

⅔ cup	seedless raspberry jam	150 mL
	Confectioner's (icing) sugar, sifted	

1. *Cinnamon Dough:* In a saucepan over medium heat, heat butter until it melts and turns golden, about 12 minutes. Transfer to a bowl and chill until hard, then beat until softened. Add confectioner's sugar, egg yolk and cinnamon, beating until light and creamy. Gradually add flour, beating until blended. Knead to form a smooth dough. Cover and chill for 1 hour.

2. *Plain Dough:* In a bowl, beat butter, confectioner's sugar, egg yolk and vanilla until light and creamy. Gradually add flour, mixing until blended. Knead to form a smooth dough. Cover and chill for about 30 minutes.

3. On a floured surface, roll out cinnamon dough to ⅛-inch (0.25 cm) thickness. Cut into 2½-inch (6 cm) rounds. Place about 1 inch (2.5 cm) apart on cookie sheet. Repeat with plain dough, then, using ½-inch (1 cm) cutter, cut the center out of the plain circles. Place on cookie sheet. Bake in preheated oven for 8 to 12 minutes or until just golden around edges. Cool for 5 minutes on sheet, then transfer to a rack and cool completely.

4. *Assembly:* Spread 1 tsp (5 mL) jam over flat side of cinnamon cookies. Top with plain cookies, bottom sides down. Press together gently. Just before serving, sprinkle with confectioner's sugar.

Coconut Cream Macaroon Sandwiches

These chewy macaroon cookies with a creamy coconut filling are, as my niece says, "awesome."

MAKES ABOUT 1 ½ DOZEN SANDWICH COOKIES

- **Preparation: 30 minutes**
- **Baking: 15 minutes**
- **Freezing: excellent (filled)**

TIPS

Coconut extract gives baked goods containing coconut a more intense coconut flavor.

Coconut milk is sold in cans. It is available in Oriental stores or grocery stores, and can be found near the evaporated milk.

- **Preheat oven to 350°F (180°C)**
- **Cookie sheet, greased or lined with parchment paper**

COOKIE

2	eggs, separated	2
Pinch	salt	Pinch
¾ cup	granulated sugar	175 mL
½ tsp	coconut extract	2 mL
1 ½ cups	sweetened flaked coconut	375 mL
¾ cup	all-purpose flour	175 mL

FILLING

1 tbsp	butter, softened	15 mL
1 ¼ cups	confectioner's (icing) sugar, sifted	300 mL
1 ½ tbsp	coconut milk	20 mL
½ tsp	coconut extract	2 mL

1. *Cookie:* In a small bowl, using an electric mixer on high speed, beat egg whites and salt until foamy. Gradually add sugar, 2 tbsp (25 mL) at a time, beating until very stiff, about 4 minutes. Set aside.

2. In a large bowl, using a wooden spoon, mix egg yolks, coconut extract, coconut and flour until blended. Add egg white mixture, mixing until thoroughly moistened.

3. Drop dough by scant tablespoonfuls (10 mL) about 2 inches (5 cm) apart on prepared cookie sheet. With a wet spatula or finger, flatten mounds slightly. Bake in preheated oven for 10 to 15 minutes or until golden. Cool for 10 minutes on sheet, then transfer to a rack and cool completely.

4. *Filling:* In a small bowl, beat butter, confectioner's sugar, coconut milk and coconut extract until smooth.

5. *Assembly:* Divide cookies into 2 batches. Spread about 1 tbsp (15 mL) filling over flat side of 1 batch. Place remaining cookies on top, flat side down. Press gently together.

Variation
Add ½ cup (125 mL) finely chopped almonds along with the coconut.

Chocolate-Filled Cashew Cookies

These cookies provide a good hit of chocolate nestled between two tender, nutty cashew cookies. Yum.

MAKES ABOUT 4 DOZEN SANDWICH COOKIES

- **Preparation: 35 minutes**
- **Baking: 14 minutes**
- **Cooking (Filling): 4 minutes**
- **Chilling: 30 minutes**
- **Freezing: excellent (filled)**

TIPS

Use a small offset spatula for spreading fillings on sandwich cookies. This will become one of your favorite baking tools.

Try not to use too much flour when rolling. It will toughen any dough. You need just enough on the surface of the dough, your hands and the rolling pin to prevent sticking. If you use a pastry cloth and rolling pin cover, you'll have no problems with the dough sticking.

- **Preheat oven to 350°F (180°C)**
- **2-inch (5 cm) round cookie cutter**
- **Cookie sheet, ungreased**

COOKIE

1 cup	butter, softened	250 mL
¾ cup	packed brown sugar	175 mL
1	egg	1
½ cup	sour cream	125 mL
1 tsp	vanilla	5 mL
3 cups	all-purpose flour	750 mL

FILLING

1½ cups	semi-sweet chocolate chips	375 mL
6 tbsp	butter	90 mL
1⅔ cups	finely chopped cashews	400 mL

1. *Cookie:* In a large bowl, using an electric mixer on medium speed, beat butter, brown sugar, egg, sour cream and vanilla until smooth. On low speed, gradually add flour, beating until dough becomes too stiff for the mixer, then finish mixing with a wooden spoon to form a smooth, soft dough. If necessary, cover and chill 1 hour for easy rolling.

2. Divide dough into halves. On floured surface, roll out 1 portion at a time to ⅛-inch (0.25 cm) thickness. Dip cutter in flour and cut into rounds. Place about 1 inch (2.5 cm) apart on prepared cookie sheet. Bake in preheated oven for 10 to 14 minutes or until golden around edges. Cool for 5 minutes on sheet, then transfer to a rack and cool completely.

3. *Filling:* In a saucepan over low heat, melt chocolate chips and butter, stirring until smooth. Remove from heat. Stir in cashews.

4. *Assembly:* Divide cookies into 2 batches. Spread about 1 tbsp (15 mL) filling over flat side of 1 batch. Place remaining cookies on top, flat side down. Chill to set filling, about 30 minutes.

Variations

Use peanuts or hazelnuts in place of the cashews.

Substitute white, milk chocolate or peanut butter chips for the semi-sweet.

Maple Leaf Sandwich Cookies

Maple is always a special flavor and it blends particularly well with walnuts.

MAKES ABOUT 3½ DOZEN SANDWICH COOKIES

- **Preparation: 30 minutes**
- **Baking: 12 minutes**
- **Freezing: excellent (filled)**

TIPS

If you don't have a maple leaf cookie cutter, use any cutter of a similar size.

A pastry cloth and rolling pin cover are a baker's dream for rolling out cookies and pastry. The dough doesn't stick and you don't have to worry about it being tough because you've added too much flour to keep it from sticking. I couldn't live without them. They're available in department stores or specialty stores that carry baking equipment.

- **Preheat oven to 325°F (160°C)**
- **2-inch (5 cm) maple leaf cookie cutter (see Tips)**
- **Cookie sheet, ungreased**

COOKIE

1 cup	butter, softened	250 mL
¾ cup	packed brown sugar	175 mL
1	egg yolk	1
½ tsp	maple extract	2 mL
2 cups	all-purpose flour	500 mL
½ cup	ground walnuts	125 mL

FILLING

¼ cup	butter, softened	50 mL
1½ cups	confectioner's (icing) sugar, sifted	375 mL
1 tbsp	milk	15 mL
½ tsp	maple extract	2 mL

1. *Cookie:* In a large bowl, using an electric mixer on medium speed, beat butter, brown sugar, egg yolk and maple extract until light and creamy, about 3 minutes. On low speed, gradually add flour, beating until blended. With a wooden spoon, stir in ground walnuts. Using your hands, knead to form a smooth dough.

2. On a floured surface, roll out dough to ⅛-inch (0.25 cm) thickness. Dip cutter in flour and cut out cookies. Place about 1 inch (2.5 cm) apart on cookie sheet. Bake in preheated oven for 8 to 12 minutes or until golden around the edges. Cool for 5 minutes on sheet, then transfer to a rack and cool completely.

3. *Filling:* In a small bowl, using an electric mixer on low speed or a wooden spoon, beat butter, confectioner's sugar, milk and maple extract until smooth.

4. *Assembly:* Divide cookies into 2 batches. Spread about 1 tbsp (15 mL) filling on top side of 1 batch. Top with remaining cookies, bottom side down. Press gently together.

Hazelnut Layer Cookies

These cookies are an Austrian specialty. They are one of my favorites — once you've tried them, you'll understand why.

MAKES ABOUT 3 DOZEN SANDWICH COOKIES

- Preparation: 30 minutes
- Baking: 11 minutes
- Freezing: excellent (unfilled)

TIPS

You can use regular (not seedless) raspberry jam, but the flavor is not as good.

The dusting of confectioner's (icing) sugar is a nice touch, but it won't last. Dust the cookies when you're ready to serve them.

You'll need about 2½ cups (625 mL) whole hazelnuts to get this quantity of ground.

Before grinding hazelnuts, toast them in a 350°F (180°C) oven for about 10 minutes, then rub them in a tea towel to remove as much of the skin as possible. It won't all come off, but what remains adds a nice color to the dough.

- **Preheat oven to 375°F (190°C)**
- **2-inch (5 cm) round cookie cutter**
- **½-inch (1 cm) round cookie cutter**
- **Cookie sheet, ungreased**

COOKIE

1 cup	butter, softened	250 mL
¾ cup	granulated sugar	175 mL
1	egg	1
2¼ cups	all-purpose flour	550 mL
2 cups	ground toasted hazelnuts (see Tips)	500 mL

FILLING

⅔ cup	seedless raspberry jam	150 mL
	Confectioner's (icing) sugar, sifted	

1. *Cookie:* In a large bowl, using an electric mixer on medium speed, beat butter, sugar and egg until light and creamy, about 3 minutes. On low speed, gradually add flour, beating until blended. With a wooden spoon, stir in hazelnuts. Using your hands, knead to form a smooth dough.

2. On a floured surface, roll out dough to ⅛-inch (0.25 cm) thickness. Dip cutter in flour and cut out 2-inch (5 cm) rounds. With a ½-inch (1 cm) cutter, cut centers out of half of the cookies. Re-roll scraps for more cookies. Place about 1 inch (2.5 cm) apart on cookie sheet. Bake in preheated oven for 7 to 11 minutes or until golden around edges. Cool for 5 minutes on sheet, then transfer to a rack to cool completely.

3. *Assembly:* Spread about 1 tsp (5 mL) jam over flat side of whole cookies. Top with cutout cookies, flat side down. Press gently together. Before serving, dust tops lightly with confectioner's sugar.

Variations

Substitute pecans or almonds for the hazelnuts.

Substitute apricot jam in place of the raspberry.

Shaped Cookies and Biscotti

Many all-time favorite cookies like biscotti, peanut butter cookies and shortbread are shaped by hand. The shapes can vary from sticks and crescents to balls and wedges, and the cookies can be left plain, dipped in chocolate, sprinkled with sugar or frosted. The dough is often chilled before shaping to make it easier to handle.

Some, like biscotti, can be quickly shaped because the dough bakes in a large portion, while others are more time-consuming because the cookies need to be shaped individually. But all are easy to make. Biscotti, unlike most cookies, require two bakings. This gives them their hard, crunchy texture, which makes them ideal for dunking. You'll discover many different flavors, textures and looks in this section, so you're bound to find some favorites.

◄ *Raspberry Pecan Ribbons*

Raspberry Pecan Ribbons

◆

These are an easy-to-make version of the ever-popular thumbprint cookie. Change the look and taste with different jams.

MAKES ABOUT 4 DOZEN COOKIES

- **Preparation: 25 minutes**
- **Baking: 19 minutes**
- **Freezing: excellent**

TIPS

A white icing drizzle can dress these cookies up. In a bowl, combine ¼ cup (50 mL) confectioner's (icing) sugar and 1 tsp (5 mL) water, adding more water, if necessary, to make a drizzling consistency.

Use a food processor to chop nuts finely.

Toast nuts for the best flavor. Be sure to cool them completely before chopping.

Pecans and walnuts can always be interchanged in recipes. It is simply a matter of taste.

- **Preheat oven to 325°F (160°C)**
- **Cookie sheet, ungreased**

1½ cups	all-purpose flour	375 mL
1 tsp	baking powder	5 mL
¼ tsp	salt	1 mL
½ cup	butter, softened	125 mL
½ cup	granulated sugar	125 mL
1	egg	1
1 tbsp	grated lemon zest	15 mL
¾ cup	finely chopped pecans	175 mL
⅓ cup	raspberry jam	75 mL

1. On a sheet of waxed paper or in a bowl, combine flour, baking powder and salt. Set aside.

2. In a large bowl, using a wooden spoon, beat butter, sugar, egg and lemon zest until light and creamy, about 3 minutes. Gradually add flour mixture, beating until blended.

3. Divide dough into thirds. Shape each into a roll 10 inches (25 cm) long. Spread pecans on a sheet of waxed paper and roll each log in the nuts until evenly coated. Place logs about 4 inches (10 cm) apart on cookie sheet. Flatten to 1½-inch (4 cm) width. Make a ½-inch (1 cm) indentation down center of each strip using a floured finger or the back of a wooden spoon. Bake in preheated oven for 15 to 19 minutes or until lightly browned around edges. Press indentation again. Cool for 15 minutes on sheet, then transfer to a rack and cool completely.

4. When cooled, fill each indentation with 2 tablespoons (25 mL) of jam, spreading along the length of the rolls to completely fill the indentations. Cut each roll into 12 or 16 pieces.

Variation
Use other soft spreads such as marmalade, or blueberry, peach, strawberry or apricot jam.

Chocolate Candy Saucers

These candy saucers are a favorite of kids young and old.

**MAKES ABOUT
16 LARGE COOKIES
OR 4 DOZEN SMALL
COOKIES**

- **Preparation: 20 minutes**
- **Baking: 15 minutes**
- **Freezing: excellent**

TIP

To easily shape the dough for saucers, use a 1/3-cup (75 mL) ice cream scoop. For regular-size cookies, drop dough by tablespoonfuls (15 mL) onto prepared cookie sheet and bake for 8 to 12 minutes.

- **Preheat oven to 350°F (180°C)**
- **Cookie sheet, greased or lined with parchment paper**

1 cup	quick-cooking rolled oats	250 mL
3/4 cup	all-purpose flour	175 mL
1/2 tsp	baking soda	2 mL
1/4 tsp	salt	1 mL
1/2 cup	butter, softened	125 mL
1/2 cup	creamy peanut butter	125 mL
3/4 cup	packed brown sugar	175 mL
1/2 cup	granulated sugar	125 mL
1	egg	1
1 cup	semi-sweet chocolate chips	250 mL
1 cup	candy-coated chocolate pieces	250 mL
3/4 cup	chopped peanuts	175 mL

1. On a sheet of waxed paper or in a bowl, combine oats, flour, baking soda and salt. Set aside.

2. In a large bowl, using an electric mixer on medium speed, beat butter, peanut butter, brown and granulated sugars and egg until smooth and creamy, about 3 minutes. On low speed, gradually add flour mixture, beating until blended. With a wooden spoon, stir in chocolate chips, candy pieces and peanuts.

3. Shape dough into balls, each about 1/3 cup (75 mL) in volume, and place about 2 inches (5 cm) apart on prepared cookie sheet. Bake in preheated oven for 11 to 15 minutes or until golden. Cool for 15 minutes on sheet, then transfer to a rack and cool completely.

Variation

For a no-nut cookie, omit the peanut butter and peanuts. Reduce the flour to 2/3 cup (150 mL).

Chocolate Crinkles

The distinct cracked top makes these cookies stand out. It just happens naturally during baking — you don't have to do anything special to achieve it.

MAKES ABOUT 3 DOZEN COOKIES

- **Preparation: 20 minutes**
- **Chilling: 2 hours**
- **Baking: 12 minutes**
- **Freezing: excellent**

TIPS

Confectioner's (icing) sugar will clump during storage. Before using, be sure to sift it (after measuring). This is especially important when it is used as a coating or in a frosting.

Use a lightly flavored oil, such as canola, in baking. Avoid strongly flavored oils, such as peanut and olive, unless specified in the recipe.

These cookies keep well and the recipe can easily be doubled to have extra on hand.

- **Preheat oven to 350°F (180°C)**
- **Cookie sheet, ungreased**

1 cup	all-purpose flour	250 mL
1 tsp	baking powder	5 mL
¼ tsp	salt	1 mL
1 cup	packed brown sugar	250 mL
¼ cup	vegetable oil	50 mL
2	squares (1 oz/28 g each) unsweetened chocolate, chopped, melted and cooled	2
2	eggs	2
½ tsp	vanilla	2 mL
¾ cup	confectioner's (icing) sugar, sifted	175 mL

1. On a sheet of waxed paper or in a bowl, combine flour, baking powder and salt. Set aside.

2. In a large bowl, whisk together brown sugar, oil, melted chocolate, eggs and vanilla until smoothly blended. With a wooden spoon, gradually stir in flour mixture, mixing until smooth. Cover and freeze for 30 minutes or refrigerate for 2 hours for easy handling.

3. Put confectioner's sugar in a small shallow dish. Shape dough into 1-inch (2.5 cm) balls. Roll balls in confectioner's sugar until evenly coated. Place about 2 inches (5 cm) apart on cookie sheet. Bake in preheated oven for 8 to 12 minutes or until set and tops are cracked and dry. Cool for 5 minutes on sheet, then transfer to a rack and cool completely.

Macadamia Ginger Macaroons

If you love coconut, you'll love these macaroons. They also contain yummy macadamia nuts and ginger.

MAKES ABOUT 3 DOZEN COOKIES

- **Preparation: 35 minutes**
- **Baking: 15 minutes**
- **Chilling: 10 minutes**
- **Freezing: excellent (without melted chocolate dip)**

TIPS

This dough is quite sticky. Moisten your hands to keep it from sticking to your fingers.

To keep coconut soft and moist, store it in the freezer.

I prefer cookie sheets without sides because I can place unbaked cookies on a piece of parchment paper and slide the paper on and off the sheet easily. While one sheet is baking, I'm putting cookies on the next piece of parchment.

- **Preheat oven to 350°F (180°C)**
- **Cookie sheet, greased or lined with parchment paper**

3 cups	sweetened flaked coconut	750 mL
½ cup	granulated sugar	125 mL
6 tbsp	all-purpose flour	90 mL
¾ tsp	ground ginger	3 mL
4	egg whites	4
⅔ cup	finely chopped macadamia nuts	150 mL
⅓ cup	finely chopped crystallized ginger	75 mL
2	squares (1 oz/28 g each) semi-sweet chocolate, chopped and melted	2

1. In a large bowl, using a wooden spoon, combine coconut, sugar, flour and ground ginger. Mix well. Add egg whites, mixing until ingredients are thoroughly moistened. Stir in nuts and crystallized ginger.

2. Shape heaping tablespoonfuls (20 mL) of mixture into rolls and place about 2 inches (5 cm) apart on prepared cookie sheet. Bake in preheated oven for 10 to 15 minutes or until golden around edges. Cool completely on sheets.

3. Dip both ends of cooled cookies in melted chocolate. Place on waxed paper. Chill until chocolate is set, about 10 minutes.

Variation

Replace macadamia nuts with an equal quantity of chopped almonds.

Hazelnut Stacks

These cookies are crisp on the outside but chewy on the inside, and rich with the luscious buttery flavor of hazelnuts.

MAKES ABOUT 20 COOKIES

- **Preparation: 30 minutes**
- **Baking: 19 minutes**
- **Freezing: excellent**

TIPS

Hazelnuts are also known as filberts.

To toast hazelnuts, preheat oven to 350°F (180°C) and place nuts on rimmed baking sheet. Bake, stirring occasionally, until golden, 8 to 10 minutes. Place in a towel and rub to remove as much of the skins as possible. Cool completely.

Store these cookies in an airtight container at room temperature for up to 5 days.

A reliable oven thermometer is a good investment. It will tell you whether your oven heat is aligned with the setting. If not, you can adjust it accordingly.

- **Preheat oven to 375°F (190°C)**
- **Cookie sheet, greased or lined with parchment paper**

1 ⅓ cups	hazelnuts, toasted (see Tips) and cooled	325 mL
¾ cup	granulated sugar, divided	175 mL
2	egg whites	2
¼ tsp	salt	1 mL
½ cup	all-purpose flour	125 mL

1. In a food processor, combine cooled toasted nuts and ¼ cup (50 mL) of the sugar. Process until very finely chopped. Set aside.

2. In a small bowl, using an electric mixer on high speed, beat egg whites and salt to soft peaks. Gradually add remaining ½ cup (125 mL) sugar, 2 tbsp (25 mL) at a time, beating to stiff peaks. With a wooden spoon, stir flour and nut mixture into egg whites, mixing just to blend.

3. With moistened fingers, shape tablespoonfuls (15 mL) of dough into pyramid-shaped mounds and place about 2 inches (5 cm) apart on prepared cookie sheet. Bake in preheated oven for 15 to 19 minutes or until lightly browned. Cool completely on sheet.

Variations

Replace hazelnuts with unblanched almonds.

Dress these up with a drizzle of melted chocolate or by dipping the bottoms in melted chocolate. You can also dust them lightly with confectioner's (icing) sugar just before serving.

Lemon Almond Balls

These are definitely one of my favorites, chewy and very nutty.

**MAKES ABOUT
4 DOZEN COOKIES**

- **Preparation: 20 minutes**
- **Baking: 17 minutes**
- **Freezing: excellent**

TIPS

If you prefer, decorate these balls. Place an almond half or candied cherry half on top of cookie before baking.

These cookies tend to stick, so parchment paper or silicone baking sheets, if you have them, are an especially good choice when making this recipe.

- **Preheat oven to 350°F (180°C)**
- **Cookie sheet, lined with parchment paper**

2²⁄₃ cups	unblanched almonds	650 mL
1²⁄₃ cups	granulated sugar, divided	400 mL
1 tbsp	grated lemon zest	15 mL
¼ tsp	salt	1 mL
2	eggs, beaten	2
½ tsp	almond extract	2 mL

1. In a food processor, process almonds and 1⅓ cups (325 mL) of the sugar until finely ground. Transfer to a large bowl. With a wooden spoon, stir in lemon zest, salt, eggs and almond extract, mixing until well blended.

2. Put remaining ⅓ cup (75 mL) sugar in a small shallow dish. With moistened hands, shape dough into 1-inch (2.5 cm) balls. Roll balls in sugar until evenly coated. Place about 2 inches (5 cm) apart on prepared cookie sheet. Bake in preheated oven for 13 to 17 minutes or until golden around edges. Cool completely on sheet.

Variation
Replace almonds with hazelnuts.

Crunchy Almond Crescents

◆

Almond paste may seem expensive, but one bite of these easy-to-make cookies will reassure you that it's well worth the price.

**MAKES ABOUT
2½ DOZEN COOKIES**

- **Preparation: 25 minutes**
- **Baking: 14 minutes**
- **Freezing: excellent**

TIPS

Parchment paper makes cleanup easy. It also solves the problem of cookies sticking to the pan. Washable silicone sheets also work well.

Store these in an airtight container between layers of waxed paper for up to 4 days.

These are a great accompaniment to a bowl of fresh fruit or sherbet.

- **Preheat oven to 375°F (190°C)**
- **Cookie sheet, greased or lined with parchment paper**

7 oz	almond paste	200 g
1 cup	granulated sugar	250 mL
2	egg whites	2
1 cup	finely chopped almonds	250 mL

1. Break almond paste into pieces. In a food processor, process almond paste and sugar until paste is pulverized. Add egg whites and process until blended.

2. Spread almonds on a sheet of waxed paper. Drop scant tablespoonfuls (10 mL) of dough onto almonds and roll until evenly coated. Shape into crescents and place about 2 inches (5 cm) apart on prepared cookie sheet. Bake in preheated oven for 10 to 14 minutes or until golden. Cool completely on sheet.

Variations

To dress up these cookies, drizzle melted chocolate on top or dip both ends in melted chocolate.

Sprinkle with confectioner's (icing) sugar just before serving.

Nutty Apricot Macaroons

If you love nuts, one taste of these cookies will transport you to heaven. They are not too sweet. Enjoy them with a dish of ice cream or sherbet, or a cup of espresso.

MAKES ABOUT 1 1/2 DOZEN COOKIES

- **Preparation: 30 minutes**
- **Cooking: 5 minutes**
- **Baking: 19 minutes**
- **Freezing: excellent**

TIPS

To toast ingredients such as coconut, almonds and pine nuts, spread in a shallow baking pan and bake at 350°F (180°C) for 5 to 10 minutes, stirring occasionally, until golden and fragrant.

For a non-alcoholic cookie, use orange juice in place of the liqueur.

Always use large eggs when baking.

- **Preheat oven to 350°F (180°C)**
- **Cookie sheet, greased or lined with parchment paper**

1/4 cup	finely chopped dried apricots	50 mL
1/4 cup	almond liqueur	50 mL
3/4 cup	toasted slivered almonds (see Tips)	175 mL
1/2 cup	toasted pine nuts	125 mL
2/3 cup	granulated sugar	150 mL
1 tbsp	all-purpose flour	15 mL
1	egg white	1
1/2 tsp	vanilla	2 mL
1/2 cup	finely chopped almonds	125 mL

1. In a small saucepan over medium heat, combine apricots and liqueur. Bring to a boil and cook, stirring occasionally, until liquid evaporates, about 5 minutes. Remove from heat. Set aside to cool.

2. In a food processor, process slivered almonds, pine nuts, sugar and flour until nuts are finely ground. Add egg white and vanilla. Process until dough forms a ball. Transfer to a bowl. With a wooden spoon, stir in reserved apricot mixture.

3. Spread finely chopped almonds in a small shallow dish. With moistened hands, shape dough into 3/4-inch (2 cm) balls. Roll balls in almonds until evenly coated. Place about 2 inches (5 cm) apart on prepared cookie sheet. Using a moistened offset spatula, flatten each to a 1 1/2-inch (4 cm) round. Bake in preheated oven for 15 to 19 minutes or until golden. Cool completely on sheet.

Variation

Replace the finely chopped almonds with finely chopped pine nuts.

Lemon Poppy Seed Balls

◆

Lemon and poppy seeds is a popular combination. It works well in these cookies.

MAKES ABOUT 4 DOZEN COOKIES

- **Preparation: 25 minutes**
- **Baking: 19 minutes**
- **Freezing: excellent**

TIP

Dress up these cookies with a drizzle of chocolate or a sprinkling of confectioner's (icing) sugar.

- **Preheat oven to 325°F (160°C)**
- **Cookie sheet, ungreased**

2½ cups	all-purpose flour	625 mL
2 tbsp	poppy seeds	25 mL
¼ tsp	salt	1 mL
1 cup	butter, softened	250 mL
⅔ cup	granulated sugar	150 mL
1	egg	1
1 tbsp	grated lemon zest	15 mL

1. On a sheet of waxed paper or in a bowl, combine flour, poppy seeds and salt. Set aside.

2. In a large bowl, using an electric mixer on medium speed, beat butter, sugar, egg and lemon zest until light and creamy, about 3 minutes. On low speed, gradually add flour mixture, beating until dough becomes too stiff for the mixer, then finish mixing with a wooden spoon until smooth. Using your hands, knead to form a smooth dough.

3. Shape dough into 1-inch (2.5 cm) balls. Place about 1 inch (2.5 cm) apart on cookie sheet. Bake in preheated oven for 15 to 19 minutes or until golden around edges. Cool for 5 minutes on sheet, then transfer to a rack and cool completely.

Variations

For another look, before baking, dip the handle end of a wooden spoon in flour and press an indentation in the center of each cookie. Fill with apricot or raspberry jam or red currant jelly, then bake as above.

For a plain cookie, omit the poppy seeds and lemon zest. Add 1 tsp (5 mL) vanilla or ½ tsp (2 mL) almond extract.

Brandy Lemon Lace Rolls

◆

Similar to brandy snaps, these candy-like cookies can be left flat or shaped into rolls while they're still warm.

MAKES ABOUT 3 DOZEN COOKIES

- **Preparation: 25 minutes**
- **Cooking: 4 minutes**
- **Baking: 7 minutes**
- **Freezing: not recommended**

TIPS

Baking just 6 cookies at a time gives you enough time to shape them before they become too cool.

Filling: Just before serving, beat 1 cup (250 mL) whipping (35%) cream with 3 tbsp (45 mL) confectioner's (icing) sugar and 1 tbsp (15 mL) brandy to stiff peaks. Pack into a pastry bag fitted with a plain nozzle and fill rolls.

If cookies cool and become too stiff to roll, warm them slightly in the oven.

These cookies are quite fragile and will crumble easily. That's okay — the crumbs are delicious sprinkled over or stirred into ice cream.

- **Preheat oven to 350°F (180°C)**
- **Cookie sheet, lined with parchment paper**

¼ cup	granulated sugar	50 mL
¼ cup	butter	50 mL
¼ cup	corn syrup	50 mL
⅓ cup	all-purpose flour	75 mL
1 tbsp	brandy	15 mL
2 tsp	grated lemon zest	10 mL
¼ tsp	ground cinnamon	1 mL

1. In a small saucepan over medium heat, bring sugar, butter and corn syrup to a boil. Remove from heat. Whisk in flour, brandy, lemon zest and cinnamon.

2. Making 6 cookies at a time, drop scant teaspoonfuls (4 mL) of batter on prepared cookie sheet. Bake in preheated oven for 5 to 7 minutes or until golden. Let stand on sheet for 1 minute or until slightly set but still soft. If you prefer flat cookies, let cool completely on sheet. To make rolls, quickly shape the soft warm cookie around the handle of a thick wooden spoon. Let cool completely, then remove and fill (see Tips).

Variation
Omit lemon zest and/or cinnamon for a plain brandy snap.

Raspberry Meringue Top Hats

This is a tender butter cookie with a jam filling hidden under a meringue top.

MAKES ABOUT 3½ DOZEN COOKIES

- **Preparation: 40 minutes**
- **Baking: 30 minutes**
- **Freezing: not recommended**

TIPS

Although recipes usually call for an electric mixer to blend ingredients, you can almost always use a wooden spoon when making cookies. It just takes more physical effort. With either method, it usually takes about 3 minutes to get a butter-and-sugar mixture light and creamy.

These cookies are best when they are first baked. The meringue will not freeze well.

If you're baking cookies that have a high amount of fat and ingredients that won't stick, you don't need to grease the cookie sheet. If in doubt, you can always use parchment paper, which I prefer because you don't have to wash the sheet between batches.

- **Preheat oven to 300°F (150°C)**
- **Cookie sheet, ungreased**

1 cup	butter, softened	250 mL
1 cup	packed brown sugar	250 mL
2	eggs, separated	2
1 tsp	vanilla	5 mL
2 cups	all-purpose flour	500 mL
¼ tsp	salt	1 mL
1 cup	finely chopped pecans	250 mL
½ cup	raspberry jam	125 mL
½ cup	granulated sugar	125 mL

1. In a large bowl, using an electric mixer on medium speed, beat butter, brown sugar, egg yolks and vanilla until light and creamy, about 3 minutes. On low speed, gradually add flour and salt, beating until blended. With a wooden spoon, stir in pecans.

2. Shape dough into 1-inch (2.5 cm) balls. Place about 1 inch (2.5 cm) apart on cookie sheet. Using a floured finger (or the flour-dipped handle end of a wooden spoon), make an indentation in the center of each ball and fill with about ½ tsp (2 mL) jam.

3. In a small bowl, beat egg whites until soft peaks form. Gradually add granulated sugar, 2 tbsp (25 mL) at a time, beating until stiff peaks form. Drop a spoonful of meringue onto the center of each cookie, covering the jam. Bake in preheated oven for 25 to 30 minutes or until golden. Cool for 5 minutes on sheet, then transfer to a rack and cool completely.

Variation

Use your favorite jam. I also like apricot and peach with these cookies. Be sure to cut up any large pieces of fruit.

Tropical Sticks

These cookies are particularly easy to make as they are shaped into four large rolls, then cut into strips after baking.

MAKES ABOUT 6 DOZEN COOKIES

- **Preparation: 25 minutes**
- **Baking: 22 minutes**
- **Freezing: excellent**

TIPS

These cookies are also delicious without the drizzle, and they store better when left plain.

When chopping nuts, I prefer to use a sharp large chef's knife rather than a food processor, which produces less uniform results. You can always purchase pre-chopped nuts to save time.

◆

- **Preheat oven to 325°F (160°C)**
- **Cookie sheet, ungreased**

COOKIE

1¾ cups	all-purpose flour	425 mL
2 tsp	baking powder	10 mL
¼ tsp	salt	1 mL
½ cup	butter, softened	125 mL
1 cup	granulated sugar	250 mL
1	egg	1
¾ cup	sweetened flaked coconut	175 mL
2 tbsp	milk	25 mL
¾ cup	chopped macadamia nuts	175 mL

DRIZZLE, OPTIONAL

1 cup	confectioner's (icing) sugar, sifted	250 mL
4 to 5 tsp	freshly squeezed lemon juice	20 to 25 mL

1. *Cookie:* Combine flour, baking powder and salt. Set aside.

2. In a large bowl, using an electric mixer on medium speed, beat butter, sugar and egg until light and creamy, about 3 minutes. On low speed, gradually add flour mixture, beating until dough becomes too stiff for the mixer, then finish mixing with a wooden spoon. Stir in coconut.

3. Divide dough into quarters. Shape each into a roll 10 inches (25 cm) long. Place 2 rolls about 2 inches (10 cm) apart on cookie sheet. Flatten to a 2½-inch (6 cm) width. Repeat with remaining 2 rolls. Brush tops of rolls with milk. Sprinkle macadamia nuts over top. Bake in preheated oven for 18 to 22 minutes or until lightly browned around edges. Cool completely on sheet.

4. *Drizzle, optional:* In a small bowl, combine confectioner's sugar and enough lemon juice to make a smooth drizzling consistency. Drizzle over strips. Let set for about 30 minutes. To make cookies, cut the rolls on a diagonal into ½-inch (1 cm) strips.

Variation

Add ½ tsp (2 mL) almond extract to the dough along with the egg and substitute almonds for the macadamia nuts. In the drizzle, replace lemon juice with milk.

Coffee Hazelnut Crescents

These cookies are similar to Crunchy Almond Crescents but with different flavoring. They are more shortbread-like in texture, but are equally loaded with nuts.

**MAKES ABOUT
4 DOZEN COOKIES**

- **Preparation: 20 minutes**
- **Baking: 19 minutes**
- **Freezing: excellent**

TIPS

Crescents will flatten slightly during baking.

Butter is a must for shortbread-like cookies. The flavor and texture it provides are unbeatable.

Instant espresso coffee powder is available in many Italian grocery stores as well as specialty coffee stores. It's a wonderful staple to have on hand for adding flavor to baked goods, as a little goes a long way.

To dip ends in chocolate, melt 3 oz (84 g) chopped semi-sweet chocolate with 1 tbsp (15 mL) butter.

- **Preheat oven to 300°F (150°C)**
- **Cookie sheet, ungreased**

1 cup	butter, softened	250 mL
½ cup	granulated sugar	125 mL
2 cups	all-purpose flour	500 mL
¼ tsp	salt	1 mL
2 tsp	instant espresso coffee powder	10 mL
1 cup	finely chopped hazelnuts	250 mL

1. In a large bowl, using an electric mixer on medium speed, beat butter and sugar until light and creamy, about 3 minutes. On low speed, gradually add flour, beating until dough becomes too stiff for the mixer, then finish mixing with a wooden spoon until smooth. Stir in salt, coffee powder and hazelnuts. Using your hands, knead to form a stiff dough.

2. Shape tablespoonfuls (15 mL) of dough into small rolls with tapered ends. Bend to form crescents. Place about 1 inch (2.5 cm) apart on cookie sheet. Bake in preheated oven for 15 to 19 minutes or until golden around edges. Cool for 5 minutes on sheet, then transfer to a rack and cool completely.

Variations

Replace hazelnuts with pecans or almonds.

Spread a coffee frosting (see filling on page 80) on top of these. Using tines of a fork, run lines down the frosting to resemble bark.

Omit the coffee powder for a plain nutty cookie.

Substitute almonds for the hazelnuts. Shape into balls rather than crescents and press an almond on top before baking.

Sesame Thins

◆

Fantastic is the best word to describe these cookies, which can easily become addictive.

**MAKES ABOUT
3 DOZEN COOKIES**

- **Preparation: 25 minutes**
- **Baking: 13 minutes**
- **Freezing: not recommended**

TIPS

Be sure not to put more than 6 cookies per sheet because they spread considerably during baking.

The dough is quite sticky. Be prepared to wash your hands often while making these cookies.

- **Preheat oven to 350°F (180°C)**
- **Cookie sheet, greased or lined with parchment paper**

½ cup	butter, softened	125 mL
¾ cup	granulated sugar	175 mL
1 tbsp	grated lemon zest	15 mL
1	egg white	1
½ tsp	vanilla	2 mL
3 tbsp	all-purpose flour	45 mL
Pinch	salt	Pinch
1½ cups	sesame seeds	375 mL

1. In a large bowl, using a wooden spoon, beat butter and sugar until light and creamy, about 3 minutes. Add lemon zest, egg white and vanilla. Mix well. Add flour, salt and sesame seeds, mixing until ingredients are well moistened.

2. Shape dough into ¾-inch (2 cm) balls. Place about 3 inches (7.5 cm) apart on prepared cookie sheet (see Tips). Press each ball flat, using a wet offset spatula or fingers. Bake in preheated oven for 9 to 13 minutes or until golden. Cool completely on cookie sheet.

Variation
Substitute ¼ cup (50 mL) black sesame seeds for an equal quantity of the white sesame seeds. They are sold in Oriental supermarkets.

Cherry Almond Butterballs

The subtle flavor of nutmeg in the coating enhances the almond flavor in the cookie.

MAKES ABOUT 4½ DOZEN COOKIES

- **Preparation: 25 minutes**
- **Baking: 20 minutes**
- **Freezing: excellent**

TIPS

Although recipes usually call for an electric mixer to blend ingredients, you can almost always use a wooden spoon when making cookies. It just takes more physical effort. With either method, it usually takes about 3 minutes to get a butter-and-sugar mixture light and creamy.

Stiff dough, like that for shortbread and shaped cookies, is best kneaded with your hands to get it smooth. If it seems too soft or sticky, add a little flour. If crumbly, add a bit more butter.

- **Preheat oven to 300°F (150°C)**
- **Cookie sheet, ungreased**

2 cups	all-purpose flour	500 mL
¼ tsp	salt	1 mL
1¼ cups	ground blanched almonds	300 mL
1 cup	butter, softened	250 mL
½ cup	granulated sugar	125 mL
½ tsp	almond extract	2 mL
27	red candied cherries, halved	27
½ cup	superfine granulated sugar	125 mL
1 tsp	ground nutmeg	5 mL

1. On a sheet of waxed paper or in a bowl, combine flour, salt and almonds. Set aside.

2. In a large bowl, using an electric mixer on medium speed, beat butter, sugar and almond extract until light and creamy, about 3 minutes. On low speed, gradually add flour mixture, beating until dough becomes too stiff for the mixer, then finish mixing with a wooden spoon until smooth. Using your hands, knead to form a smooth dough.

3. Shape tablespoonfuls (15 mL) of dough into balls. Press a cherry half into the center. Fold dough around cherry to enclose it. Place about 1 inch (2.5 cm) apart on cookie sheet. Bake in preheated oven for 16 to 20 minutes or until set and lightly golden. Cool for 5 minutes on sheet, then transfer to a rack placed over a sheet of waxed paper.

4. Combine superfine sugar and nutmeg in a small shallow dish. Roll warm balls in sugar mixture. Place on a rack and cool completely.

Variations

Replace nutmeg with cinnamon.

Roll cookies in plain confectioner's (icing) sugar for a different look.

Toffee Almond Cookies

The combination of crunchy toffee bits in a soft tender cookie is unbeatable. These won't last long.

MAKES ABOUT 4 DOZEN COOKIES

- **Preparation: 25 minutes**
- **Baking: 12 minutes**
- **Freezing: excellent**

TIPS

Toffee bits are available in bags where bakery ingredients like chocolate chips are sold. They also can be purchased in bulk, where available. Over time, they tend to pick up moisture, which softens them, so check before using to ensure they still have a fresh crunchy texture.

Don't overbake, unless you prefer a very crisp cookie.

- **Preheat oven to 350°F (180°C)**
- **Cookie sheet, lined with parchment paper**

2 cups	all-purpose flour	500 mL
1 1/4 tsp	baking powder	6 mL
1/4 tsp	baking soda	1 mL
1/4 tsp	salt	1 mL
3/4 cup	butter, softened	175 mL
1/2 cup	granulated sugar	125 mL
1/2 cup	packed brown sugar	125 mL
1	egg	1
1 tsp	vanilla	5 mL
2/3 cup	finely chopped almonds	150 mL
1/2 cup	toffee bits	125 mL

1. On a sheet of waxed paper or in a bowl, combine flour, baking powder, baking soda and salt. Set aside.

2. In a large bowl, using an electric mixer on medium speed, beat butter, granulated and brown sugars, egg and vanilla until light and creamy, about 3 minutes. On low speed, gradually add flour mixture, beating until blended. With a wooden spoon, stir in almonds and toffee bits.

3. Shape dough into 1-inch (2.5 cm) balls. Place about 2 inches (5 cm) apart on prepared cookie sheet. With the bottom of a glass dipped in granulated sugar, press flat into 1 1/2-inch (4 cm) circles. Bake in preheated oven for 8 to 12 minutes or until golden around edges. Cool for 5 minutes on sheet, then transfer to a rack and cool completely.

Variation

Flatten cookies with a fork or potato masher dipped in sugar for a different look.

Peanut Butter Cookies

No cookie book is complete without this classic. There are many versions of it, but this is the one I was brought up on and is still my favorite. The cinnamon is my mother's creative touch.

**MAKES ABOUT
5 DOZEN COOKIES**

- **Preparation: 25 minutes**
- **Baking: 16 minutes**
- **Freezing: excellent**

TIPS

Use creamy rather than crunchy peanut butter for these cookies. There's lots of crunch from the added peanuts.

A reliable oven thermometer is a good investment. It will tell you whether your oven heat is aligned with the setting. If not, you can adjust it accordingly.

- **Preheat oven to 375°F (190°C)**
- **Cookie sheet, ungreased**

2⅓ cups	all-purpose flour	575 mL
1 tsp	baking soda	5 mL
¼ tsp	salt	1 mL
½ tsp	ground cinnamon	2 mL
1 cup	butter, softened	250 mL
1 cup	creamy peanut butter	250 mL
1 cup	granulated sugar	250 mL
1 cup	packed brown sugar	250 mL
2	eggs	2
¾ cup	chopped dry roasted peanuts	175 mL

1. On a sheet of waxed paper or in a bowl, combine flour, baking soda, salt and cinnamon. Set aside.

2. In a large bowl, using an electric mixer on medium speed, beat butter, peanut butter, and granulated and brown sugars until blended. Add eggs, one at a time, mixing well after each addition, and beat until mixture is light and creamy, about 3 minutes. On low speed, gradually add flour mixture, beating until blended. With a wooden spoon, stir in peanuts.

3. Shape dough into 1-inch (2.5 cm) balls. Place about 2 inches (5 cm) apart on cookie sheet. Using a fork dipped in sugar or flour, press flat, forming a crisscross pattern. Bake in preheated oven for 12 to 16 minutes or until set and golden. Cool for 5 minutes on sheet, then transfer to a rack and cool completely.

Variations

Omit the peanuts for a plain peanut butter cookie.

Substitute honey-roasted peanuts for the regular ones. They add a nice flavor to these cookies.

Try these as sandwich cookies, filled with banana ice cream or strawberry jam.

Pineapple Macadamia Wedges

◆

Not only do these taste good, their different shape makes them a particularly nice addition to cookie trays.

**MAKES ABOUT
4 DOZEN COOKIES**

- **Preparation: 25 minutes**
- **Baking: 19 minutes**
- **Freezing: excellent**

TIPS

The macadamia nuts can be replaced with almonds or Brazil nuts, but the flavor of the cookies will be quite different.

Dried pineapple is often sold in bulk in the snack food section.

- **Preheat oven to 350°F (180°C)**
- **Cookie sheet, greased or lined with parchment paper**

COOKIE

1 cup	butter, softened	250 mL
²/₃ cup	granulated sugar	150 mL
1 tsp	vanilla	5 mL
2 cups	all-purpose flour	500 mL
¼ tsp	salt	1 mL
1 cup	finely chopped macadamia nuts	250 mL
¾ cup	chopped dried pineapple	175 mL

DRIZZLE, OPTIONAL

¾ cup	confectioner's (icing) sugar, sifted	175 mL
1 tbsp	pineapple juice	15 mL

1. *Cookie:* In a large bowl, using an electric mixer on medium speed, beat butter, sugar and vanilla until light and creamy, about 3 minutes. On low speed, gradually add flour and salt, beating until dough becomes too stiff for the mixer, then finish mixing with a wooden spoon until smooth. Stir in nuts and pineapple. Using your hands, knead to form a smooth dough.

2. Divide dough into sixths. Shape each into a ball. Place 3 balls on prepared cookie sheet. Flatten each to a 5-inch (12.5 cm) round. Smooth the edge then, using a fork dipped in flour, press around edge to make a pattern. Cut each round into 8 wedges (like cutting a pie), leaving the circle intact. Repeat with remaining dough. Bake in preheated oven for 15 to 19 minutes or until light golden. Cool for 5 minutes on sheet. Re-cut rounds into wedges. Transfer to a rack and cool completely.

3. *Drizzle, optional:* In a bowl, combine confectioner's sugar and juice to make a drizzling consistency. Drizzle over cooled cookie wedges. Let drizzle set, about 30 minutes.

Variation

Replace pineapple with dried cranberries. Use orange juice in the drizzle.

Crunchy Date and Nut Balls

◆

These small, bite-size cookies have a tender yet crunchy texture.

**MAKES ABOUT
3½ DOZEN COOKIES**

- **Preparation: 25 minutes**
- **Chilling: 30 minutes**
- **Baking: 12 minutes**
- **Freezing: excellent**

TIPS

These cookies retain their ball shape during baking rather than spreading and flattening.

Dates keep cookies moist and chewy, in addition to adding sweetness and delicious flavor.

When chopping dates, spray the blade of your knife with cooking spray to prevent sticking.

- **Preheat oven to 375°F (190°C)**
- **Cookie sheet, ungreased**

1¼ cups	all-purpose flour	300 mL
½ tsp	baking powder	2 mL
½ tsp	baking soda	2 mL
¼ tsp	salt	1 mL
½ cup	butter, softened	125 mL
¾ cup	packed brown sugar	175 mL
1	egg	1
1 tsp	vanilla	5 mL
2 cups	corn flakes cereal, slightly crushed	500 mL
1 cup	chopped dates	250 mL
½ cup	chopped walnuts	125 mL

1. On a sheet of waxed paper or in a bowl, combine flour, baking powder, baking soda and salt. Set aside.

2. In a large bowl, using an electric mixer on medium speed, beat butter, brown sugar, egg and vanilla until light and creamy, about 3 minutes. On low speed, gradually add flour mixture, beating until blended. With a wooden spoon, stir in cereal, dates and walnuts. Cover and chill for 30 minutes for easy handling.

3. Shape dough into 1-inch (2.5 cm) balls. Place about 2 inches (5 cm) apart on cookie sheet. Bake in preheated oven for 8 to 12 minutes or until set and golden around edges. Cool for 5 minutes on sheet, then transfer to a rack and cool completely.

Variation

Replace ¼ cup (50 mL) dates with dried cranberries or chopped dried apricots.

Mini Cranberry Cookie Cakes

These have a soft cake-like texture and look like mini muffins. The cranberries give them a pleasant tart flavor.

MAKES ABOUT 20 COOKIES

- **Preparation: 25 minutes**
- **Baking: 20 minutes**
- **Freezing: excellent**

TIPS

For best results, use light-colored muffin pans. The darker ones cook more quickly. If your pans are nonstick black, check the cakes after 12 minutes or decrease the temperature to 325° (160°C).

If you're putting these in a box for gift giving or on a cookie tray after baking, place them in small festive paper cups.

- **Preheat oven to 350°F (180°C)**
- **Mini muffin pans, greased and floured**

COOKIE

½ cup	butter, softened	125 mL
½ cup	granulated sugar	125 mL
2	eggs	2
1 tsp	grated lemon zest	5 mL
⅔ cup	all-purpose flour	150 mL
½ cup	dried cranberries	125 mL

TOPPING

2 tbsp	sliced almonds	25 mL
1 tbsp	granulated sugar	15 mL

1. *Cookie:* In a large bowl, using an electric mixer on medium speed, beat butter and sugar until light and creamy, about 3 minutes. Add eggs, one at a time, beating well after each addition. Add lemon zest. On low speed, gradually add flour, beating until blended. With a wooden spoon, stir in cranberries. Spoon dough into prepared muffin pan, pressing into pan.

2. *Topping:* In a small bowl, combine almonds and sugar. Sprinkle about ½ tsp (2 mL) over each cookie. Using your finger, press in lightly so mixture sticks to the dough. Bake in preheated oven for 15 to 20 minutes or until golden around edges. Cool for 15 minutes in pan, then transfer to a rack and cool completely.

Variations

Replace lemon zest with ¼ tsp (1 mL) almond extract. Substitute sliced unblanched hazelnuts for the almonds.

Four-Nut Biscotti

Enjoy several looks from one recipe. Leave these plain, drizzle chocolate over the top or dip the ends in melted semi-sweet or white chocolate.

MAKES ABOUT 4½ DOZEN BISCOTTI

- **Preparation: 25 minutes**
- **Baking: 1 hour**
- **Cooling: 15 minutes**
- **Freezing: excellent**

TIPS

This dough is quite soft and a bit sticky, hence the floured hands and use of a spoon instead of an electric mixer.

A sharp serrated knife works best for cutting biscotti.

The glaze gives the biscotti nice appearance and taste, but it can be omitted.

Use any combination of nuts you like, keeping the total amount to 2 cups (500 mL).

- **Preheat oven to 350°F (180°C)**
- **Cookie sheet, greased or lined with parchment paper**

BISCOTTI

3½ cups	all-purpose flour	875 mL
½ tsp	baking powder	2 mL
½ tsp	salt	2 mL
1 cup	butter, softened	250 mL
1 cup	granulated sugar	250 mL
⅔ cup	packed brown sugar	150 mL
3	eggs	3
1 tsp	almond extract	5 mL
½ cup	each coarsely chopped hazelnuts, pecans, pistachios and slivered almonds	125 mL

GLAZE

1	egg	1
2 tbsp	water	25 mL
¼ cup	turbinado or coarse sugar	50 mL

1. *Biscotti:* On a sheet of waxed paper or in a bowl, combine flour, baking powder and salt. Set aside.

2. In a large bowl, using a wooden spoon, beat butter and granulated and brown sugars until blended. Add eggs, one at a time, beating well after each addition. Mix in almond extract. Gradually add flour mixture, mixing until smooth. Stir in nuts.

3. Spoon mixture into 2 lengths on prepared cookie sheet. With floured hands, shape each into a roll about 14 inches (35 cm) long. Flatten rolls to 4 inches (10 cm) wide, leaving top slightly rounded.

4. *Glaze:* In a small bowl, beat egg and water until blended. Brush over top of rolls. Sprinkle with sugar. Bake in preheated oven for 25 to 30 minutes or until lightly browned around edges. Cool for 15 minutes on sheet, then transfer to a cutting board. Cut into ½-inch (1 cm) slices. Place upright about ½ inch (1 cm) apart on cookie sheet. Return to oven. Turn off oven and leave 30 minutes to dry. Cool for 5 minutes on sheet, then transfer to a rack and cool completely.

Gingersnaps

This spicy cookie has definitely withstood the test of time. This variation is crisp and thin with a pleasantly mild ginger flavor.

MAKES ABOUT 6½ DOZEN COOKIES

- **Preparation: 25 minutes**
- **Chilling: 2 hours**
- **Baking: 14 minutes**
- **Freezing: excellent**

TIPS

Turbinado sugar is a coarse raw sugar. It is available in many grocery stores, bulk stores and natural foods stores. You can substitute coarse white sugar for sprinkling over cookies.

If ground white pepper isn't available, use ¼ tsp (1 mL) freshly ground black pepper. You will notice black specks in the dough.

- **Preheat oven to 350°F (180°C)**
- **Cookie sheet, ungreased**

3¾ cups	all-purpose flour	925 mL
1¼ tsp	baking powder	6 mL
¼ tsp	salt	1 mL
2 tbsp	ground ginger	25 mL
1 tbsp	ground cinnamon	15 mL
½ tsp	ground white pepper	2 mL
¼ tsp	ground cloves	1 mL
1½ cups	butter, softened	375 mL
1¾ cups	packed brown sugar	425 mL
1	egg	1
1 tbsp	grated fresh gingerroot	15 mL
2 tsp	grated lemon zest	10 mL
¼ cup	turbinado sugar	50 mL

1. On a sheet of waxed paper or in a bowl, combine flour, baking powder, salt, ginger, cinnamon, pepper and cloves. Set aside.

2. In a large bowl, using an electric mixer on medium speed, beat butter, brown sugar, egg, gingerroot and lemon zest until smooth and creamy. On low speed, gradually add flour mixture, beating until dough becomes too stiff for the mixer, then finish mixing with a wooden spoon until smooth. Cover and chill dough for 2 hours for easy handling.

3. Shape teaspoonfuls (5 mL) of dough into balls. Place about 1 inch (2.5 cm) apart on cookie sheet. With the bottom of a glass dipped in flour, press down firmly on each to form thin rounds. Sprinkle turbinado sugar evenly over tops. Bake in preheated oven for 10 to 14 minutes or until crisp and golden. Cool for 5 minutes on sheet, then transfer to a rack and cool completely.

Variation

If you are a fan of the chocolate-ginger combo, omit the sprinkled sugar and instead sandwich 2 cookies together with melted chocolate.

Cranberry Almond Biscotti

These biscotti are not too sweet and not too hard. The crisp, tender texture makes them enjoyable without needing to be dunked.

MAKES ABOUT 4 DOZEN BISCOTTI

- **Preparation: 25 minutes**
- **Baking: 58 minutes**
- **Cooling: 15 minutes**
- **Freezing: excellent**

TIPS

A sharp serrated knife works best for cutting biscotti.

These biscotti look and taste great with the ends dipped in white chocolate.

Although these biscotti don't need to be dunked, they are nice served in the Italian fashion, with a glass of sweet wine.

- **Preheat oven to 325°F (160°C)**
- **Cookie sheet, greased or lined with parchment paper**

2¼ cups	all-purpose flour	550 mL
1½ tsp	baking powder	7 mL
¼ tsp	salt	1 mL
½ cup	butter, softened	125 mL
¾ cup	granulated sugar	175 mL
2	eggs	2
1 tbsp	grated orange zest	15 mL
1 tbsp	orange juice	15 mL
1 cup	dried cranberries	250 mL
½ cup	slivered almonds	125 mL

1. On a sheet of waxed paper or in a bowl, combine flour, baking powder and salt. Set aside.

2. In a large bowl, using an electric mixer on medium speed, beat butter and sugar until blended. Add eggs, one at a time, beating well after each addition. Beat in orange zest and juice. On low speed, gradually add flour mixture, beating until dough becomes too stiff for the mixer, then finish mixing with a wooden spoon until smooth. Stir in cranberries and almonds.

3. Divide dough into halves. Shape each into a roll 12 inches (30 cm) long. Place about 4 inches (10 cm) apart on prepared cookie sheet. Flatten rolls to 2½ inches (6 cm) wide, leaving top slightly rounded. Bake in preheated oven for 35 to 40 minutes or until firm and golden around edges. Cool for 15 minutes on sheet, then transfer to a cutting board. Cut into ½-inch (1 cm) slices. Place cut side down on cookie sheet. Bake for 8 minutes. Turn slices over and bake for 5 to 10 minutes or until crisp and golden. Cool for 5 minutes on sheet, then transfer to a rack and cool completely.

Variations

Replace cranberries with chopped dried apricots.

Replace almonds with hazelnuts or pistachios.

Replace orange zest and juice with lemon.

Lemon Poppy Seed Biscotti

◆

A real digression from traditional nutty biscotti, these tender, crisp sticks are delicious with afternoon tea.

MAKES ABOUT 2½ DOZEN BISCOTTI

- **Preparation: 20 minutes**
- **Baking: 50 minutes**
- **Cooling: 15 minutes**
- **Freezing: excellent**

TIPS

Store poppy seeds in the freezer to retain their freshness. They develop an unpleasant rancid flavor with age.

Some people prefer thicker slices, about ¾-inch (2 cm). The choice is yours. Thick ones will take a little longer to dry in the second baking.

- **Preheat oven to 350°F (180°C)**
- **Cookie sheet, greased or lined with parchment paper**

2 cups	all-purpose flour	500 mL
1½ tsp	baking powder	7 mL
¼ tsp	salt	1 mL
½ cup	butter, softened	125 mL
¾ cup	granulated sugar	175 mL
2	eggs	2
2 tbsp	grated lemon zest	25 mL
1 tbsp	lemon juice	15 mL
⅓ cup	poppy seeds	75 mL

1. On a sheet of waxed paper or in a bowl, combine flour, baking powder and salt. Set aside.

2. In a large bowl, using an electric mixer on medium speed, beat butter and sugar until light and creamy, about 3 minutes. Add eggs, one at a time, beating well after each addition. Add lemon zest and juice. On low speed, gradually add flour mixture, beating until blended. With a wooden spoon, stir in poppy seeds.

3. Divide dough into halves. Shape each into a roll 7 inches (17.5 cm) long. Place about 4 inches (10 cm) apart on prepared cookie sheet. Flatten rolls to 3 inches (7.5 cm) wide, leaving top slightly rounded. Bake in preheated oven for 25 to 30 minutes or until lightly browned. Cool for 15 minutes on sheet, then transfer to a cutting board. Cut into ½-inch (1 cm) slices. Place upright on cookie sheet. Bake for 15 to 20 minutes or until crisp and golden. Cool for 5 minutes on sheet, then transfer to a rack and cool completely.

Variation
Replace lemon zest and juice with orange or lime.

Coconut Pecan Biscotti

Biscotti means "twice cooked" in Italian. This gives them their characteristic dry, crisp texture. They're a perfect hostess gift because they keep very well.

MAKES ABOUT 2½ DOZEN BISCOTTI

- **Preparation: 25 minutes**
- **Baking: 55 minutes**
- **Cooling: 15 minutes**
- **Freezing: excellent**

TIP

Biscotti keep very well. Store in an airtight container at room temperature for up to 2 weeks or freeze for up to 6 months.

- **Preheat oven to 350°F (180°C)**
- **Cookie sheet, greased or lined with parchment paper**

2¼ cups	all-purpose flour	550 mL
1½ tsp	baking powder	7 mL
¼ tsp	salt	1 mL
½ cup	butter, softened	125 mL
¾ cup	granulated sugar	175 mL
2	eggs	2
1 tsp	vanilla	5 mL
1 cup	coarsely chopped pecans	250 mL
⅔ cup	sweetened flaked coconut	150 mL

1. On a sheet of waxed paper or in a bowl, combine flour, baking powder and salt. Set aside.

2. In a large bowl, using an electric mixer on medium speed, beat butter and sugar until light and creamy, about 3 minutes. Add eggs, one at time, beating well after each addition. Add vanilla. On low speed, gradually add flour mixture, mixing until blended. With a wooden spoon, stir in pecans and coconut.

3. Divide dough into halves. Shape each into a roll 8 inches (20 cm) long. Place about 4 inches (10 cm) apart on prepared cookie sheet. Flatten rolls to 2½ inches (6 cm) wide, leaving top slightly rounded. Bake in preheated oven for 30 to 35 minutes or until firm and golden around edges. Cool for 15 minutes on sheet, then transfer to a cutting board. Reduce oven temperature to 325°F (160°C). Cut rolls into ½-inch (1 cm) slices. Place upright on cookie sheet. Bake for 15 to 20 minutes or until crisp and golden. Cool for 5 minutes on sheet, then transfer to a rack and cool completely.

Variation

Replace pecans with almonds and vanilla with ½ tsp (2 mL) almond extract.

Chocolate-Wrapped Ginger Biscotti

A dark chocolate dough wraps around a lighter ginger dough to form an attractive two-toned biscotti.

**MAKES ABOUT
2½ DOZEN BISCOTTI**

- **Preparation: 40 minutes**
- **Baking: 55 minutes**
- **Cooling: 15 minutes**
- **Freezing: excellent**

TIPS

To distribute cocoa evenly and avoid streaks in a dough, knead the dough with your hands on a lightly floured surface.

Cocoa tends to lump during storage. Before mixing, even the smallest amount should be sifted to remove the lumps as they won't disappear during baking.

A sharp serrated knife works best for cutting biscotti.

- **Preheat oven to 375°F (190°C)**
- **Cookie sheet, greased or lined with parchment paper**

2 cups	all-purpose flour	500 mL
2 tsp	baking powder	10 mL
¼ tsp	salt	1 mL
⅓ cup	butter, softened	75 mL
⅔ cup	granulated sugar	150 mL
2	eggs	2
2 tbsp	unsweetened cocoa powder, sifted	25 mL
¼ cup	finely chopped crystallized ginger	50 mL
½ cup	miniature semi-sweet chocolate chips	125 mL
¼ tsp	ground ginger	1 mL

1. On a sheet of waxed paper or in a bowl, combine flour, baking powder and salt. Set aside.

2. In a large bowl, using an electric mixer on medium speed, beat butter and sugar until light and creamy, about 3 minutes. Add eggs, one at a time, beating well after each addition. On low speed, gradually add flour mixture, beating until blended. Divide dough into halves. With a wooden spoon, stir cocoa powder and crystallized ginger into 1 portion and, using your hands, knead until thoroughly integrated. Add mini chocolate chips and ground ginger to the other portion and, using your hands, knead until thoroughly integrated.

3. Divide each portion into halves to make 4 portions. Between two sheets of waxed paper, roll 1 portion of chocolate dough into an 8- by 6-inch (20 by 15 cm) rectangle. Remove top sheet of waxed paper. Shape 1 portion of light dough into a roll 8 inches (20 cm) long. Place roll in the center of chocolate dough and wrap chocolate dough around it. Repeat with remaining dough and place the 2 rolls about 4 inches (10 cm) apart on prepared cookie sheet. Flatten slightly, leaving top slightly rounded.

4. Bake in preheated oven for 35 to 40 minutes or until set. Cool for 15 minutes on sheet, then transfer to a cutting board. Reduce oven temperature to 325°F (160°C). Cut rolls into ½-inch (1 cm) slices. Place upright on cookie sheet. Bake for 10 to 15 minutes or until crisp and center is light golden. Cool for 5 minutes on sheet, then transfer to a rack and cool completely.

Maple Walnut Biscotti

◆

Maple extract has a wonderful real maple flavor that is ideal for baking. Because cookies don't require much liquid, you can't use maple syrup to provide that taste.

MAKES ABOUT 2½ DOZEN BISCOTTI

- **Preparation: 20 minutes**
- **Baking: 50 minutes**
- **Cooling: 15 minutes**
- **Freezing: excellent**

TIPS

When grinding nuts in a food processor, add a little flour or sugar from your recipe to keep them from clumping.

Be sure biscotti are thoroughly dry and cool before packing or they will soften during storage.

- **Preheat oven to 350°F (180°C)**
- **Cookie sheet, greased or lined with parchment paper**

2 cups	all-purpose flour	500 mL
⅓ cup	ground walnuts	75 mL
1¼ tsp	baking powder	6 mL
¼ tsp	salt	1 mL
2	eggs	2
½ cup	packed brown sugar	125 mL
¼ cup	granulated sugar	50 mL
½ cup	vegetable oil	125 mL
1 tsp	maple extract	5 mL
1 cup	coarsely chopped walnuts	250 mL

1. On a sheet of waxed paper or in a bowl, combine flour, ground walnuts, baking powder and salt. Set aside.

2. In a large bowl, using a wooden spoon, beat eggs, brown and granulated sugars, oil and maple extract until smoothly blended. Add flour mixture, stirring until smooth. Add walnuts. Using your hands, knead to form a smooth dough.

3. Divide dough into halves. Shape each into a roll 8 inches (20 cm) long. Place about 4 inches (10 cm) apart on prepared cookie sheet. Flatten rolls to 3 inches (7.5 cm) wide, leaving top slightly rounded. Bake in preheated oven for 25 to 30 minutes or until light golden. Cool for 15 minutes on sheet, then transfer to a cutting board. Cut into ½-inch (1 cm) slices. Place cut side down on cookie sheet. Bake for 10 minutes. Turn slices over and bake for 5 to 10 minutes or until crisp and golden. Cool for 5 minutes on sheet, then transfer to a rack and cool completely.

Variations

Replace walnuts with pecans.

Omit maple extract. Add 1 tbsp (15 mL) instant espresso coffee powder along with the flour mixture.

Chocolate Cappuccino Biscotti

◆

Now you can eat your cappuccino and drink it, too. In fact, these biscotti go very well with cappuccino. These are a little smaller than some biscotti, but that makes them a particularly nice afternoon pick-me-up.

MAKES ABOUT 4 DOZEN BISCOTTI

- **Preparation: 30 minutes**
- **Baking: 35 minutes**
- **Cooling: 15 minutes**
- **Freezing: excellent**

TIP

Turbinado is a raw cane sugar. If you don't have it, use another coarse-textured brown sugar, such as Demerara or muscovado.

- **Preheat oven to 375°F (190°C)**
- **Cookie sheet, greased or lined with parchment paper**

BISCOTTI

2½ cups	all-purpose flour	625 mL
1½ tsp	baking powder	7 mL
¼ tsp	salt	1 mL
2 tbsp	instant espresso coffee powder	25 mL
1 tsp	ground cinnamon	5 mL
½ cup	butter, softened	125 mL
1 cup	granulated sugar	250 mL
2	eggs	2
2 tbsp	coffee liqueur	25 mL
3	squares (1 oz/28 g each) semi-sweet chocolate, finely chopped	3

GLAZE

1	egg, lightly beaten	1
2 tbsp	turbinado sugar	25 mL

1. *Biscotti:* On a sheet of waxed paper or in a bowl, combine flour, baking powder, salt, espresso powder and cinnamon. Set aside.

2. In a large bowl, using an electric mixer on medium speed, beat butter and granulated sugar until light and creamy, about 3 minutes. Add eggs, one at a time, beating well after each addition. Add liqueur. On low speed, gradually add flour mixture, beating until dough becomes too stiff for the mixer, then finish mixing with a wooden spoon until smooth. Stir in chopped chocolate. Using your hands, knead to form a smooth dough.

3. Divide dough into halves. Shape each into a roll 12 inches (30 cm) long. Place about 4 inches (10 cm) apart on prepared cookie sheet. Flatten rolls to 2 inches (5 cm) wide, leaving top slightly rounded.

4. *Glaze:* Brush top of rolls with beaten egg. Sprinkle turbinado sugar evenly over top. Bake in preheated oven for 20 minutes or until set and lightly browned around edges. Cool for 15 minutes on sheet, then transfer to a cutting board. Cut into ½-inch (1 cm) slices. Stand upright on cookie sheet. Bake for 10 to 15 minutes or until crisp and golden. Cool for 5 minutes on sheet, then transfer to a rack and cool completely.

Cake Mix Cookies

The convenience of a cake mix gives you a jump-start on baking a batch of delicious cookies. The cake mix makes the batter hold even the crunchiest, chunkiest ingredients. Because many of the ingredients are pre-measured, it eliminates much of the need for measuring, which also saves on washing up. The pre-measured ingredients also reduce the room for error. I'm sure once you've tried a few of the cookie recipes made with a cake mix, you'll agree they're quick, easy and delicious — a perfect choice for spur-of-the-moment treats. Keep one chocolate and one white cake mix on hand for whenever you feel the urge to make homemade cookies.

◄ *Spicy Oatmeal Raisin Cookies*

Spicy Oatmeal Raisin Cookies

Once a favorite, always a favorite.

MAKES ABOUT 4 DOZEN COOKIES

- **Preparation: 15 minutes**
- **Baking: 12 minutes**
- **Freezing: excellent**

TIPS

Use quick-cooking oats to make cookies. You can use large-flake old-fashioned oats for a more "oaty" taste, but the texture will change slightly.

Don't let cookies remain on the baking sheet longer than 5 minutes. They will continue to cook and be more difficult to remove.

- **Preheat oven to 375°F (190°C)**
- **Cookie sheet, greased or lined with parchment paper**

1	pkg (18.25 oz/515 g) white cake mix	1
1 cup	quick-cooking rolled oats	250 mL
2 tsp	ground cinnamon	10 mL
1 tsp	ground nutmeg	5 mL
2	eggs	2
1/2 cup	vegetable oil	125 mL
1 cup	raisins	250 mL

1. In a large bowl, using an electric mixer on low speed, beat cake mix, oats, cinnamon, nutmeg, eggs and oil for 1 minute or just until blended. With a wooden spoon, stir in raisins.

2. Drop dough by tablespoonfuls (15 mL) about 2 inches (5 cm) apart on prepared cookie sheet. Flatten slightly with fingers or an offset spatula. Bake in preheated oven for 8 to 12 minutes or until lightly browned. Cool for 5 minutes on sheet, then transfer to a rack and cool completely.

Variation

Replace raisins with dried cranberries or a mixture of other dried fruits, such as chopped papaya, pineapple, mango and dates. Adjust spice to suit your own taste.

Gingerbread Shapes

Don't limit these to the festive season. With different cookie-cutter shapes and decorations, you can make gingerbread a year-round treat.

MAKES ABOUT 2 DOZEN COOKIES

- **Preparation: 30 minutes**
- **Chilling: 3 hours**
- **Baking: 12 minutes**
- **Freezing: excellent (not decorated)**

TIPS

Use Royal Icing (see recipe, page 250) or a prepared icing to frost these cookies.

If making gingerbread people cookies, press raisins for eyes and colorful candies for buttons in dough before baking.

If you're baking ahead, don't add the decorations. Cool and store the cookies in a container with a loose-fitting lid. They are ready to decorate when you are.

- **Preheat oven to 375°F (190°C)**
- **4-inch (10 cm) cookie cutter**
- **Cookie sheet, greased or lined with parchment paper**

1	pkg (18.25 oz/515 g) spice cake mix	1
3/4 cup	all-purpose flour	175 mL
2 tsp	ground ginger	10 mL
2	eggs	2
1/3 cup	vegetable oil	75 mL
1/3 cup	molasses	75 mL
	Vanilla frosting, optional (see Tips)	

1. In a large bowl, using a wooden spoon, combine cake mix, flour, ginger, eggs, oil and molasses, mixing until smooth (dough will be soft). Cover and refrigerate until firm enough to handle, about 3 hours.

2. On a lightly floured surface, roll out dough to 1/4-inch (0.5 cm) thickness. Cut with cookie cutter dipped in flour. Place on prepared cookie sheet (see Tips). Bake in preheated oven for 8 to 12 minutes or until edges start to brown. Cool for 5 minutes on sheet, then transfer to a rack and cool completely.

Variation

There are different sizes of gingerbread people cutters and various shapes of different sizes that you can use to make these cookies. Decrease baking time if you are using smaller cutters and increase time for larger ones.

Chocolate Macadamia Nut Oatmeal Cookies

Loaded with chocolate and luscious macadamia nuts, these cookies are a real treat.

MAKES ABOUT 5 DOZEN COOKIES

- **Preparation: 20 minutes**
- **Baking: 15 minutes**
- **Freezing: excellent**

TIP

Use large-flake old-fashioned oats for a more "oaty" taste. Be sure not to use instant oatmeal, which doesn't work in baking because it's too fine.

- **Preheat oven to 375°F (190°C)**
- **Cookie sheet, greased or lined with parchment paper**

1	pkg (18.25 oz/515 g) white cake mix	1
½ cup	quick-cooking rolled oats	125 mL
2	eggs	2
½ cup	butter, melted	125 mL
1 tsp	vanilla	5 mL
1½ cups	coarsely chopped macadamia nuts	375 mL
1½ cups	semi-sweet chocolate chunks or chips	375 mL

1. In a large bowl, using an electric mixer on low speed, beat cake mix, oats, eggs, melted butter and vanilla for 1 minute or just until smooth. With a wooden spoon, stir in nuts and chocolate chunks.

2. Drop dough by tablespoonfuls (15 mL) about 2 inches (5 cm) apart on prepared cookie sheet. Bake in preheated oven for 10 to 15 minutes or until light golden. Cool for 5 minutes on sheet, then transfer to a rack and cool completely.

Variation

Substitute pecans for macadamia nuts and white chocolate chunks for the semi-sweet.

Peanut Butter Cookies

An old-fashioned favorite that is easier to prepare with the use of a cake mix.

**MAKES ABOUT
4 DOZEN COOKIES**

- **Preparation: 20 minutes**
- **Baking: 14 minutes**
- **Freezing: excellent**

- **Preheat oven to 375°F (190°C)**
- **Cookie sheet, greased or lined with parchment paper**

1 cup	creamy peanut butter	250 mL
2	eggs	2
1 tbsp	milk	15 mL
1	pkg (18.25 oz/515 g) white cake mix	1
	Granulated sugar	

1. In a large bowl, combine peanut butter, eggs, milk and half of the cake mix, mixing well. Add remaining cake mix. Blend well, then use your hands to form a smooth dough.

2. Shape dough into 1-inch (2.5 cm) balls. Place about 2 inches (5 cm) apart on prepared cookie sheet. Press flat with a fork dipped in sugar. Bake in preheated oven for 10 to 14 minutes or until set. Cool for 5 minutes on sheet, then transfer to a rack and cool completely.

Cereal Crisps

Cereal never tasted so good. There's a lot of crunch packed into every bite of these delicious cookies. It won't be hard to convince kids to eat their breakfast cereal.

**MAKES ABOUT
4 DOZEN COOKIES**

- **Preparation: 20 minutes**
- **Baking: 12 minutes**
- **Freezing: excellent**

- **Preheat oven to 375°F (190°C)**
- **Cookie sheet, greased or lined with parchment paper**

1	pkg (18.25 oz/515 g) white cake mix	1
1	egg	1
1/2 cup	water	125 mL
1/2 cup	vegetable oil	125 mL
1 1/4 cups	crisp rice cereal	300 mL
3/4 cup	corn flakes cereal	175 mL
1/2 cup	unsweetened flaked coconut	125 mL
1/2 cup	chopped walnuts	125 mL

1. In a large bowl, using an electric mixer on low speed, beat cake mix, egg, water and oil just until smooth. With a wooden spoon, stir in rice cereal, corn flakes cereal, coconut and walnuts.

2. Drop dough by tablespoonfuls (15 mL) about 2 inches (5 cm) apart on prepared cookie sheet. Bake in preheated oven for 8 to 12 minutes or until lightly browned around edges. Cool for 5 minutes on sheet, then transfer to a rack and cool completely.

Lemon Crisps

Crisp and lemony — this is a wonderful plain cookie to enjoy with a cup of tea.

MAKES ABOUT 4 DOZEN COOKIES

- **Preparation: 20 minutes**
- **Baking: 12 minutes**
- **Freezing: excellent**

TIPS

When grating the zest for lemons and oranges, use only the colored part. The white pith underneath has a bitter flavor.

You can also mix this dough using an electric mixer on low speed for 1 minute.

- **Preheat oven to 350°F (180°C)**
- **Cookie sheet, greased or lined with parchment paper**

1	pkg (18.25 oz/515 g) lemon cake mix	1
1	egg	1
½ cup	butter, melted	125 mL
1 tsp	grated lemon zest	5 mL
	Granulated sugar	

1. In a large bowl, using a wooden spoon, combine cake mix, egg, melted butter and lemon zest, mixing until well blended.

2. Place granulated sugar in small shallow dish. Shape dough into 1-inch (2.5 cm) balls. Roll balls in granulated sugar until evenly coated. Place about 2 inches (5 cm) apart on prepared cookie sheet. Press flat with bottom of a glass dipped in sugar. Bake in preheated oven 8 to 12 minutes or until lightly browned around edges. Cool for 5 minutes on sheet, then transfer to a rack and cool completely.

Variation

Make these into sandwich cookies by putting 2 cookies together with lemon frosting or raspberry jam between.

Chunky Chocolate Pecan Cookies

A good choice for the cookie jar.

MAKES ABOUT 4½ DOZEN COOKIES

- **Preparation: 20 minutes**
- **Baking: 15 minutes**
- **Freezing: excellent**

- **Preheat oven to 375°F (190°C)**
- **Cookie sheet, greased or lined with parchment paper**

1	pkg (18.25 oz/515 g) white cake mix	1
2	eggs	2
½ cup	butter, melted	125 mL
1 tsp	vanilla	5 mL
1½ cups	semi-sweet chocolate chunks or chips	375 mL
1¼ cups	coarsely chopped pecans	300 mL

1. In a bowl, beat cake mix, eggs, melted butter and vanilla just until smooth. Stir in chocolate chunks and pecans.

2. Drop dough by tablespoonfuls (15 mL) about 2 inches (5 cm) apart on prepared cookie sheet. Bake in preheated oven for 10 to 15 minutes or until light golden. Cool for 5 minutes on sheet, then transfer to a rack and cool completely.

Refrigerator Nut Wafers

With a roll of dough in the refrigerator, fresh-baked cookies are only minutes away.

MAKES ABOUT 7 DOZEN COOKIES

- **Preparation: 20 minutes**
- **Chilling: 4 hours**
- **Baking: 11 minutes**
- **Freezing: excellent**

- **Cookie sheet, greased or lined with parchment paper**

1	pkg (18.25 oz/515 g) white cake mix	1
1	egg	1
½ cup	butter, melted	125 mL
1 tbsp	water	15 mL
1 tsp	vanilla	5 mL
1½ cups	chopped pecans or hazelnuts	375 mL

1. In a bowl, combine cake mix, egg, melted butter, water and vanilla. Add pecans and knead to form a smooth dough. Divide dough into halves. Shape each into a roll 2 inches (5 cm) in diameter. Wrap and chill until firm, about 4 hours.

2. Fifteen minutes before you're ready to bake, preheat oven to 375°F (190°C). Cut rolls into ⅛-inch (0.25 cm) slices. Place about 1 inch (2.5 cm) apart on prepared cookie sheet. Bake in preheated oven for 7 to 11 minutes or until lightly browned around the edges. Cool for 5 minutes on sheet, then transfer to a rack and cool completely.

Chocolate Caramel Pecan Cookies

Pecans and chocolate chips always go well together in cookies.

MAKES ABOUT 4 DOZEN COOKIES

- **Preparation: 20 minutes**
- **Baking: 12 minutes**
- **Freezing: excellent**

- **Preheat oven to 375°F (190°C)**
- **Cookie sheet, greased or lined with parchment paper**

1	pkg (18.25 oz/515 g) white cake mix	1
2	eggs	2
½ cup	butter, melted	125 mL
6	squares (1 oz/28 g each) semi-sweet chocolate, chopped	6
25	individual soft caramels, quartered	25
¾ cup	chopped pecans	175 mL

1. In a bowl, beat cake mix, eggs and melted butter for 1 minute or just until smooth. Stir in chocolate, caramels and pecans.

2. Drop dough by tablespoonfuls (15 mL) about 2 inches (5 cm) apart on prepared cookie sheet. Flatten slightly with fingers or an offset spatula. Bake in preheated oven for 8 to 12 minutes or until lightly browned. Cool for 5 minutes on sheet, then transfer to a rack and cool completely.

Double Chocolate Dreams

A chocoholic's dream. Try them warm from the oven, but be prepared to make a second batch.

MAKES ABOUT 4 DOZEN COOKIES

- **Preparation: 20 minutes**
- **Baking: 12 minutes**
- **Freezing: excellent**

- **Preheat oven to 375°F (190°C)**
- **Cookie sheet, greased or lined with parchment paper**

1	pkg (18.25 oz/515 g) devil's food cake mix	1
2	eggs	2
½ cup	vegetable oil	125 mL
2 cups	semi-sweet chocolate chips	500 mL
¾ cup	chopped nuts, your choice	175 mL

1. In a large bowl, using a wooden spoon, combine cake mix, eggs and oil, mixing until well blended. Dough will be stiff. Stir in chocolate chips and nuts.

2. Drop dough by tablespoonfuls (15 mL) about 2 inches (5 cm) apart on prepared cookie sheet. Bake in preheated oven for 8 to 12 minutes or just until set. Cool for 5 minutes on sheet, then transfer to a rack and cool completely.

Almond Crisps

This is a plain crisp cookie with a delightful almond flavor.

MAKES ABOUT 4 DOZEN COOKIES

- **Preparation: 25 minutes**
- **Baking: 12 minutes**
- **Freezing: excellent**

TIPS

Although recipes usually call for an electric mixer to blend ingredients, you can almost always use a wooden spoon when making cookies. This batter can also be mixed using an electric mixer on low speed for 1 minute.

Use unblanched almonds for an attractive appearance. The flecks of brown skin add a nice flavor, too.

Cooled baked cookies can be frozen in airtight plastic bags for up to 6 months.

- **Preheat oven to 375°F (190°C)**
- **Cookie sheet, greased or lined with parchment paper**

1	pkg (18.25 oz/515 g) white cake mix	1
1 cup	very finely chopped or ground almonds	250 mL
1	egg	1
½ cup	butter, melted	125 mL
1 tbsp	water	15 mL
1 tsp	almond extract	5 mL
	Granulated sugar	
	Whole almonds, optional	

1. In a large bowl, using a wooden spoon, combine cake mix, almonds, egg, melted butter, water and almond extract until blended, about 1 minute.

2. Shape dough into 1-inch (2.5 cm) balls. Place about 2 inches (5 cm) apart on prepared cookie sheet. Press flat with bottom of glass dipped in sugar. If desired, press an almond on top of each cookie. Bake in preheated oven for 8 to 12 minutes or until lightly browned. Cool for 5 minutes on sheet, then transfer to a rack and cool completely.

Variations

Replace almonds with hazelnuts or pecans.

Replace almond extract with vanilla.

Hazelnut Biscotti

Double baking makes biscotti extra crunchy, so they are ideal for dunking into your favorite drink. Because they are very firm and dry, they stay fresh and are unlikely to break during shipping, which makes them a good choice if you want to mail a homemade gift.

MAKES ABOUT 3½ DOZEN BISCOTTI

- **Preparation: 15 minutes**
- **Baking: 35 minutes**
- **Cooling: 15 minutes**
- **Freezing: excellent**

TIPS

Use a sharp serrated knife for cutting biscotti.

Parchment paper makes easy work of transferring the biscotti to a cutting board.

Store biscotti in airtight containers for up to 3 weeks.

- **Preheat oven to 350°F (180°C)**
- **Cookie sheet, greased or lined with parchment paper**

1	pkg (18.25 oz/515 g) white cake mix	1
⅔ cup	all-purpose flour	150 mL
⅓ cup	ground hazelnuts	75 mL
2	eggs	2
½ cup	vegetable oil	125 mL
1 tbsp	grated lemon zest	15 mL
⅔ cup	coarsely chopped hazelnuts	150 mL

1. In a large bowl, using an electric mixer on low speed, beat cake mix, flour, ground hazelnuts, eggs, oil and lemon zest for 1 minute or until blended. With a wooden spoon, stir in chopped hazelnuts. Using your hands, knead to form a smooth dough.

2. Divide dough into halves. On a prepared cookie sheet, shape each into a 10- by 3-inch (25 cm by 8 cm) rectangle, approximately ½ inch (1 cm) thick. Bake in preheated oven for 15 minutes until firm and golden. Cool for 15 minutes on sheet, then transfer to a cutting board. Cut into ½-inch (1 cm) slices. Place cut side down on cookie sheet. Bake for 10 minutes. Turn slices over and bake for 5 to 10 minutes or until crisp and golden. Cool for 5 minutes on sheet, then transfer to a rack and cool completely.

Variations

Use your favorite nut. Pecans and almonds work well in these cookies.

Omit lemon zest.

Rum Balls

There are many recipes for this classic no-bake treat. It's nice to make while another recipe is in the oven — or in the summer, when you don't want to turn on the oven.

**MAKES ABOUT
5 DOZEN COOKIES**

- **Preparation: 20 minutes**
- **Standing: 1 hour**
- **Freezing: excellent**

TIPS

An excellent way to use leftover cake, if that ever happens. Keep this recipe in mind if you have the opportunity to bake an extra cake when preparing another cake recipe.

Prepare these balls several days ahead to let flavors develop.

Place in small paper cups for serving or gift giving.

- **Cookie sheet lined with waxed paper**

1	pkg (18.25 oz/515 g) chocolate cake mix, baked and cooled	1
1 cup	finely chopped walnuts	250 mL
4 tsp	rum	20 mL
2 cups	confectioner's (icing) sugar, sifted	500 mL
¼ cup	unsweetened cocoa powder, sifted	50 mL
	Finely chopped nuts or chocolate sprinkles	

1. In a large bowl, crumble cake. With a fork, stir cake until crumbs are fine and uniform in size. Add walnuts, rum, confectioner's sugar and cocoa. With a wooden spoon, stir until thoroughly blended.

2. Spread nuts or sprinkles in a small shallow dish. Shape heaping tablespoonfuls (20 mL) of dough into 1-inch (2.5 cm) balls. Roll balls in nuts or sprinkles, pressing firmly to adhere coating. Place on prepared cookie sheet. Let stand for about 1 hour, until set. Store in an airtight container in refrigerator.

Variations

Rum can be replaced with 1 tsp (5 mL) rum extract.

Use pecans or almonds in place of the walnuts.

Chocolate Peanut Butter Cookies

These cookies are just like peanuts — you can't stop at just one.

MAKES ABOUT 4 DOZEN COOKIES

- **Preparation: 20 minutes**
- **Baking: 12 minutes**
- **Freezing: excellent**

- **Preheat oven to 350°F (180°C)**
- **Cookie sheet, greased or lined with parchment paper**

1	pkg (18.25 oz/515 g) devil's food cake mix	1
1 cup	creamy peanut butter	250 mL
2	eggs	2
¼ cup	milk	50 mL
1 cup	peanut butter chips	250 mL
¾ cup	chopped peanuts	175 mL

1. In a large bowl, using a wooden spoon, combine cake mix, peanut butter, eggs and milk, mixing until blended. Stir in peanut butter chips and peanuts.

2. Drop dough by tablespoonfuls (15 mL) about 2 inches (5 cm) apart on prepared cookie sheet. Bake in preheated oven for 8 to 12 minutes or until set. Cool for 5 minutes on sheet, then transfer to a rack and cool completely.

Crunchy Chocolate Dreams

The taste of these rich, dark cookies resembles a chocolate bar.

MAKES ABOUT 4 DOZEN

- **Preparation: 20 minutes**
- **Baking: 12 minutes**
- **Freezing: excellent**

- **Preheat oven to 375°F (190°C)**
- **Cookie sheet, greased or lined with parchment paper**

1	pkg (18.25 oz/515 g) devil's food cake mix	1
2	eggs	2
½ cup	vegetable oil	125 mL
1 cup	semi-sweet chocolate chips	250 mL
¾ cup	chopped walnuts	175 mL
¾ cup	crunchy toffee bits	175 mL

1. In a large bowl, using a wooden spoon, combine cake mix, eggs and oil, mixing until well blended (dough will be stiff). Stir in chocolate chips, walnuts and toffee bits.

2. Drop dough by tablespoonfuls (15 mL) about 2 inches (5 cm) apart on prepared cookie sheet. Bake in preheated oven for 8 to 12 minutes or until firm around edges. Cool for 5 minutes on sheet, then transfer to a rack and cool completely.

Crispy Chocolate Chunk Cookies

The addition of crispy rice cereal gives these cookies a pleasingly chewy texture that complements the chocolate.

**MAKES ABOUT
4 DOZEN COOKIES**

- **Preparation: 20 minutes**
- **Baking: 12 minutes**
- **Freezing: excellent**

- **Preheat oven to 375°F (190°C)**
- **Cookie sheet, greased or lined with parchment paper**

1	pkg (18.25 oz/515 g) devil's food cake mix	1
2	eggs	2
½ cup	butter, melted	125 mL
6	squares (1 oz/28 g each) semi-sweet chocolate, coarsely chopped	6
1½ cups	crisp rice cereal	375 mL

1. In a large bowl, using an electric mixer on low speed, beat cake mix, eggs and melted butter for 1 minute or just until smooth. With a wooden spoon, stir in chocolate and cereal.

2. Drop dough by tablespoonfuls (15 mL) about 2 inches (5 cm) apart on prepared cookie sheet. Flatten slightly with fingers. Bake in preheated oven for 8 to 12 minutes or until set. Cool for 5 minutes on sheet, then transfer to a rack and cool completely.

Double Chocolate Chewies

This versatile chocolate cookie lends itself to a variety of additions, such as chips, nuts and dried fruit.

**MAKES ABOUT
4 DOZEN COOKIES**

- **Preparation: 20 minutes**
- **Baking: 12 minutes**
- **Freezing: excellent**

- **Preheat oven to 375°F (190°C)**
- **Cookie sheet, greased or lined with parchment paper**

1	pkg (18.25 oz/515 g) devil's food cake mix	1
1	egg	1
⅓ cup	water	75 mL
¼ cup	butter, melted	50 mL
1½ cups	white chocolate chips	375 mL
½ cup	dried cranberries	125 mL
½ cup	slivered almonds	125 mL

1. In a large bowl, using an electric mixer on low speed, beat cake mix, egg, water and melted butter for 1 minute or just until smooth. With a wooden spoon, stir in chocolate chips, cranberries and almonds.

2. Drop dough by tablespoonfuls (15 mL) about 2 inches (5 cm) apart on prepared cookie sheet. Bake in preheated oven for 8 to 12 minutes or just until softly set. Cool for 5 minutes on sheet, then transfer to a rack and cool completely.

Chocolate Cookies

Chocolate is such a popular ingredient, it deserves a section of its own. You'll find cookies containing chocolate in other chapters of this book, but there the luscious chocolate flavor is secondary. Here, chocolate dominates. Some of the cookies are downright decadent and will satisfy even the most committed chocoholic.

I guarantee there's a cookie in this chapter for every chocolate-lover you know. They range from plain and simple to those loaded with chocolate-compatible ingredients, such as nuts, cereals, caramels and dried fruits, which add texture and taste. The chocolate flavors run the gamut from deep dark to creamy milk and, from time to time, are accented with buttery white chocolate.

Different flavors will suit different preferences, but all are delicious. Packaged in a fancy box or tin, they make a welcome gift with the personal touch you just don't get from a box of store-bought chocolates. The hardest part of this chapter was eliminating some of my many favorites that I just couldn't fit in.

◄ *Chocolate Chunk Pecan Cookies and Toffee Chocolate Almond Chippers*

Chocolate Chunk Pecan Cookies

Chocolate has to be a cookie's best friend. This rich, buttery dough, studded with chocolate and pecans, bakes into a delicious cookie with a soft, chewy texture.

MAKES ABOUT 5 DOZEN COOKIES

- **Preparation: 25 minutes**
- **Baking: 12 minutes**
- **Freezing: excellent**

TIPS

Don't overbake chocolate chip cookies if you like them chewy. With longer baking, they are still very edible but they have a crispier texture.

Although recipes usually call for an electric mixer to blend ingredients, you can almost always use a wooden spoon when making cookies. It just takes more physical effort. With either method, it usually takes about 3 minutes to get a butter-and-sugar mixture light and creamy.

- **Preheat oven to 375°F (190°C)**
- **Cookie sheet, ungreased**

2¼ cups	all-purpose flour	550 mL
1 tsp	baking soda	5 mL
½ tsp	salt	2 mL
1 cup	butter, softened	250 mL
¾ cup	granulated sugar	175 mL
¾ cup	packed brown sugar	175 mL
2	eggs	2
1 tsp	vanilla	5 mL
15	squares (1 oz/28 g each) semi-sweet chocolate, coarsely chopped	15
1 cup	coarsely chopped pecans	250 mL

1. On a sheet of waxed paper or in a bowl, combine flour, baking soda and salt. Set aside.

2. In a large bowl, using an electric mixer on medium speed, beat butter and granulated and brown sugars until light and creamy, about 3 minutes. Add eggs, one at a time, beating well after each addition. Beat in vanilla. On low speed, gradually add flour mixture, beating until blended. With a wooden spoon, stir in chocolate and pecans.

3. Drop dough by tablespoonfuls (15 mL) about 2 inches (5 cm) apart on cookie sheet. Bake in preheated oven for 8 to 12 minutes or until golden around edges. Cool for 5 minutes on sheet, then transfer to a rack and cool completely.

Variations

Omit the pecans for a version that doesn't contain nuts.

Replace chopped chocolate with 2½ cups (625 mL) chocolate chips.

Toffee Chocolate Almond Chippers

When you have a craving for something sweet and you can't decide between a cookie and a candy bar, these cookies fit the bill.

MAKES ABOUT 3 DOZEN COOKIES

- **Preparation: 25 minutes**
- **Baking: 16 minutes**
- **Freezing: excellent**

TIPS

I like to use Skor bars, which are available in bulk. Heath bars are another good choice for this recipe.

If you bake most chocolate chip cookies until they are golden around the edges but still pale in the center, they will be soft and chewy. Bake until they are a light golden color overall, and they will be crisp. Try some both ways the next time you make a batch and decide your preference.

Chill the chocolate bars for easy chopping. You can also put them in a heavy plastic bag and smash them with a meat mallet.

- **Preheat oven to 350°F (180°C)**
- **Cookie sheet, lined with parchment paper**

1 ½ cups	all-purpose flour	375 mL
¾ tsp	baking soda	3 mL
¼ tsp	salt	1 mL
½ cup	butter, softened	125 mL
½ cup	packed brown sugar	125 mL
¼ cup	granulated sugar	50 mL
1	egg	1
2 tbsp	milk	25 mL
½ tsp	almond extract	2 mL
4	(1.4 oz/39 g each) chocolate-covered toffee bars, chopped	4
1 cup	semi-sweet chocolate chips	250 mL
1 cup	slivered almonds	250 mL

1. On a sheet of waxed paper or in a bowl, combine flour, baking soda and salt. Set aside.

2. In a large bowl, using an electric mixer on medium speed, beat butter, brown and granulated sugars, egg, milk and almond extract until light and creamy, about 3 minutes. On low speed, gradually add flour mixture, beating until blended. With a wooden spoon, stir in toffee bars, chocolate chips and almonds.

3. Drop dough by tablespoonfuls (15 mL) about 2 inches (5 cm) apart on prepared cookie sheet. Bake in preheated oven for 12 to 16 minutes or until golden. Cool for 5 minutes on sheet, then transfer to a rack and cool completely.

Variations

Substitute pecans or cashews for the almonds.

For a milder chocolate taste, use milk chocolate chips.

If you prefer a deeper chocolate flavor, add 2 tbsp (25 mL) cocoa powder to the dry ingredients.

Turn these into sandwich cookies with a filling of chocolate or butterscotch ripple ice cream.

Double Chocolate Chunk Cookies

These are so good warm you should be prepared to make a double batch if you serve them that way. The chocolate flavor permeates the dough and the chunks provide a great finish.

MAKES ABOUT 4 DOZEN COOKIES

- **Preparation: 25 minutes**
- **Baking: 12 minutes**
- **Freezing: excellent**

TIPS

Cocoa tends to clump in storage. Before using, sift it with other dry ingredients.

You can use brown and granulated sugar interchangeably. Brown sugar contains molasses, so it is moist and has a slight caramel flavor. Because it is moister, brown sugar will clump and dry out, while granulated sugar will stay granular, which makes it easier to mix.

- **Preheat oven to 375°F (190°C)**
- **Cookie sheet, greased or lined with parchment paper**

1 ½ cups	all-purpose flour	375 mL
½ cup	unsweetened cocoa powder, sifted	125 mL
1 tsp	baking soda	5 mL
¼ tsp	salt	1 mL
1 cup	butter, softened	250 mL
¾ cup	packed brown sugar	175 mL
⅔ cup	granulated sugar	150 mL
1	egg	1
1 tsp	vanilla	5 mL
6	squares (1 oz/28 g each) bittersweet chocolate, cut in chunks	6
6	squares (1 oz/28 g each) semi-sweet chocolate, cut in chunks	6
1 cup	coarsely chopped pecans	250 mL

1. On a sheet of waxed paper or in a bowl, combine flour, cocoa, baking soda and salt. Set aside.

2. In a large bowl, using an electric mixer on medium speed, beat butter and brown and granulated sugars until light and creamy, about 3 minutes. Add egg and vanilla, beating until blended. On low speed, gradually add flour mixture, beating until blended. With a wooden spoon, stir in bittersweet and semi-sweet chocolate and pecans.

3. Drop dough by tablespoonfuls (15 mL) about 2 inches (5 cm) apart on prepared cookie sheet. Bake in preheated oven for 8 to 12 minutes or until set. Cool for 5 minutes on sheet, then transfer to a rack and cool completely.

Variations

Use all semi-sweet chocolate.

Replace half of the chocolate with white chocolate.

Use 1 cup (250 mL) semi-sweet chocolate chips in place of the chunks.

Judie's Chocolate Chip Cookies

Many, many people in her hometown love my sister's chocolate chip cookies. And I have to admit, they are pretty darn good.

MAKES ABOUT 5 DOZEN COOKIES

- **Preparation: 25 minutes**
- **Baking: 12 minutes**
- **Freezing: excellent**

TIPS

I usually bake with butter because I like its flavor and because shortening usually contains unhealthy trans fats. However, my niece's kids have difficulty digesting butter, so I've included her mother's recipe for these delicious cookies. Make them using shortening that doesn't contain hydrogenated oils.

Remember, cookies continue to bake when they come out of the oven. If you aren't sure, bake them for a little less time than you think is right.

Nuts are always an option in chocolate chip cookies. Sometimes I use half the batter, then add nuts to the remaining half.

If you do omit the nuts, you can replace them with more chocolate chips.

- **Preheat oven to 375°F (190°C)**
- **Cookie sheet, ungreased**

1¾ cups	all-purpose flour	425 mL
½ cup	quick-cooking rolled oats	125 mL
1 tsp	baking soda	5 mL
½ tsp	salt	2 mL
1 cup	non-hydrogenated shortening (see Tips)	250 mL
1¼ cups	packed brown sugar	300 mL
2	eggs	2
2½ cups	semi-sweet chocolate chips	625 mL
1 cup	chopped pecans, optional	250 mL

1. On a sheet of waxed paper or in a bowl, combine flour, oats, baking soda and salt. Set aside.

2. In a large bowl, using an electric mixer on medium speed, beat shortening, brown sugar and eggs until light and creamy, about 3 minutes. On low speed, gradually add flour mixture, beating until blended. With a wooden spoon, stir in chocolate chips and pecans, if using.

3. Drop dough by tablespoonfuls (15 mL) about 2 inches (5 cm) apart on cookie sheet. Bake in preheated oven for 8 to 12 minutes or until golden around edges. Cool for 5 minutes on sheet, then transfer to a rack and cool completely.

Variations

Replace chocolate chips with 10 squares (1 oz/28 g each) chocolate, chopped.

Replace pecans with slivered almonds.

Peanut Fudgies

These cookies are like a chewy brownie that's loaded with chips and peanuts.

MAKES ABOUT 3½ DOZEN COOKIES

- Preparation: 30 minutes
- Cooking: 4 minutes
- Baking: 13 minutes
- Freezing: excellent

TIPS

Use a sharp chef's knife to chop nuts, and do it on a wooden board, or pulse them in a food processor. If you prefer, look for nuts that are already chopped.

If you're not using nuts soon after purchase, store them in the freezer to prevent rancidity.

- **Preheat oven to 350°F (180°C)**
- **Cookie sheet, greased or lined with parchment paper**

2¼ cups	semi-sweet chocolate chips, divided	550 mL
½ cup	butter	125 mL
⅔ cup	all-purpose flour	150 mL
½ tsp	baking soda	2 mL
2	eggs	2
¾ cup	packed brown sugar	175 mL
1¼ cups	chopped honey-roasted peanuts	300 mL
1 cup	peanut butter chips	250 mL

1. In a small saucepan, over low heat, melt 1¼ cups (300 mL) chocolate chips and butter, stirring until smooth. Remove from heat. Set aside to cool.

2. On a sheet of waxed paper or in a bowl, combine flour and baking soda. Set aside.

3. In a large bowl, using a wooden spoon, beat eggs and brown sugar until well blended. Stir in cooled chocolate mixture. Gradually add flour mixture, mixing until smooth. Stir in peanuts, peanut butter chips and remaining 1 cup (250 mL) chocolate chips.

4. Drop dough by tablespoonfuls (15 mL) about 2 inches (5 cm) apart on prepared cookie sheet. Bake in preheated oven for 9 to 13 minutes or until set around edges but slightly soft in the center. Cool for 5 minutes on sheet, then transfer to a rack and cool completely.

Variation

Other nuts, like cashews, pecans or hazelnuts, are also great in this recipe.

Chocolate Cherry Mounds

These luscious mounds are a slightly firmer version of melted chocolate with nuts and cherries. Rich and delicious.

MAKES ABOUT 4½ DOZEN COOKIES

- **Preparation: 30 minutes**
- **Cooking: 4 minutes**
- **Baking: 15 minutes**
- **Freezing: excellent**

TIP

Toasting nuts before baking improves their flavor. Spread them out on a rimmed baking sheet and bake at 350°F (180°C) for about 10 minutes or until fragrant and lightly browned. If nuts are chopped, they'll take less time. Cool before using.

- **Preheat oven to 325°F (160°C)**
- **Cookie sheet, ungreased**

1 cup	all-purpose flour	250 mL
1 tsp	baking powder	5 mL
¼ tsp	salt	1 mL
12	squares (1 oz/28 g each) semi-sweet chocolate, divided into 2 groups of 6 and chopped	12
4	squares (1 oz/28 g each) unsweetened chocolate, chopped	4
6 tbsp	butter	90 mL
1 cup	granulated sugar	250 mL
3	eggs	3
1½ tsp	vanilla	7 mL
1½ cups	coarsely chopped pecans	375 mL
¾ cup	chopped dried cherries	175 mL

1. On a sheet of waxed paper or in a bowl, combine flour, baking powder and salt. Set aside.

2. In a large saucepan over low heat, combine 6 squares of the semi-sweet chocolate, the unsweetened chocolate and butter, stirring until melted and smooth. Remove from heat. With a wooden spoon, stir in sugar. Add eggs, one at a time, beating well after each addition. Stir in vanilla. Gradually add flour mixture, stirring until smooth. Add pecans, cherries and remaining chopped semi-sweet chocolate, mixing until thoroughly blended.

3. Drop by tablespoonfuls (15 mL) about 2 inches (5 cm) apart on cookie sheet. Bake in preheated oven for 11 to 15 minutes or until set. Cool for 5 minutes on sheet, then transfer to a rack and cool completely.

Variations

Any kind of nut works well in these cookies.

Replace cherries with dried cranberries. There's no need to chop cranberries because they are smaller.

Omit cherries and add 1 tbsp (15 mL) instant espresso coffee powder to the dough along with the flour.

Chocolate Peanut Crisps

This is a soft brownie-like cookie with crisp cereal and lots of crunchy nuts.

MAKES ABOUT 4 DOZEN COOKIES

- **Preparation: 25 minutes**
- **Cooking: 4 minutes**
- **Baking: 11 minutes**
- **Freezing: excellent**

TIPS

You can also use your microwave oven to melt chocolate. Place in a microwave-safe bowl and heat at high power for 1 minute. Stir and microwave for 10 to 20 seconds longer or until softened. Stir until smooth.

Chopping chocolate before melting ensures it will melt smoothly and easily.

- **Preheat oven to 375°F (190°C)**
- **Cookie sheet, ungreased**

4	squares (1 oz/28 g each) semi-sweet chocolate, chopped	4
1 1/4 cups	all-purpose flour	300 mL
3/4 tsp	baking soda	3 mL
1/4 tsp	salt	1 mL
1/2 cup	butter, softened	125 mL
1/2 cup	packed brown sugar	125 mL
1/4 cup	granulated sugar	50 mL
1	egg	1
1 1/2 tsp	vanilla	7 mL
1 1/2 cups	coarsely chopped honey-roasted peanuts	375 mL
1 cup	semi-sweet chocolate chips	250 mL
1 cup	crisp rice cereal	250 mL

1. In a small saucepan over low heat, melt chocolate, stirring until smooth. Remove from heat. Set aside to cool.

2. On a sheet of waxed paper or in a bowl, combine flour, baking soda and salt. Set aside.

3. In a large bowl, using an electric mixer on medium speed, beat butter, brown and granulated sugars, egg and vanilla until light and creamy, about 3 minutes. Beat in melted chocolate until smooth. On low speed, gradually add flour mixture, beating until blended. With a wooden spoon, stir in peanuts, chocolate chips and cereal.

4. Drop dough by tablespoonfuls (15 mL) about 2 inches (5 cm) apart on cookie sheet. Bake in preheated oven for 7 to 11 minutes or until puffed and set around edges but slightly soft in center. Cool for 5 minutes on sheet, then transfer to a rack and cool completely.

Variations

Use regular peanuts rather than honey-roasted.

Use salted or unsalted peanuts, whichever you prefer.

Triple Chocolate Fudge Cookies

These cookies are soft and almost fudge-like. Chocolate-lovers will thoroughly enjoy the intense chocolate flavor.

MAKES ABOUT 5 DOZEN COOKIES

- **Preparation: 25 minutes**
- **Baking: 11 minutes**
- **Freezing: excellent**

TIPS

When storing soft cookies, be sure they have cooled completely. Separate each layer with waxed paper and store in airtight containers.

Don't store soft cookies with crisp cookies, as neither will retain their desired texture.

- **Preheat oven to 375°F (190°C)**
- **Cookie sheet, ungreased**

2¼ cups	all-purpose flour	550 mL
½ cup	unsweetened cocoa powder, sifted	125 mL
1 tsp	baking soda	5 mL
¼ tsp	salt	1 mL
1 cup	butter, softened	250 mL
¾ cup	packed brown sugar	175 mL
¾ cup	granulated sugar	175 mL
2	eggs	2
1 tsp	vanilla	5 mL
1 cup	semi-sweet chocolate chips	250 mL
1 cup	white chocolate chips	250 mL
1 cup	milk chocolate chips	250 mL

1. On a sheet of waxed paper or in a bowl, combine flour, cocoa, baking soda and salt. Set aside.

2. In a large bowl, using an electric mixer on medium speed, beat butter and brown and granulated sugars until light and creamy, about 3 minutes. Add eggs, one at a time, beating well after each addition. Beat in vanilla. On low speed, gradually add flour mixture, beating until blended. With a wooden spoon, stir in semi-sweet, white and milk chocolate chips.

3. Drop dough by tablespoonfuls (15 mL) about 2 inches (5 cm) apart on cookie sheet. Bake in preheated oven for 7 to 11 minutes or until puffed and set around edges but slightly soft in center. Cool for 5 minutes on sheet, then transfer to a rack and cool completely.

Variation

Vary the kind of chocolate chips, keeping total amount to 3 cups (750 mL).

Marbled Chocolate Puffs

These are light, puffy meringues with a great hit of chocolate. The cooked meringue is well worth the extra preparation time because it allows you to use melted chocolate in a meringue cookie, which is delicious and unusual.

MAKES ABOUT 3½ DOZEN COOKIES

- **Preparation: 20 minutes**
- **Cooking: 4 minutes**
- **Baking: 40 minutes**
- **Freezing: not recommended**

TIPS

Don't fold the chocolate and meringue too much. It will marble more as you spoon it out.

If you don't have a double boiler, look for a metal bowl that will fit inside a pot and extend about halfway down into the pot.

These meringues will be crispy outside but chewy inside.

- **Preheat oven to 275°F (140°C)**
- **Cookie sheet greased or lined with parchment paper**

3	squares (1 oz/28 g each) bittersweet chocolate, chopped	3
4	egg whites	4
1 cup	granulated sugar	250 mL
½ tsp	vanilla	2 mL

1. In a small saucepan, over low heat, melt chocolate, stirring until smooth. Remove from heat. Set aside to cool slightly.

2. In a metal bowl or the top of a double boiler, combine egg whites and sugar. Place bowl over a pot of simmering (not boiling) water so the bowl is just above, not touching, the water. Whisk egg white mixture until it is translucent and hot, about 4 minutes. Transfer to a large bowl. Using an electric mixer on high speed, beat until stiff, shiny peaks form, about 4 minutes. Beat in vanilla. Drizzle with melted chocolate and, with a spatula, gently fold chocolate into the meringue just until slightly marbled.

3. Drop meringue in large mounds about 2 inches (5 cm) apart on prepared cookie sheet. Bake in preheated oven for 35 to 40 minutes or until outside is crisp and dry. Cool completely on sheet.

Soft and Chewy Chocolate Indulgences

These decadent cookies are loaded with chocolate flavor and are simply irresistible while still warm.

MAKES ABOUT 3 DOZEN COOKIES

- **Preparation: 25 minutes**
- **Baking: 12 minutes**
- **Freezing: excellent**

TIPS

Cookies should be set around the edges but a little soft in the center when you take them out of the oven. They continue to cook while cooling on the cookie sheet.

Use real vanilla for baking. It has a wonderful true flavor you don't get in artificial versions.

- **Preheat oven to 350°F (180°C)**
- **Cookie sheet, greased or lined with parchment paper**

1 ½ cups	all-purpose flour	375 mL
¾ cup	unsweetened cocoa powder, sifted	175 mL
½ tsp	baking soda	2 mL
½ tsp	salt	2 mL
1 cup	butter, softened	250 mL
1 cup	packed brown sugar	250 mL
½ cup	granulated sugar	125 mL
2	eggs	2
1 ½ tsp	vanilla	7 mL
2 cups	semi-sweet chocolate chips	500 mL

1. On a sheet of waxed paper or in a bowl, combine flour, cocoa, baking soda and salt. Set aside.

2. In a large bowl, using an electric mixer on medium speed, beat butter and brown and granulated sugars until light and creamy, about 3 minutes. Add eggs, one at a time, beating well after each addition. Beat in vanilla. On low speed, gradually add flour mixture, beating until blended. With a wooden spoon, stir in chocolate chips.

3. Drop dough by heaping tablespoonfuls (20 mL) about 2 inches (5 cm) apart on prepared cookie sheet. Bake in preheated oven for 8 to 12 minutes or just until set. Cool for 5 minutes on sheet, then transfer to a rack and cool completely.

Variation
Replace semi-sweet chocolate chips with milk chocolate chips.

Chocolate Chunk Walnut Oat Cookies

◆

Ground oats give these cookies a taste and texture unlike any others. They are thicker than most, with a great "oaty" taste. Not really crisp or chewy, they are soft but not cakey.

MAKES ABOUT 4 DOZEN COOKIES

- **Preparation: 25 minutes**
- **Baking: 12 minutes**
- **Freezing: excellent**

TIPS

Use quick-cooking or large-flake old-fashioned rolled oats, as you prefer.

To freeze these cookies to bake later, drop the dough on sheet as described and freeze until firm. Transfer to a freezer bag. When ready to bake, place on cookie sheet. Let thaw for about 10 minutes, then bake 15 to 20 minutes.

- **Preheat oven to 375°F (190°C)**
- **Cookie sheet, ungreased**

2 cups	rolled oats (see Tips)	500 mL
2½ cups	semi-sweet chocolate chips, divided	625 mL
2 cups	all-purpose flour	500 mL
1 tsp	baking powder	5 mL
1 tsp	baking soda	5 mL
½ tsp	salt	2 mL
1 cup	butter, softened	250 mL
1 cup	granulated sugar	250 mL
1 cup	packed brown sugar	250 mL
2	eggs	2
1 tsp	vanilla	5 mL
1 cup	chopped walnuts	250 mL

1. In a food processor or blender, process oats and ½ cup (125 mL) of the chocolate chips until ground to a fine powder. Place on a sheet of waxed paper or in a bowl. Add flour, baking powder, baking soda and salt, and mix to blend. Set aside.

2. In a large bowl, using an electric mixer on medium speed, beat butter and granulated and brown sugars until light and creamy, about 3 minutes. Add eggs, one at a time, beating well after each addition. Beat in vanilla. On low speed, gradually add flour mixture, beating until blended. With a wooden spoon, stir in remaining 2 cups (500 mL) chocolate chips and walnuts.

3. Drop dough by tablespoonfuls (15 mL) about 2 inches (5 cm) apart on cookie sheet. Bake in preheated oven for 8 to 12 minutes or until golden. Cool for 5 minutes on sheet, then transfer to a rack and cool completely.

Variations

Any nut is great in this cookie. Try almonds, pecans or cashews.

Add 1 tsp (5 mL) ground cinnamon to the flour mixture.

Chocolate Peanut Butter Cashew Crisps

Awesome! What more is there to say?

MAKES ABOUT 3 DOZEN COOKIES

- **Preparation: 25 minutes**
- **Baking: 14 minutes**
- **Freezing: excellent**

TIPS

I prefer combining the dry ingredients on a piece of waxed paper instead of dirtying a bowl. Then I use the paper as a funnel when adding them to the butter mixture.

Nuts have a high fat content, which can cause them to become rancid fairly quickly. Store them in the freezer to keep them fresh.

Don't overbeat cookie dough. The more air you incorporate into the dough, the lighter and more cake-like the texture will become. Cookies should be chewy or crisp.

- **Preheat oven to 350°F (180°C)**
- **Cookie sheet, ungreased**

1¾ cups	all-purpose flour	425 mL
½ tsp	baking soda	2 mL
¼ tsp	salt	1 mL
½ cup	butter, softened	125 mL
½ cup	crunchy peanut butter	125 mL
½ cup	granulated sugar	125 mL
½ cup	packed brown sugar	125 mL
1	egg	1
¼ cup	corn syrup	50 mL
1½ cups	semi-sweet chocolate chips	375 mL
1 cup	crisp rice cereal	250 mL
½ cup	coarsely chopped cashews	125 mL

1. On a sheet of waxed paper or in a bowl, combine flour, baking soda and salt. Set aside.

2. In a large bowl, using an electric mixer on medium speed, beat butter, peanut butter, granulated and brown sugars, egg and corn syrup until light and creamy, about 3 minutes. On low speed, gradually add flour mixture, beating until blended. With a wooden spoon, stir in chocolate chips, cereal and cashews.

3. Drop dough by heaping tablespoonfuls (20 mL) about 2 inches (5 cm) apart on cookie sheet. Bake in preheated oven for 10 to 14 minutes or until golden. Cool for 5 minutes on sheet, then transfer to a rack and cool completely.

Variations

Substitute any kind of nut for the cashews.

Replace cashews with flaked coconut.

Nutty Chocolate Candy Cookies

No flour and no eggs! These cookies are chewy, chocolaty and nutty — halfway between a cookie and a candy. However you describe them, they certainly are delicious.

MAKES ABOUT 3½ DOZEN COOKIES

- **Preparation: 30 minutes**
- **Cooking: 5 minutes**
- **Baking: 12 minutes**
- **Freezing: excellent**

TIPS

It's hard to tell when chocolate cookies are done because there's no golden color to give you a clue. If you touch the top lightly, they will feel set. Remember, cookies will continue to cook after being removed from the oven.

A reliable oven thermometer is a good investment. It will tell you whether your oven heat is aligned with the setting. If not, you can adjust it accordingly.

- **Preheat oven to 350°F (180°C)**
- **Cookie sheet, greased or lined with parchment paper**

1	can (14 oz/396 g OR 300 mL) sweetened condensed milk	1
2	squares (1 oz/28 g each) unsweetened chocolate, chopped	2
2	squares (1 oz/28 g each) bittersweet chocolate, chopped	2
1 tbsp	butter	15 mL
½ tsp	almond extract	2 mL
1 cup	unsweetened flaked coconut	250 mL
¾ cup	slivered almonds	175 mL
½ cup	coarsely chopped hazelnuts	125 mL
½ cup	coarsely chopped pecans	125 mL

1. In a large saucepan over low heat, heat condensed milk, unsweetened and bittersweet chocolate and butter, stirring until chocolate is melted and mixture is smooth. Remove from heat. With a wooden spoon, stir in almond extract, coconut, almonds, hazelnuts and pecans.

2. Drop dough by tablespoonfuls (15 mL) about 2 inches (5 cm) apart on prepared cookie sheet. Bake in preheated oven for 8 to 12 minutes or until set. Cool completely on sheet.

Variations

Replace one of the nuts, or the coconut, with dried cranberries or chopped dried apricots.

Use your favorite kinds of nuts. I like a mixture, but you can also use 1¾ cups (425 mL) of a single variety.

Chocolate Walnut Raisin Clusters

A hint of spice enhances the flavor of this cookie, which is filled with chewy, chunky ingredients and great chocolate flavor.

MAKES ABOUT 4 DOZEN COOKIES

- **Preparation: 25 minutes**
- **Baking: 12 minutes**
- **Freezing: excellent**

TIPS

This recipe has a lot of extra ingredients for such a small quantity of dough. Mix well to ensure that all are coated with some dough.

Keep your spices fresh — their flavor weakens with storage. It's a good idea to replace spices about every 6 months for optimum flavor.

- **Preheat oven to 350°F (180°C)**
- **Cookie sheet, ungreased**

1 cup	all-purpose flour	250 mL
1 tsp	baking soda	5 mL
¼ tsp	salt	1 mL
1 tsp	ground cinnamon	5 mL
½ cup	butter, softened	125 mL
½ cup	granulated sugar	125 mL
¼ cup	packed brown sugar	50 mL
1	egg	1
1½ cups	semi-sweet chocolate chips	375 mL
1½ cups	coarsely chopped walnuts	375 mL
1½ cups	raisins	375 mL
½ cup	sunflower seeds	125 mL

1. On a sheet of waxed paper or in a bowl, combine flour, baking soda, salt and cinnamon. Set aside.

2. In a large bowl, using an electric mixer on medium speed, beat butter, granulated and brown sugars and egg until light and creamy, about 3 minutes. On low speed, gradually add flour mixture, beating until blended. With a wooden spoon, stir in chocolate chips, walnuts, raisins and sunflower seeds.

3. Drop dough by tablespoonfuls (15 mL) about 2 inches (5 cm) apart on cookie sheet. Bake in preheated oven for 8 to 12 minutes or until golden. Cool for 5 minutes on sheet, then transfer to a rack and cool completely.

Variations

Omit sunflower seeds.

For a less chunky cookie, reduce the chocolate, walnuts and raisins to 1 cup (250 mL) each.

Chocolate-Dipped Brownie Mounds

Bite-size brownies dipped in chocolate are easy to make from a roll of refrigerator chocolate cookie dough.

MAKES ABOUT 4 DOZEN COOKIES

- **Preparation: 35 minutes**
- **Chilling: 2 hours**
- **Baking: 14 minutes**
- **Freezing: excellent (not dipped)**

TIPS

If chocolate mixture thickens before you have all the cookies dipped, rewarm it slightly to soften.

You can buy coating chocolate, which hardens quickly, in small wafer shapes. They make dipping easy. Look for them in bulk and cake decorating stores.

If freezing, do not dip the cookies in chocolate until you're ready to serve.

To get perfectly round cookies, pack the dough into an appropriate-size used roll from waxed paper, plastic wrap or aluminum foil. Once chilled, simply cut tube open.

◆

- **Cookie sheet, greased or lined with parchment paper**

COOKIE

1 ½ cups	all-purpose flour	375 mL
⅓ cup	unsweetened cocoa powder, sifted	75 mL
½ tsp	baking powder	2 mL
½ tsp	baking soda	2 mL
¼ tsp	salt	1 mL
½ cup	butter, softened	125 mL
¾ cup	granulated sugar	175 mL
1	egg	1

CHOCOLATE DIP

5	squares (1 oz/28 g each) semi-sweet chocolate, chopped	5
1 tsp	vegetable oil	5 mL

1. *Cookie:* On a sheet of waxed paper or in a bowl, combine flour, cocoa, baking powder, baking soda and salt. Set aside.

2. In a large bowl, using an electric mixer on medium speed, beat butter, sugar and egg until light and creamy, about 3 minutes. On low speed, gradually add flour mixture, beating until blended. Divide dough into thirds. Shape each into a roll 12 inches (30 cm) long. Wrap and chill until firm, at least 2 hours.

3. When you're ready to bake, preheat oven to 350°F (180°C). Cut rolls into ¾-inch (2 cm) slices. Place cut side down about 1 inch (2.5 cm) apart on prepared cookie sheet. Bake in preheated oven for 10 to 14 minutes or until set around edges but still soft in the center. Cool for 5 minutes on sheet, then transfer to a rack and cool completely.

4. *Chocolate Dip:* In a small saucepan on low heat, melt chocolate and oil, stirring until smooth. Remove from heat. Transfer to a small bowl for easy dipping. Dip side of each cookie into chocolate, covering half the cookie. Set on a rack placed over a sheet of waxed paper. Chill 20 minutes to set chocolate.

Variation

Dip some of the cookies in melted white chocolate.

Chocolate Chunk Oatmeal Cookies

These cookies are particularly good for after-school snacks and lunch-box treats.

MAKES ABOUT 5 DOZEN COOKIES

- **Preparation: 25 minutes**
- **Baking: 14 minutes**
- **Freezing: excellent**

TIPS

Always check cookies halfway through the baking time to see how they are browning. If they are browning faster at the back of the oven, turn the cookie sheet around.

When using an electric mixer, scrape down the sides of the bowl often so all the ingredients are properly blended.

- **Preheat oven to 325°F (160°C)**
- **Cookie sheet, ungreased**

1¾ cups	all-purpose flour	425 mL
1½ tsp	baking powder	7 mL
1 tsp	baking soda	5 mL
½ tsp	salt	2 mL
1 tsp	ground cinnamon	5 mL
¾ cup	butter, softened	175 mL
1¾ cups	packed brown sugar	425 mL
2	eggs	2
3 tbsp	milk	45 mL
1½ tsp	vanilla	7 mL
2 cups	quick-cooking rolled oats	500 mL
10	squares (1 oz/28 g each) semi-sweet chocolate, chopped	10
1½ cups	coarsely chopped pecans	375 mL
1 cup	sweetened flaked coconut	250 mL

1. On a sheet of waxed paper or in a bowl, combine flour, baking powder, baking soda, salt and cinnamon. Set aside.

2. In a large bowl, using an electric mixer on medium speed, beat butter and brown sugar until light and creamy, about 3 minutes. Add eggs, one at a time, beating well after each addition. Beat in milk and vanilla. On low speed, gradually add flour mixture, beating until blended. With a wooden spoon, stir in oats, chocolate, pecans and coconut.

3. Drop dough by tablespoonfuls (15 mL) about 2 inches (5 cm) apart on cookie sheet. Bake in preheated oven for 10 to 14 minutes or until golden around edges. Cool for 5 minutes on sheet, then transfer to a rack and cool completely.

Variation

Substitute large-flake old-fashioned oats for the quick-cooking. They will provide a more homey appearance and a slightly drier, but oatier, taste.

Chocolate Chip Oatmeal Toffee Cookies

With their deep chocolate flavor, these cookies remind me of a candy bar disguised as a cookie.

MAKES ABOUT 5 DOZEN COOKIES

- **Preparation: 25 minutes**
- **Baking: 12 minutes**
- **Freezing: excellent**

TIPS

For a crisp cookie, bake 10 to 14 minutes.

Toffee bits don't keep very well. They soften and lose their crunchiness with age, so don't stock up on them.

Skor toffee bits are available in bulk and in packages where the chocolate chips are displayed. Heath is another well-known brand.

- **Preheat oven to 375°F (190°C)**
- **Cookie sheet, greased or lined with parchment paper**

1¾ cups	all-purpose flour	425 mL
1 tsp	baking soda	5 mL
¼ tsp	salt	1 mL
½ tsp	ground cinnamon	2 mL
1¼ cups	butter, softened	300 mL
1 cup	packed brown sugar	250 mL
½ cup	granulated sugar	125 mL
2	eggs	2
2 tbsp	milk	25 mL
2½ cups	quick-cooking rolled oats	625 mL
1½ cups	semi-sweet chocolate chips	375 mL
1 cup	milk chocolate chips	250 mL
¾ cup	toffee bits	175 mL

1. On a sheet of waxed paper or in a bowl, combine flour, baking soda, salt and cinnamon. Set aside.

2. In a large bowl, using an electric mixer on medium speed, beat butter and brown and granulated sugars until light and creamy, about 3 minutes. Add eggs, one at a time, beating well after each addition. Beat in milk. On low speed, gradually add flour mixture, beating until blended. With a wooden spoon, stir in oats, semi-sweet and milk chocolate chips and toffee bits.

3. Drop dough by tablespoonfuls (15 mL) about 2 inches (5 cm) apart on prepared cookie sheet. Bake in preheated oven for 8 to 12 minutes or until golden. Cool for 5 minutes on sheet, then transfer to a rack and cool completely.

Variations

Replace toffee bits with chopped nuts.

Replace milk chocolate chips with semi-sweet or white chocolate chips, or butterscotch chips.

Chocolate Orange Oatmeal Cookies

Here's a sweet, crisp, chocolaty cookie with a hint of orange. It makes a great ice cream sandwich with orange or chocolate ice cream.

MAKES ABOUT 4 DOZEN COOKIES

- Preparation: 25 minutes
- Baking: 12 minutes
- Freezing: excellent

TIPS

Although recipes usually call for an electric mixer to blend ingredients, you can almost always use a wooden spoon when making cookies. It just takes more physical effort. With either method, it usually takes about 3 minutes to get a butter-and-sugar mixture light and creamy.

When baking, always set your timer for the minimum time recommended. You can always bake a little longer, but you can't fix an overbaked product.

- **Preheat oven to 375°F (190°C)**
- **Cookie sheet, ungreased**

¾ cup	all-purpose flour	175 mL
½ tsp	baking soda	2 mL
¼ tsp	salt	1 mL
½ cup	butter, softened	125 mL
¾ cup	granulated sugar	175 mL
½ cup	packed brown sugar	125 mL
1	egg	1
1 tbsp	grated orange zest	15 mL
1¼ cups	quick-cooking rolled oats	300 mL
1 cup	semi-sweet chocolate chips	250 mL
1 cup	white chocolate chips	250 mL
1 cup	slivered almonds	250 mL

1. On a sheet of waxed paper or in a bowl, combine flour, baking soda and salt. Set aside.

2. In a large bowl, using an electric mixer on medium speed, beat butter, granulated and brown sugars, egg and orange zest until light and creamy, about 3 minutes. On low speed, gradually add flour mixture, beating until blended. With a wooden spoon, stir in oats, semi-sweet and white chocolate chips and almonds.

3. Drop dough by tablespoonfuls (15 mL) about 2 inches (5 cm) apart on cookie sheet. Bake in preheated oven for 8 to 12 minutes or until golden. Cool for 5 minutes on sheet, then transfer to a rack and cool completely.

Variations

Replace almonds with dried cranberries.

Replace both kinds of chocolate chips with 2 cups (500 mL) chopped bittersweet chocolate.

If you prefer, make this recipe into bars. Press the dough into a greased 13- by 9-inch (3 L) cake pan and bake at 350°F (180°C) for 30 to 35 minutes or until golden.

Milk Chocolate Peanut Butter Cookies

These cookies have a mild peanut butter taste with lots of chocolate. They're perfect with a glass of milk for an after-school treat.

**MAKES ABOUT
5 DOZEN COOKIES**

- **Preparation: 20 minutes**
- **Baking: 15 minutes**
- **Freezing: excellent**

TIP

Check the best-before date on peanut butter. It can go rancid quickly if not properly stored.

- **Preheat oven to 350°F (180°C)**
- **Cookie sheet, ungreased**

2½ cups	all-purpose flour	625 mL
1 tsp	baking soda	5 mL
1 cup	butter, softened	250 mL
¾ cup	creamy peanut butter	175 mL
1 cup	granulated sugar	250 mL
1 cup	packed brown sugar	250 mL
2	eggs	2
3 cups	milk chocolate chips	750 mL

1. On a sheet of waxed paper or in a bowl, combine flour and baking soda. Set aside.

2. In a large bowl, using an electric mixer on medium speed, beat butter, peanut butter and granulated and brown sugars until light and creamy, about 3 minutes. Add eggs, one at a time, beating well after each addition. On low speed, gradually add flour mixture, beating until blended. With a wooden spoon, stir in chocolate chips.

3. Drop dough by tablespoonfuls (15 mL) about 2 inches (5 cm) apart on cookie sheet. Bake in preheated oven for 11 to 15 minutes or until light golden. Cool for 5 minutes on sheet, then transfer to a rack and cool completely.

Variation
Add 1 cup (250 mL) peanuts along with the chocolate chips.

Fabulous Florentines

Florentines, a chewy cookie made with almonds and candied citrus peel, are one of my favorite cookies, so I worked hard to come up with the best recipe. The blend of dark chocolate and orange with crunchy almonds is amazing. I enjoyed these so much, I lost count of the number of times I tested them.

**MAKES ABOUT
4 DOZEN COOKIES**

- **Preparation: 35 minutes**
- **Baking: 11 minutes**
- **Freezing: not recommended**

TIPS

These are delicious served in, with or as a garnish for a scoop of orange sherbet or ice cream. They actually make great ice cream sandwiches as well.

Caution — these spread considerably during baking, so keep the amount of dough per cookie small and leave ample room between the cookies. Bake only 6 cookies per sheet.

- **Preheat oven to 350°F (180°C)**
- **Cookie sheet, greased or lined with parchment paper**

6 tbsp	butter	90 mL
¼ cup	whipping (35%) cream	50 mL
1 tbsp	corn syrup	15 mL
½ cup	granulated sugar	125 mL
2 tbsp	all-purpose flour	25 mL
1 tsp	grated orange zest	5 mL
1 cup	slivered almonds, finely chopped	250 mL
½ cup	finely chopped candied orange peel	125 mL
8	squares (1 oz/28 g each) bittersweet chocolate, chopped, melted and cooled	8

1. In a medium saucepan, combine butter, whipping cream and corn syrup. With a wooden spoon, stir in sugar, flour and orange zest, mixing until smooth. Over medium-high heat, bring mixture to a boil, stirring frequently. Remove from heat. Stir in almonds and candied orange peel.

2. Drop dough by 1½ teaspoonfuls (7 mL) about 3 inches (7.5 cm) apart on prepared cookie sheet. Flatten slightly with the back of a spoon or an offset spatula. Bake in preheated oven for 9 to 11 minutes or just until set and light golden. Cool for 1 minute on sheet then, with a wide spatula, transfer to a rack and cool completely.

3. When cool, using a small offset spatula, spread melted chocolate over the flat side of each cookie. Return to rack, chocolate side up, and leave until chocolate sets, about 1 hour.

Variations

Replace candied orange peel with mixed candied peel.

Try white chocolate on some of the cookies. Some of each looks nice in a box or on a tray.

Chocolate Toffee Nut Cookies

◆

This crisp cookie is loaded with chocolate and toffee bits.

MAKES ABOUT 5 DOZEN COOKIES

- **Preparation: 30 minutes**
- **Baking: 15 minutes**
- **Freezing: excellent**

TIPS

Whenever a dough contains caramel, it's a good idea to use parchment paper, or another nonstick surface such as silicone sheets, because caramel is very sticky.

You can replace all or part of the all-purpose flour called for in any cookie recipe with an equal quantity of whole wheat flour.

Unbleached and regular all-purpose flours are interchangeable. What you use depends on your preference.

- **Preheat oven to 350°F (180°C)**
- **Cookie sheet, greased or lined with parchment paper**

2¾ cups	all-purpose flour	675 mL
1 tsp	baking soda	5 mL
¼ tsp	salt	1 mL
1½ cups	butter, melted and cooled slightly	375 mL
1 cup	packed brown sugar	250 mL
½ cup	granulated sugar	125 mL
2	eggs	2
1½ tsp	vanilla	7 mL
2¼ cups	semi-sweet chocolate chips	550 mL
6	squares (1 oz/28 g each) bittersweet chocolate, chopped	6
¾ cup	chopped pecans	175 mL
¾ cup	toffee bits	175 mL

1. On a sheet of waxed paper or in a bowl, combine flour, baking soda and salt. Set aside.

2. In a large bowl, using an electric mixer on medium speed, beat melted butter and brown and granulated sugars until light and creamy, about 3 minutes. Add eggs, one at a time, beating well after each addition. Beat in vanilla. On low speed, gradually add flour mixture, beating until blended. With a wooden spoon, stir in chocolate chips, chocolate chunks, pecans and toffee bits.

3. Drop dough by tablespoonfuls (15 mL) about 2 inches (5 cm) apart on prepared cookie sheet. Bake in preheated oven for 11 to 15 minutes or until light golden. Cool for 5 minutes on sheet, then transfer to a rack and cool completely.

Variation

Replace some or all of the semi-sweet chocolate chips with milk chocolate chips or white chocolate chips.

Chocolate Cinnamon Wheels

Pretty to look at and fun to eat. In this refrigerator cookie, which slices into attractive spirals, a chocolate walnut filling is rolled inside a shortbread dough.

MAKES ABOUT 2 DOZEN COOKIES

- **Preparation: 35 minutes**
- **Chilling: 4 hours**
- **Baking: 18 minutes**
- **Freezing: excellent**

TIPS

If you prefer, use a wooden spoon because the small amount of dough is easily mixed.

Slice this roll using a sharp, thin, non-serrated knife. The slices are a bit thicker than most refrigerator cookies because of the filling.

• **Cookie sheet, greased or lined with parchment paper**

DOUGH

1/3 cup	butter, softened	75 mL
1/2 cup	granulated sugar	125 mL
1	egg	1
1/4 tsp	salt	1 mL
1 1/2 cups	all-purpose flour	375 mL

FILLING

1 1/4 cups	miniature semi-sweet chocolate chips	300 mL
3/4 cup	finely chopped walnuts	175 mL
1/4 cup	packed brown sugar	50 mL
2 tsp	ground cinnamon	10 mL
3 tbsp	butter, melted	45 mL

1. *Dough:* In a large bowl, using an electric mixer on medium speed, beat butter, sugar and egg until light and creamy, about 3 minutes. On low speed, gradually add salt and flour, mixing until blended. Using your hands, knead to form a smooth dough. Between 2 sheets of waxed paper, roll out dough to a 12- by 10-inch (30 cm by 25 cm) rectangle.

2. *Filling:* In a bowl, combine chocolate chips, walnuts, brown sugar, cinnamon and melted butter. Mix well. Chips should melt slightly from the warm butter. If they don't, microwave the mixture for 10 seconds to soften.

3. Remove top sheet of waxed paper from dough. With an offset spatula, spread filling evenly over dough, leaving a 1/2-inch (1 cm) border on one long side. Starting with the opposite long side and using the bottom sheet of waxed paper to help you, roll up the dough jelly-roll fashion. Press edge to seal and, using your hands, mold roll into nicely rounded shape. Wrap and chill until firm, at least 4 hours.

4. Fifteen minutes before you're ready to bake, preheat oven to 350°F (180°C). Cut roll into 1/2-inch (1 cm) slices. Place about 2 inches (5 cm) apart on prepared cookie sheet. Bake in preheated oven for 14 to 18 minutes or until light golden. Cool for 5 minutes on sheet, then transfer to a rack and cool completely.

Mini Chocolate Hazelnut Biscotti

These small, crunchy chocolate biscotti with an abundance of hazelnuts are perfect dippers for a cup of steaming coffee or hot chocolate.

**MAKES ABOUT
10 DOZEN BISCOTTI**

- Preparation: 30 minutes
- Baking: 1 hour
- Cooling: 10 minutes
- Freezing: excellent

TIP

Because biscotti have a hard, dry texture, they store particularly well. Be sure to bake them thoroughly. If they aren't dry enough, they will soften and become chewy when stored.

- **Preheat oven to 325°F (160°C)**
- **Cookie sheet, greased or lined with parchment paper**

2¾ cups	all-purpose flour	675 mL
2½ tsp	baking powder	12 mL
¼ tsp	salt	1 mL
⅔ cup	butter, softened	150 mL
1 cup	granulated sugar	250 mL
3	eggs	3
2 cups	semi-sweet chocolate chips, melted and cooled	500 mL
1 cup	finely chopped hazelnuts	250 mL
4	squares (1 oz/28 g each) semi-sweet chocolate, chopped	4

1. On a sheet of waxed paper or in a bowl, combine flour, baking powder and salt. Set aside.

2. In a large bowl, using an electric mixer on medium speed, beat butter and sugar until light and creamy, about 3 minutes. Add eggs, one at a time, beating well after each addition. On low speed, beat in melted chocolate until blended. Gradually add flour mixture, beating until blended. With a wooden spoon, stir in hazelnuts and chocolate.

3. Divide dough into quarters. Shape each into a roll about 15 inches (37.5 cm) long. Place about 4 inches (10 cm) apart on prepared cookie sheet. Flatten rolls to 1½ inch (4 cm) wide, leaving top slightly rounded. Bake in preheated oven for 25 to 30 minutes or until set. Cool for 10 minutes on cookie sheet. Transfer rolls to a cutting board. Cut warm biscotti into ½-inch (1 cm) slices. Stand upright about ½ inch (1 cm) apart on cookie sheet. Return to oven and bake 25 to 30 minutes or until dry and crisp and hazelnuts just start to turn golden. Cool for 5 minutes on sheet, then transfer to a rack and cool completely.

Variations

Dip the ends in melted chocolate for a fancier look.

Substitute pecans or almonds for the hazelnuts.

Chocolate Chip Almond Crisps

Ground rice cereal gives these cookies an interesting taste and texture that will keep people guessing about what they contain. A ground chocolate candy bar adds to the mystery.

**MAKES ABOUT
7 DOZEN COOKIES**

- **Preparation: 30 minutes**
- **Baking: 14 minutes**
- **Freezing: excellent**

TIPS

For soft cookies, don't flatten the dough balls.

This dough has a texture similar to that of a stiff shortbread dough, which is why it's easier to work it with your hands than to continue mixing with the mixer.

- **Preheat oven to 375°F (190°C)**
- **Cookie sheet, greased or lined with parchment paper**

4 cups	crisp rice cereal	1 L
3	(1.4 oz/39 g each) crunchy chocolate-covered toffee bars, chopped	3
2 cups	all-purpose flour	500 mL
1 tsp	baking powder	5 mL
1 tsp	baking soda	5 mL
¼ tsp	salt	1 mL
1 cup	butter, softened	250 mL
1 cup	packed brown sugar	250 mL
¾ cup	granulated sugar	175 mL
2	eggs	2
2 cups	semi-sweet chocolate chips	500 mL
1½ cups	finely chopped almonds	375 mL

1. In a food processor, process cereal until ground. Add toffee bars and process until ground. Add flour, baking powder, baking soda and salt. Process to blend. Transfer to a sheet of waxed paper or a bowl. Set aside.

2. In a large bowl, using an electric mixer on medium speed, beat butter and brown and granulated sugars until light and creamy, about 3 minutes. Add eggs, one at a time, beating well after each addition. On low speed, gradually add flour mixture, beating until blended. Using your hands, knead to form a smooth dough. With a wooden spoon, stir in chocolate chips and almonds.

3. Shape dough into 1-inch (2.5 cm) balls. Place about 2 inches (5 cm) apart on prepared cookie sheet. With a floured fork, press balls to flatten. Bake in preheated oven for 10 to 14 minutes or until golden around edges. Cool for 5 minutes on sheet, then transfer to a rack and cool completely.

Variation

Use your favorite chips to replace the semi-sweet chocolate. Milk, white or a mixture of chocolate chips is nice.

Fudge Drops

These yummy drops are crisp on the outside with a chewy middle. They have lots of chocolate, nuts and coconut throughout.

MAKES ABOUT 2½ DOZEN COOKIES

- **Preparation: 25 minutes**
- **Cooking: 4 minutes**
- **Baking: 16 minutes**
- **Freezing: not recommended**

TIPS

For a marbled appearance, fold mixture just slightly. It will blend more when dropped on the cookie sheet. If you prefer a chocolate look, blend in the chocolate more thoroughly.

These cookies will flatten slightly while they bake, which gives them their unique texture.

- **Preheat oven to 350°F (180°C)**
- **Cookie sheet, greased or lined with parchment paper**

1 cup	semi-sweet chocolate chips	250 mL
2	egg whites	2
Pinch	salt	Pinch
½ tsp	vinegar	2 mL
½ tsp	vanilla	2 mL
½ cup	granulated sugar	125 mL
½ cup	unsweetened flaked coconut	125 mL
½ cup	chopped pecans	125 mL

1. In a small saucepan over low heat, melt chocolate chips, stirring until smooth. Set aside to cool.
2. In a small bowl, using an electric mixer on high speed, beat egg whites, salt, vinegar and vanilla until frothy. Gradually add sugar, 2 tbsp (25 mL) at a time, beating until stiff, shiny peaks form. With a spatula, fold in coconut and nuts gently but thoroughly. Fold in melted chocolate just until mixture is lightly marbled (see Tips).
3. Drop mixture by tablespoonfuls (15 mL) about 2 inches (5 cm) apart on prepared cookie sheet. Bake in preheated oven for 12 to 16 minutes or until dry on top. Cool completely on sheet.

Variation

Replace semi-sweet chocolate chips with milk chocolate chips for a milder chocolate taste.

Chewy Chocolate Walnut Strips

This easy-to-make cookie doesn't require much time for shaping. The dough is shaped into large logs, then cut into strips when cool.

**MAKES ABOUT
4 DOZEN COOKIES**

- **Preparation: 30 minutes**
- **Baking: 18 minutes**
- **Freezing: excellent**

TIP

Baking powder and baking soda don't last forever. Check the expiry date. If they haven't been used within the past 6 months, replace them. It's disappointing to bake cookies that don't rise because of old leavening.

- **Preheat oven to 350°F (180°C)**
- **Cookie sheet, greased or lined with parchment paper**

2 cups	all-purpose flour	500 mL
½ cup	unsweetened cocoa powder, sifted	125 mL
½ tsp	baking soda	2 mL
¼ tsp	salt	1 mL
¾ cup	butter, softened	175 mL
¾ cup	granulated sugar	175 mL
½ cup	packed brown sugar	125 mL
2	eggs	2
2 cups	semi-sweet chocolate chips	500 mL
¾ cup	chopped walnuts	175 mL
4	squares (1 oz/28 g each) semi-sweet chocolate, chopped, melted and cooled	4

1. On a sheet of waxed paper or in a bowl, combine flour, cocoa, baking soda and salt. Set aside.

2. In a large bowl, using an electric mixer on medium speed, beat butter and granulated and brown sugars until light and creamy, about 3 minutes. Add eggs, one at a time, beating well after each addition. On low speed, gradually add flour mixture, beating until blended. With a wooden spoon, stir in chocolate chips and walnuts.

3. Divide dough into quarters. Shape each into a strip about 12 inches (30 cm) long. Place about 4 inches (10 cm) apart on prepared cookie sheet. Bake in preheated oven for 14 to 18 minutes or until set. Cool for 5 minutes on sheet, then transfer to a rack and cool completely.

4. Drizzle melted chocolate on top of cookie strips. Set aside until chocolate is set, about 30 minutes, then with a sharp knife cut into 1-inch (2.5 cm) slices.

Variations

Use white chocolate for the drizzle, or do half with white and half with semi-sweet.

Omit the nuts or use your favorite.

Chocolate Rum Balls

This recipe is a must for your collection of no-bakes.

MAKES ABOUT 3 DOZEN COOKIES

- **Preparation: 20 minutes**
- **Standing: 1 hour**
- **Freezing: excellent**

TIPS

Chocolate shot is also called chocolate vermicelli or chocolate sprinkles. It is available where cake decorating supplies are sold and in bulk stores.

Let balls ripen at least one day before eating. They will improve with standing.

- **Cookie sheet lined with waxed paper**

2¼ cups	chocolate wafer crumbs	550 mL
1 cup	confectioner's (icing) sugar, sifted	250 mL
¾ cup	finely chopped walnuts	175 mL
2 tbsp	unsweetened cocoa powder, sifted	25 mL
¼ cup	butter, melted	50 mL
¼ cup	dark rum	50 mL
3 tbsp	corn syrup	45 mL
¾ cup	chocolate shot (see Tips)	175 mL

1. In a large bowl, combine wafer crumbs, confectioner's sugar, walnuts and cocoa. Mix well.

2. In a small bowl, using a wooden spoon, combine melted butter, rum and corn syrup. Mix well. Add to crumb mixture. Mix, then, using your hands, knead until mixture holds together.

3. Spread chocolate shot in a small shallow dish. Shape dough into 1-inch (2.5 cm) balls. Roll in chocolate shot to cover thoroughly. Place on waxed paper. Set aside until dry, about 1 hour. Store in airtight container in the refrigerator.

Variations

Replace rum with brandy.

Replace rum with 1 tbsp (15 mL) rum extract.

Roll balls in toasted or plain medium flaked or shredded coconut or finely chopped nuts. It's nice to do a variety of coatings for the one batch.

Chocolate Toffee Peanut Mounds

These cookies couldn't be easier to make or more delicious.

MAKES ABOUT 2 DOZEN COOKIES

- Preparation: 15 minutes
- Cooking: 4 minutes
- Chilling: 1 hour
- Freezing: not recommended

- **Cookie sheet lined with waxed paper**

6	squares (1 oz/28 g each) semi-sweet chocolate, chopped	6
1 cup	coarsely chopped toffee-coated peanuts	250 mL
½ cup	dried cranberries	125 mL

1. In a medium saucepan over low heat, melt chocolate, stirring constantly. Remove from heat. With a wooden spoon, stir in peanuts and cranberries until all ingredients are coated.
2. Drop mixture by tablespoonfuls (15 mL) about 1 inch (2.5 cm) apart on waxed paper. Chill until chocolate is set, about 1 hour.

Chocolate Cashew Crunchies

The combination of sweet and salty in these no-bake treats is irresistible.

MAKES ABOUT 4 DOZEN COOKIES

- Preparation: 15 minutes
- Cooking: 4 minutes
- Chilling: 1 hour
- Standing: 2 hours
- Freezing: not recommended

TIPS

Once the chocolate is firm, store cookies in airtight container with waxed paper between layers. They may develop a whitish coating when cold. It will disappear at room temperature.

Use the thinner pretzel sticks. If using knots, break them into smaller pieces.

- **Cookie sheet lined with waxed paper**

12	squares (1 oz/28 g each) bittersweet chocolate, chopped	12
2 tbsp	butter	25 mL
1½ cups	coarsely chopped cashews	375 mL
1½ cups	salted pretzel sticks, broken into ¾-inch (2 cm) pieces	375 mL
2	squares (1 oz/28 g each) white chocolate, chopped and melted	2

1. In a large saucepan over low heat, melt chocolate and butter, stirring until smooth. Remove from heat and let cool for 10 minutes. With a wooden spoon, stir in cashews and pretzels until all ingredients are coated.
2. Drop mixture by tablespoonfuls (15 mL) about 1 inch (2.5 cm) apart on waxed paper. Chill until chocolate is set, about 1 hour.
3. Drizzle white chocolate over cookies. Let stand until chocolate is set, about 2 hours.

Variation
Use white chocolate in place of bittersweet for the mounds, and drizzle with dark chocolate.

Crunchy Chocolate Nut Cookies

These cookies are similar to macaroons, but made with nuts rather than the usual coconut. They make a great Valentine's gift, one that is much more personal than a store-bought box of chocolates.

MAKES ABOUT 2½ DOZEN COOKIES

- **Preparation: 35 minutes**
- **Baking: 19 minutes**
- **Cooking: 4 minutes**
- **Standing: 2 hours**
- **Freezing: excellent (not dipped)**

TIPS

Instead of using a pastry bag, you can drop the mixture from a spoon onto the cookie sheet. With moistened fingers, shape top of cookie into a teardrop.

If you're freezing these cookies, leave them plain, then dip them in chocolate just before using.

- **Preheat oven to 325°F (160°C)**
- **Cookie sheet, lined with parchment paper**
- **Pastry bag with ½-inch (1 cm) round tip**

2	egg whites	2
Pinch	cream of tartar	Pinch
Pinch	salt	Pinch
1 cup	granulated sugar	250 mL
⅓ cup	unsweetened cocoa powder, sifted	75 mL
¾ cup	ground hazelnuts	175 mL
¾ cup	ground unblanched almonds	175 mL
4	squares (1 oz/28 g each) white chocolate, chopped	4

1. In a small bowl, using an electric mixer on high speed, beat egg whites, cream of tartar and salt to soft peaks. Gradually add sugar, 2 tbsp (25 mL) at a time, beating until stiff, shiny peaks form. On low speed, beat in cocoa just until combined. With a wooden spoon, stir in hazelnuts and almonds.

2. Place mixture in pastry bag. Pipe small kisses, about 2 teaspoonfuls (10 mL) each, about 1 inch (2.5 cm) apart on prepared cookie sheet. Bake in preheated oven for 15 to 19 minutes or until set and surface seems dry. Cool for 5 minutes on sheet, then transfer to a rack and cool completely.

3. In a small saucepan over low heat, melt white chocolate, stirring until smooth. Transfer mixture to a small bowl for easy dipping. Dip bottom third of each cookie in melted chocolate. Place on sheet of waxed paper and leave until chocolate is set, about 2 hours.

Variations

To make "snowcaps," dip top of cookie, rather than bottom, in melted white chocolate.

Use semi-sweet rather than white chocolate for dipping.

Good for You, Too

Just because they are loaded with nutritious ingredients doesn't mean you have to shop in natural foods stores to make the cookies in this chapter. With ingredients such as whole grain cereals, dried fruits and even vegetables, these cookies are definitely good for you. And although they aren't designed for specialty diets, you'll find some recipes that are free of ingredients people may find troublesome, such as eggs, nuts and lactose, the sugar found in dairy products that can cause digestive problems in sensitive individuals. To keep calories lower without sacrificing flavor, I've tried to reduce sugar and fat while increasing dietary fiber. In most cases, I've used unbleached rather than bleached flour and tried to include at least some whole wheat flour, for its pleasant nutty flavor, as well as its superior nutritional profile.

These cookies qualify as high-energy foods that will satisfy hearty appetites with a minimum of guilt. Most of the recipes are easy-to-make drop cookies, and they freeze and travel well. That means you can have them ready for your favorite outdoor activity — hiking, camping or biking. You can also serve them for an after-school or lunch-box treat or for a quick energy boost any time of the day.

◄ *Cherry Mandelbrot*

Cherry Mandelbrot

◆

Mandelbrot or almond bread is shaped and baked like a loaf. Similar to biscotti, it is then sliced and re-baked to make crisp cookies. This version is lower in fat and provides more dietary fiber than most.

MAKES ABOUT 3 DOZEN COOKIES

- **Preparation: 30 minutes**
- **Baking: 42 minutes**
- **Cooling: 10 minutes**
- **Oven cooling: 45 minutes**
- **Freezing: excellent**

TIPS

Use a sharp serrated knife to cut the semi-baked cookies.

Store mandelbrot in airtight container at room temperature for up to 1 month.

- **Preheat oven to 350°F (180°C)**
- **Two 9- by 5-inch (2 L) loaf pans, lined with parchment paper**
- **Cookie sheet, ungreased**

1 cup	unbleached all-purpose flour	250 mL
1 cup	whole wheat flour	250 mL
1/4 cup	wheat germ	50 mL
2 tsp	baking powder	10 mL
1/4 tsp	salt	1 mL
1/2 tsp	ground cinnamon	2 mL
2 tbsp	butter, softened	25 mL
3/4 cup	granulated sugar	175 mL
2 tbsp	vegetable oil	25 mL
2	eggs	2
1	egg white	1
1 tbsp	grated orange zest	15 mL
1/4 cup	orange juice	50 mL
2 tbsp	lower-fat plain yogurt	25 mL
1/2 cup	sliced almonds	125 mL
1/2 cup	dried cherries	125 mL

1. On a sheet of waxed paper or in a bowl, combine all-purpose and whole wheat flours, wheat germ, baking powder, salt and cinnamon. Set aside.

2. In a large bowl, using a wooden spoon, beat butter, sugar, oil, eggs, egg white, orange zest, orange juice and yogurt until smooth. Gradually add flour mixture, beating until blended. Stir in almonds and cherries.

3. Divide dough into halves and place in prepared pans. Bake in preheated oven for 25 to 30 minutes or until tops are golden. Cool for 10 minutes in pan, then transfer to a cutting board. Cut into 1/2-inch (1 cm) slices. Place upright about 1 inch (2.5 cm) apart on cookie sheet. Bake for 8 to 12 minutes or until golden. Turn oven off and leave in oven for 40 to 45 minutes or until crisp.

Variation

Replace almonds with coarsely chopped hazelnuts or Brazil nuts and cherries with dried cranberries.

Cranberry Apricot Oat Cookies

Ground oats give these cookies a wonderful rich taste.

MAKES ABOUT 3 DOZEN COOKIES

- **Preparation: 25 minutes**
- **Baking: 15 minutes**
- **Freezing: excellent**

TIPS

You can successfully substitute a soft non-hydrogenated margarine for the butter in these cookies.

Substitute ½ cup (125 mL) whole wheat flour for the all-purpose for a slightly drier but nicely flavored cookie.

- **Preheat oven to 325°F (160°C)**
- **Cookie sheet, greased or lined with parchment paper**

1½ cups	quick-cooking rolled oats	375 mL
½ cup	unbleached all-purpose flour	125 mL
½ cup	whole wheat flour	125 mL
½ tsp	baking powder	2 mL
½ tsp	baking soda	2 mL
1½ tsp	ground cinnamon	7 mL
½ cup	butter, softened	125 mL
1 cup	packed brown sugar	250 mL
1	egg	1
¾ cup	dried cranberries	175 mL
¾ cup	chopped dried apricots	175 mL

1. In a food processor, process oats until they have the consistency of fine flour. On a sheet of waxed paper or in a bowl, combine ground oats, all-purpose and whole wheat flours, baking powder, baking soda and cinnamon. Set aside.

2. In a large bowl, using an electric mixer on medium speed, beat butter, brown sugar and egg until light and creamy, about 3 minutes. With a wooden spoon, stir in flour mixture, cranberries and apricots.

3. Drop dough by tablespoonfuls (15 mL) about 2 inches (5 cm) apart on prepared cookie sheet. Bake in preheated oven for 11 to 15 minutes or until lightly browned. Cool for 5 minutes on sheet, then transfer to a rack and cool completely.

Variation

Replace dried cranberries with an equal quantity of raisins or chopped dates.

Oatmeal Raisin Cookies

♦

Here's a lighter, lower-fat version of a classic cookie.

MAKES ABOUT 4½ DOZEN COOKIES

- **Preparation: 25 minutes**
- **Baking: 11 minutes**
- **Freezing: excellent**

TIPS

Cookies that are low in fat don't keep as well as those containing more fat. These are best eaten within 2 days or frozen.

Apple butter replaces some of the fat and also gives these cookies a nice flavor. It is sold in the health food sections of grocery stores and in many European and Mennonite stores.

- **Preheat oven to 375°F (190°C)**
- **Cookie sheet, greased or lined with parchment paper**

3 cups	quick-cooking rolled oats	750 mL
½ cup	chopped pecans	125 mL
2 cups	unbleached all-purpose flour	500 mL
1 tsp	baking soda	5 mL
½ tsp	baking powder	2 mL
¼ tsp	salt	1 mL
1 tsp	ground cinnamon	5 mL
½ tsp	ground cloves	2 mL
1½ cups	packed brown sugar	375 mL
½ cup	apple butter	125 mL
2	eggs	2
¼ cup	vegetable oil	50 mL
1½ cups	raisins	375 mL

1. On a large rimmed baking sheet, spread out oats and pecans. Bake in preheated oven, stirring occasionally, for 5 to 8 minutes or until lightly browned. Remove from oven. Set aside to cool.

2. On a sheet of waxed paper or in a bowl, combine flour, baking soda, baking powder, salt, cinnamon and cloves. Set aside.

3. In a large bowl, using an electric mixer on medium speed, beat brown sugar, apple butter, eggs and oil until very light and fluffy, about 5 minutes. On low speed, gradually add flour mixture, beating until blended. With a wooden spoon, stir in oat mixture and raisins.

4. Drop dough by tablespoonfuls (15 mL) about 2 inches (5 cm) apart on prepared cookie sheet. Press down with a floured fork. Bake in preheated oven for 7 to 11 minutes or until lightly browned. Cool for 5 minutes on sheet, then transfer to a rack and cool completely.

Variations

Replace raisins with dried cranberries.

Replace apple butter with plum butter.

Carrot Cake Cookies

You'll love this bite-size take on carrot cake.

**MAKES ABOUT
2½ DOZEN COOKIES**

- **Preparation: 30 minutes**
- **Baking: 13 minutes**
- **Freezing: excellent**

TIPS

Peel the carrots before grating. If peel is left on, it may react with the leavening and create green specks in the cookies.

Check your spices regularly as they don't last forever. I replace mine every 6 months. You can buy small amounts in bulk of those you don't use frequently.

- **Preheat oven to 350°F (180°C)**
- **Cookie sheet, greased or lined with parchment paper**

1¼ cups	unbleached all-purpose flour	300 mL
½ tsp	baking powder	2 mL
¼ tsp	salt	1 mL
¾ tsp	ground cinnamon	3 mL
¼ tsp	ground nutmeg	1 mL
½ cup	butter, softened	125 mL
½ cup	packed brown sugar	125 mL
1	egg	1
¾ cup	peeled, grated carrot	175 mL
¾ cup	raisins	175 mL
¾ cup	chopped pecans	175 mL
½ cup	unsweetened flaked coconut	125 mL

1. On sheet of waxed paper or in a bowl, combine flour, baking powder, salt, cinnamon and nutmeg. Set aside.

2. In a large bowl, using an electric mixer on medium speed, beat butter, brown sugar and egg until light and creamy, about 3 minutes. On low speed, gradually add flour mixture, beating until blended. With a wooden spoon, stir in carrot, raisins, pecans and coconut.

3. Drop dough by tablespoonfuls (15 mL) about 2 inches (5 cm) apart on prepared cookie sheet. Bake in preheated oven for 9 to 13 minutes or until lightly browned. Cool for 5 minutes on sheet, then transfer to a rack and cool completely.

Variations

Replace raisins with dried cranberries.

Omit the nuts.

Replace carrot with grated zucchini.

Applesauce Hermits

Here's an old-fashioned favorite spice cookie made healthier with whole wheat flour and less sugar and fat than the traditional version.

MAKES ABOUT 2½ DOZEN COOKIES

- **Preparation: 25 minutes**
- **Baking: 17 minutes**
- **Freezing: excellent**

TIPS

If your raisins have dried out, pour boiling water over them and leave for 5 minutes to soften. Drain and pat dry with paper towels before using.

I like to line cookie sheets with parchment paper. You can easily slip it on and off a cookie sheet without sides. There's no need to wash the sheet and the cookies don't stick.

Replace the butter with a soft, non-hydrogenated margarine, if you prefer.

- **Preheat oven to 325°F (160°C)**
- **Cookie sheet, greased or lined with parchment paper**

¾ cup	whole wheat flour	175 mL
⅔ cup	unbleached all-purpose flour	150 mL
1½ tsp	baking powder	7 mL
1 tsp	ground cinnamon	5 mL
¼ tsp	ground cloves	1 mL
¼ tsp	ground nutmeg	1 mL
⅓ cup	butter, softened	75 mL
⅔ cup	packed brown sugar	150 mL
1	egg	1
¼ cup	unsweetened applesauce	50 mL
1 cup	raisins	250 mL

1. On a sheet of waxed paper or in a bowl, combine whole wheat and all-purpose flours, baking powder, cinnamon, cloves and nutmeg. Set aside.

2. In a large bowl, using an electric mixer on medium speed, beat butter, brown sugar, egg and applesauce until light and creamy, about 3 minutes. On low speed, gradually add flour mixture, beating until blended. With a wooden spoon, stir in raisins.

3. Drop dough by tablespoonfuls (15 mL) about 2 inches (5 cm) apart on prepared cookie sheet. Bake in preheated oven for 13 to 17 minutes or until lightly browned. Cool for 5 minutes on sheet, then transfer to a rack and cool completely.

Variations

Replace applesauce with an equal quantity of milk or yogurt.

Use any combination of chopped dried fruit, such as dates, apricots, cranberries or figs, in place of the raisins.

Spicy Zucchini Cookies

I guarantee that kids prefer their vegetables in cookies rather than cooked or in a salad.

MAKES ABOUT 3½ DOZEN COOKIES

- **Preparation: 30 minutes**
- **Baking: 16 minutes**
- **Freezing: excellent**

TIPS

These cookies are soft and cake-like. Store them in an airtight container.

Never store crisp cookies with soft ones. The crisp ones will soften and the soft ones will dry out.

It isn't necessary to peel the zucchini, unless you expect negative comments about the green flecks.

- **Preheat oven to 350°F (180°C)**
- **Cookie sheet, greased or lined with parchment paper**

1¾ cups	unbleached all-purpose flour	425 mL
2 tsp	baking powder	10 mL
¼ tsp	salt	1 mL
1 tsp	ground cinnamon	5 mL
¼ tsp	ground nutmeg	1 mL
½ cup	butter, softened	125 mL
1 cup	packed brown sugar	250 mL
1	egg	1
¼ cup	milk	50 mL
1½ cups	grated zucchini	375 mL
¾ cup	raisins	175 mL
½ cup	chopped walnuts	125 mL

1. On a sheet of waxed paper or in a bowl, combine flour, baking powder, salt, cinnamon and nutmeg. Set aside.

2. In a large bowl, using an electric mixer on medium speed, beat butter, brown sugar and egg until light and creamy, about 3 minutes. On low speed, add flour mixture alternately with milk, making 3 additions of dry ingredients and 2 of liquid, beating until blended. With a wooden spoon, stir in zucchini, raisins and walnuts.

3. Drop dough by tablespoonfuls (15 mL) about 2 inches (5 cm) apart on prepared cookie sheet. Bake in preheated oven for 12 to 16 minutes or until lightly browned. Cool for 5 minutes on sheet, then transfer to a rack and cool completely.

Variations

Omit the nuts or replace them with an equal quantity of flaked coconut.

Add 1 tbsp (15 mL) grated orange zest and replace milk with an equal quantity of orange juice.

Crunchy Apricot Oat Drops

Not only are these cookies easy to make, but they are nutritious and delicious as well.

MAKES ABOUT 3 DOZEN COOKIES

- **Preparation: 30 minutes**
- **Baking: 12 minutes**
- **Freezing: excellent**

TIPS

Do not use light or whipped margarine when baking. These products are lower in fat and often contain water, which may result in baked goods that aren't acceptable.

When baking, always place cookie dough on a cool sheet. Cookies will spread too much if the sheet is warm.

Always set your timer for the minimum time suggested. You can always bake longer, if necessary.

- **Preheat oven to 350°F (180°C)**
- **Cookie sheet, greased or lined with parchment paper**

¾ cup	unbleached all-purpose flour	175 mL
½ tsp	baking soda	2 mL
¼ tsp	salt	1 mL
½ tsp	ground cinnamon	2 mL
½ cup	butter, softened	125 mL
¾ cup	packed brown sugar	175 mL
1	egg	1
¾ cup	quick-cooking rolled oats	175 mL
⅓ cup	wheat germ	75 mL
1 cup	crisp rice cereal	250 mL
¾ cup	chopped dried apricots	175 mL
⅓ cup	unsweetened flaked coconut	75 mL
¼ cup	sunflower seeds	50 mL

1. On a sheet of waxed paper or in a bowl, combine flour, baking soda, salt and cinnamon. Set aside.

2. In a large bowl, using an electric mixer on medium speed, beat butter, brown sugar and egg until light and creamy, about 3 minutes. On low speed, gradually add flour mixture, beating until blended. With a wooden spoon, stir in oats and wheat germ. Add cereal, apricots, coconut and sunflower seeds. Mix well.

3. Drop dough by tablespoonfuls (15 mL) about 2 inches (5 cm) apart on prepared cookie sheet. Bake in preheated oven for 8 to 12 minutes or until golden. Cool for 5 minutes on sheet, then transfer to a rack and cool completely.

Variation

Replace apricots with dried cranberries, raisins or chopped dates.

Multigrain Madness

Crunchy grains and seeds give these hearty cookies great texture and taste.

MAKES ABOUT 2 DOZEN COOKIES

- **Preparation: 25 minutes**
- **Baking: 15 minutes**
- **Freezing: excellent**

TIPS

Use candy-coated chocolate pieces such as M&M's.

Store cookies in layers separated by waxed paper in airtight containers.

These cookies freeze well for up to 3 months.

To make small cookies, drop by tablespoonfuls (15 mL) and bake for 8 to 12 minutes.

- **Preheat oven to 350°F (180°C)**
- **Cookie sheet, greased or lined with parchment paper**

1¼ cups	unbleached all-purpose flour	300 mL
½ cup	wheat germ	125 mL
½ tsp	baking soda	2 mL
½ tsp	ground cinnamon	2 mL
⅔ cup	butter, softened	150 mL
½ cup	granulated sugar	125 mL
½ cup	packed brown sugar	125 mL
1	egg	1
⅓ cup	vegetable oil	75 mL
¼ cup	liquid honey	50 mL
2¼ cups	quick-cooking rolled oats	550 mL
1 cup	candy-coated chocolate pieces (see Tips)	250 mL
1 cup	raisins	250 mL
½ cup	sunflower seeds	125 mL

1. On a sheet of waxed paper or in a bowl, combine flour, wheat germ, baking soda and cinnamon. Set aside.

2. In a large bowl, using an electric mixer on medium speed, beat butter, granulated and brown sugars and egg until light and creamy, about 3 minutes. Add oil and honey, beating until blended. On low speed, gradually add flour mixture, beating until blended. With a wooden spoon, stir in oats, candy pieces, raisins and sunflower seeds.

3. Drop dough by ¼ cupfuls (50 mL) about 4 inches (10 cm) apart on prepared cookie sheet. Bake in preheated oven for 11 to 15 minutes or until lightly browned. Cool for 5 minutes on sheet, then transfer to a rack and cool completely.

Variations

Replace half of the sunflower seeds with flax seeds.

For an even healthier cookie, replace the candy pieces with dried fruits such as cranberries or chopped apricots or dates.

Refrigerator Spicy Almond Crisps

There's no egg in these cookies and the honey gives them a great flavor.

MAKES ABOUT 9 DOZEN COOKIES

- **Preparation: 30 minutes**
- **Chilling: 4 hours**
- **Baking: 12 minutes**
- **Freezing: excellent**

TIPS

Bake longer if you like crisp cookies and for less time if you prefer them softer.

Store whole wheat flour in the freezer to retain its freshness. It doesn't keep as long as white flour. It has a shelf life of 6 months compared to 1 year for white flour.

Make sure you have at least 2 inches (5 cm) between your cookie sheet and the sides of your oven so the air can circulate properly to ensure even baking.

- **Cookie sheet, ungreased**

2 cups	unbleached all-purpose flour	500 mL
2 cups	whole wheat flour	500 mL
1½ tsp	baking soda	7 mL
½ tsp	salt	2 mL
2 tsp	ground cinnamon	10 mL
2 tsp	ground cloves	10 mL
2 tsp	ground ginger	10 mL
1 cup	butter, softened	250 mL
1 cup	granulated sugar	250 mL
¾ cup	liquid honey	175 mL
1½ cups	finely chopped unblanched almonds	375 mL

1. On a sheet of waxed paper or in a bowl, combine all-purpose and whole wheat flours, baking soda, salt, cinnamon, cloves and ginger. Set aside.

2. In a large bowl, using an electric mixer on medium speed, beat butter, sugar and honey until smooth, about 3 minutes. On low speed, gradually add flour mixture, beating until blended. With a wooden spoon, stir in almonds. Divide dough into halves. Shape each into a roll 14 inches (35 cm) long. Wrap and chill until firm, at least 4 hours.

3. Fifteen minutes before you're ready to bake, preheat oven to 375°F (190°C). Cut rolls into ¼-inch (0.5) slices. Place about 1 inch (2.5 cm) apart on cookie sheet. Bake in preheated oven for 8 to 12 minutes or until set and lightly browned. Cool for 5 minutes on sheet, then transfer to a rack and cool completely.

Variation
Substitute pecans, walnuts or hazelnuts for the almonds.

Mixed Seed and Fruit Spice Cookies

◆

Flax seeds give these cookies a wonderful crunch and unique flavor, while adding nutritional value.

MAKES ABOUT 3 DOZEN COOKIES

- **Preparation: 30 minutes**
- **Baking: 12 minutes**
- **Freezing: excellent**

TIPS

Store flax seeds in freezer to prevent rancidity.

Flax seeds are a good source of soluble fiber and omega-3 fatty acids. Consumption of omega-3 fatty acids has been linked with lower rates of heart disease and stroke.

- **Preheat oven to 350°F (180°C)**
- **Cookie sheet, greased or lined with parchment paper**

1 ¼ cups	unbleached all-purpose flour	300 mL
½ cup	ground flax seeds	125 mL
½ tsp	baking powder	2 mL
½ tsp	baking soda	2 mL
¼ tsp	salt	1 mL
½ tsp	ground cinnamon	2 mL
½ tsp	ground cloves	2 mL
½ tsp	ground nutmeg	2 mL
⅓ cup	butter, softened	75 mL
⅔ cup	packed brown sugar	150 mL
1	egg	1
⅓ cup	corn syrup	75 mL
2 tbsp	milk	25 mL
¾ cup	chopped dried apricots	175 mL
¾ cup	dried cranberries	175 mL
⅓ cup	sunflower seeds	75 mL
¼ cup	sesame seeds	50 mL
¼ cup	flax seeds	50 mL

1. Combine flour, ground flax seeds, baking powder, baking soda, salt, cinnamon, cloves and nutmeg. Set aside.

2. In a large bowl, using an electric mixer on medium speed, beat butter, brown sugar, egg, corn syrup and milk until smooth and creamy. On low speed, gradually add flour mixture, beating until blended. With a wooden spoon, stir in apricots, cranberries and sunflower, sesame and flax seeds.

3. Drop dough by tablespoonfuls (15 mL) about 2 inches (5 cm) apart on prepared cookie sheet. Bake in preheated oven for 8 to 12 minutes or until lightly browned. Cool for 5 minutes on sheet, then transfer to a rack and cool completely.

Variation

Substitute other dried fruit, such as raisins, or chopped dried mango or dates, for the apricots and cranberries.

Cherry Fruit Logs

Nicely spiced, these cookies are similar to gingerbread with the addition of dried fruits. They are easy to shape, too.

MAKES ABOUT 4 DOZEN COOKIES

- **Preparation: 30 minutes**
- **Chilling: 1 hour**
- **Baking: 15 minutes**
- **Freezing: excellent**

TIPS

Use a sharp serrated knife to cut these cookies.

Don't overbake or the cookies will be crisp rather than chewy.

The recipe makes a large quantity, but the cookies keep well and freeze well.

If you prefer, substitute soft, non-hydrogenated margarine for the butter.

- **Cookie sheet, greased or lined with parchment paper**

1 cup	unbleached all-purpose flour	250 mL
1 cup	whole wheat flour	250 mL
1 tsp	baking soda	5 mL
1/4 tsp	salt	1 mL
1 tsp	ground cinnamon	5 mL
1/2 tsp	ground ginger	2 mL
1/4 tsp	ground cloves	1 mL
1/2 cup	butter, softened	125 mL
1 cup	packed brown sugar	250 mL
1	egg	1
3 tbsp	molasses	45 mL
3 tbsp	cold strong coffee	45 mL
3/4 cup	chopped dried cherries	175 mL
1/2 cup	chopped dried apricots	125 mL
1/3 cup	chopped crystallized ginger	75 mL

1. On a sheet of waxed paper or in a bowl, combine all-purpose and whole wheat flours, baking soda, salt, cinnamon, ginger and cloves. Set aside.

2. In a large bowl, using an electric mixer on medium speed, beat butter, brown sugar, egg, molasses and coffee until smooth and creamy. On low speed, gradually add flour mixture, beating until blended. With a wooden spoon, stir in cherries, apricots and crystallized ginger. Cover and chill for 1 hour.

3. Fifteen minutes before you're ready to bake, preheat oven to 350°F (180°C). Divide dough into quarters. Shape each into a roll 12 inches (30 cm) long. Place 4 inches (10 cm) apart on prepared cookie sheet. Flatten to 2 inches (5 cm) wide. Bake in preheated oven for 10 to 15 minutes or until starting to brown around edges but still soft. Cool on sheets for 10 minutes, then transfer to a cutting board. Cut diagonally into 1-inch (2.5 cm) slices. Transfer to a rack and cool completely.

Variation

Substitute other dried fruits, such as raisins, cranberries or chopped dates or figs, for the cherries.

Mini Hazelnut Biscotti

The honey flavor is especially nice in these small crisp biscotti. They are lower in fat than most biscotti and perfect to dip in coffee or tea.

MAKES ABOUT 5 DOZEN BISCOTTI

- **Preparation: 20 minutes**
- **Baking: 45 minutes**
- **Cooling: 15 minutes**
- **Freezing: excellent**

TIPS

Be prepared — this dough is very stiff, so you will need to work it with your hands to get it smooth.

Use a sharp serrated knife to cut biscotti.

Although recipes usually call for an electric mixer to blend ingredients, you can almost always use a wooden spoon when making cookies. It just takes more physical effort. With either method, it usually takes about 3 minutes to get a butter-and-sugar mixture light and creamy.

- **Preheat oven to 350°F (180°C)**
- **Cookie sheet, greased or lined with parchment paper**

2 cups	unbleached all-purpose flour	500 mL
2/3 cup	granulated sugar	150 mL
1/2 cup	ground hazelnuts	125 mL
1/2 tsp	baking powder	2 mL
1/2 tsp	baking soda	2 mL
1/4 tsp	salt	1 mL
1 tsp	ground cinnamon	5 mL
3/4 cup	whole hazelnuts	175 mL
1/3 cup	liquid honey	75 mL
2 tsp	grated orange zest	10 mL
1/3 cup	orange juice	75 mL

1. In a large bowl, combine flour, sugar, ground hazelnuts, baking powder, baking soda, salt, cinnamon and whole hazelnuts. Mix to blend.

2. Add honey and orange zest and juice. With a wooden spoon, stir until blended, then, using your hands, knead to form a smooth, stiff dough.

3. Divide dough into halves. Shape each into a roll 15 inches (37.5 cm) long. Place about 2 inches (5 cm) apart on prepared cookie sheet. Bake in preheated oven for 25 to 30 minutes or until set and golden. Cool for 15 minutes on sheet, then transfer to a cutting board. Cut diagonally into 1/2-inch (1 cm) slices. Place upright about 1 inch (2.5 cm) apart on cookie sheet. Bake for 15 minutes until crisp and golden. Cool for 5 minutes on sheet, then transfer to a rack and cool completely.

Variation
Substitute almonds or Brazil nuts for the hazelnuts.

Chocolate Hazelnut Meringues

◆

The brown sugar adds color and flavor to these chewy meringues. The chocolate and nut topping makes them very attractive — and tasty, too.

MAKES ABOUT 3½ DOZEN COOKIES

- **Preparation: 25 minutes**
- **Baking: 32 minutes**
- **Freezing: not recommended**

TIPS

If you prefer, grate the chocolate on a fine grater rather than chopping it.

Bake 25 to 30 minutes for chewy meringues or 30 to 35 minutes for crisp ones.

- **Preheat oven to 275°F (140°C)**
- **Cookie sheet, lined with parchment paper**

1¼ cups	finely chopped toasted hazelnuts, divided	300 mL
2 tbsp	all-purpose flour	25 mL
4	egg whites	4
¼ tsp	cream of tartar	1 mL
Pinch	salt	Pinch
1½ cups	packed brown sugar	375 mL
1½	squares (1 oz/28 g each) semi-sweet chocolate, finely chopped (see Tips)	1½

1. On a sheet of waxed paper or in a bowl, combine 1 cup (250 mL) of the hazelnuts and flour. Mix well. Set aside.

2. In a small bowl, using an electric mixer on high speed, beat egg whites, cream of tartar and salt until soft peaks form. Gradually add brown sugar, 2 tbsp (25 mL) at a time, beating until stiff peaks form. With a spatula, fold in nut mixture gently but thoroughly.

3. Drop batter by scant tablespoonfuls (10 mL) about 1 inch (2.5 cm) apart on prepared cookie sheet. Bake in preheated oven for 25 to 30 minutes or until firm. Remove from oven and sprinkle chocolate on top of cookies. Bake for 2 minutes to soften chocolate. Sprinkle remaining ¼ cup (50 mL) hazelnuts over chocolate. Cool completely on sheet.

Variations

Substitute an equal quantity of chopped pecans for the hazelnuts.

Add 2 tsp (10 mL) instant espresso coffee powder along with the brown sugar for a nice coffee meringue.

Chewy Cranberry Apricot Balls

If you like to snack on dried fruits and nuts, these are for you.

**MAKES ABOUT
5 DOZEN COOKIES**

- **Preparation: 20 minutes**
- **Cooking: 15 minutes**
- **Standing: 1 hour**
- **Freezing: excellent**

TIP

Store these and Coconut Apricot Balls in an airtight container in refrigerator.

- **Cookie sheet, lined with waxed paper**

1 1/4 cups	chopped dried apricots	300 mL
2/3 cup	dried cranberries	150 mL
3/4 cup	corn syrup	175 mL
2 1/2 cups	sweetened flaked coconut	625 mL
1 cup	finely chopped pecans	250 mL
3/4 cup	granulated sugar, optional	175 mL

1. Over medium heat, bring apricots, cranberries and corn syrup to a boil. Cover, reduce heat and simmer, stirring often, until thickened, 10 to 15 minutes. Remove from heat. Stir in coconut and pecans and mix well. Cool until easy to handle, about 30 minutes.

2. Shape into 3/4-inch (2 cm) balls. If using, spread sugar in a small shallow dish and roll balls in it until coated. Place on waxed paper. Let stand until dry, about 1 hour.

Coconut Apricot Balls

These balls make a nice dessert with ice cream or sherbet or a great snack because they aren't too sweet.

**MAKES ABOUT
2 1/2 DOZEN COOKIES**

- **Preparation: 20 minutes**
- **Standing: overnight**
- **Freezing: excellent**

TIP

It's easier to roll these balls if you moisten your hands.

- **Cookie sheet, lined with waxed paper**

1 cup	chopped dried apricots	250 mL
1/2 cup	chopped dates	125 mL
1/2 cup	dried cranberries	125 mL
1 tbsp	grated orange zest	15 mL
3 tbsp	orange juice	45 mL
1 2/3 cups	sweetened flaked coconut, divided	400 mL
3/4 cup	finely chopped pecans	175 mL

1. In a bowl, combine apricots, dates, cranberries and orange zest and juice. Mix well. Cover and let stand for at least 1 hour.

2. Transfer mixture to a food processor and process until finely chopped. Return to bowl. Add 1 cup (250 mL) of the coconut and pecans. Mix until ingredients are thoroughly moistened.

3. Place remaining coconut in a small shallow dish. Shape mixture into 3/4-inch (2 cm) balls and roll in coconut, pressing firmly. Place on waxed paper. Let stand overnight to dry.

Not Just for Kids

Kids enjoy making cookies that contain their favorite ingredients. That's why recipes in this section include different kinds of cereal, chocolate chips, marshmallows, caramels, potato chips and peanut butter. These cookies are relatively quick and easy to make so kids can quickly arrive at the best part — tasting. For many recipes, you don't even need to turn on the oven.

In addition to creating something delicious to eat, making cookies is a perfect opportunity to enjoy quality family time. It also helps to develop simple practical skills, such as measuring, counting, chopping and mixing, as well as personal qualities such as self-confidence and responsibility. Let your kids choose the recipes they want to make and help with the shopping. They will be thrilled to be able to prepare their own lunch-box treats and after-school snacks. The recipes are foolproof and guarantee results that kids can proudly share with their families and friends.

◄ *Peanut Butter and Banana Sandwich Cookies*

Peanut Butter and Banana Sandwich Cookies

This no-egg sandwich cookie is as much fun to make as it is to eat.

MAKES ABOUT 2 DOZEN COOKIES

- **Preparation: 35 minutes**
- **Baking: 14 minutes**
- **Freezing: not recommended**

TIPS

These cookies are also excellent left plain without a frosting.

The cookies are crisp and crunchy but will soften a little after they are filled. If you prefer a crisp cookie, fill them no more than a day ahead.

The riper the banana, the better the flavor. The banana should be soft and ripe for easy mixing. If it isn't, mash it with a fork before mixing.

- **Preheat oven to 350°F (180°C)**
- **Cookie sheet, greased or lined with parchment paper**

COOKIE

1 cup	butter, softened	250 mL
1 cup	granulated sugar	250 mL
1/2 cup	thinly sliced ripe banana (1 banana)	125 mL
2 1/3 cups	all-purpose flour	575 mL
1/2 tsp	baking soda	2 mL
1/4 tsp	salt	1 mL
1 cup	chopped peanuts	250 mL

FROSTING

1/4 cup	butter, softened	50 mL
3 tbsp	creamy peanut butter	45 mL
3 cups	confectioner's (icing) sugar, sifted	750 mL
1/4 cup	milk	50 mL

1. *Cookie:* In a large bowl, combine butter, sugar, banana, flour, baking soda and salt. Using an electric mixer on low speed, beat until smooth, scraping the bowl often. With a wooden spoon, stir in peanuts.

2. Drop dough by tablespoonfuls (15 mL) about 2 inches (5 cm) apart on prepared cookie sheet. Bake in preheated oven for 10 to 14 minutes or until golden around edges. Cool for 5 minutes on sheet, then transfer to a rack and cool completely.

3. *Frosting:* In a medium bowl, using an electric mixer on medium speed, beat butter and peanut butter until smooth, about 1 minute. Gradually add confectioner's sugar and milk, beating to a smooth, spreadable consistency. Spread about 1 tbsp (15 mL) frosting on flat side of half of the cookies. Place remaining cookies on top, flat side down. Press gently together.

Variation

If you prefer a non-peanut cookie, substitute pecans. Omit peanut butter in the frosting and increase the butter to 1/3 cup (75 mL).

Chocolate-Covered Raisin Crunchies

Try these cookies with kids who claim to not like raisins. The raisins are in disguise.

MAKES ABOUT 4 DOZEN COOKIES

- **Preparation: 25 minutes**
- **Baking: 13 minutes**
- **Freezing: excellent**

TIPS

To shape drop cookies, fill a tablespoon (15 mL) with dough, then push it off onto the cookie sheet using another spoon or small spatula.

Kids may like to make frozen cookie mounds. Drop the dough on the cookie sheet as above, then freeze until firm. Transfer the pucks to a freezer bag. When ready to use, place on the cookie sheet. Cover with waxed paper and thaw for 30 to 45 minutes at room temperature, then bake as directed.

- **Preheat oven to 350°F (180°C)**
- **Cookie sheet, greased or lined with parchment paper**

1²⁄₃ cups	all-purpose flour	400 mL
1¹⁄₂ cups	quick-cooking rolled oats	375 mL
1¹⁄₂ tsp	baking powder	7 mL
¹⁄₂ tsp	baking soda	2 mL
¹⁄₄ tsp	salt	1 mL
²⁄₃ cup	butter, softened	150 mL
²⁄₃ cup	granulated sugar	150 mL
²⁄₃ cup	packed brown sugar	150 mL
2	eggs	2
1¹⁄₂ cups	crisp rice cereal	375 mL
1 cup	chocolate-covered raisins	250 mL
¹⁄₂ cup	flaked coconut	125 mL

1. On a sheet of waxed paper or in a bowl, combine flour, oats, baking powder, baking soda and salt. Set aside.

2. In a large bowl, using an electric mixer on medium speed or a wooden spoon, beat butter and granulated and brown sugars until light and creamy, about 3 minutes. Add eggs, one at a time, beating well after each addition. Gradually add flour mixture, beating until blended. With a wooden spoon, stir in cereal, raisins and coconut, mixing until thoroughly blended.

3. Drop dough by tablespoonfuls (15 mL) about 2 inches (5 cm) apart on prepared cookie sheet. Bake in preheated oven for 9 to 13 minutes or until golden. Cool for 5 minutes on sheet, then transfer to a rack and cool completely.

Variations

Replace chocolate-covered raisins with chocolate-covered peanuts or chocolate chips.

Replace rice cereal with crushed corn flakes cereal.

No-Bake Chinese Noodle Crunchies

Children from preschool to teens will enjoy making these cookies.

MAKES ABOUT 3 DOZEN COOKIES

- **Preparation: 15 minutes**
- **Cooking: 4 minutes**
- **Chilling: 1 hour**
- **Freezing: not recommended**

TIPS

It's important to use low heat and stir constantly when melting chips to ensure they don't burn. You can also melt chocolate mixtures in a double boiler.

Be sure your chips are fresh. If they have a whitish coating on them they don't melt as easily.

- **Cookie sheet lined with waxed paper**

1 cup	butterscotch chips	250 mL
½ cup	creamy peanut butter	125 mL
2 cups	chopped chow mein noodles	500 mL
1 cup	peanuts	250 mL
1 cup	miniature marshmallows	250 mL

1. In a medium saucepan over low heat, melt butterscotch chips and peanut butter, stirring with a wooden spoon until smooth. Remove from heat. Add noodles and peanuts. Mix well. Add marshmallows, stirring until thoroughly coated.

2. Drop mixture by tablespoonfuls (15 mL) on waxed paper. Chill until set, about 1 hour.

Variation

Use your favorite chip. Chocolate is also great with the peanut butter.

No-Bake Chocolate Peanut Drops

It's hard to find a kid who doesn't like peanut butter and chocolate in any form — bars, candy, ice cream or cake. Add these scrumptious cookies to the list.

**MAKES ABOUT
5 DOZEN COOKIES**

- **Preparation: 15 minutes**
- **Cooking: 4 minutes**
- **Chilling: 2 hours**
- **Freezing: not recommended**

- **Cookie sheet lined with waxed paper**

½ cup	butter	125 mL
⅓ cup	unsweetened cocoa powder, sifted	75 mL
1	can (14 oz/396 g OR 300 mL) sweetened condensed milk	1
½ cup	creamy peanut butter	125 mL
2½ cups	quick-cooking rolled oats	625 mL
1 cup	coarsely chopped peanuts	250 mL
½ cup	sunflower seeds	125 mL
½ cup	dried cranberries	125 mL

1. In a large saucepan over low heat, cook butter, cocoa and condensed milk, stirring with a wooden spoon until smooth. Remove from heat. Stir in peanut butter until smooth. Add oats, peanuts, sunflower seeds and cranberries. Mix well.
2. Drop dough by tablespoonfuls (15 mL) on waxed paper. Refrigerate until firm, about 2 hours.

No-Bake Chewy Caramel Balls

You don't have to be a kid to love these chewy balls.

**MAKES ABOUT
4 DOZEN BALLS**

- **Preparation: 20 minutes**
- **Cooking: 8 minutes**
- **Standing: 1 hour**
- **Freezing: excellent**

TIP
When making these balls, lightly butter your hands to make rolling easier.

- **Cookie sheet lined with waxed paper**

9 oz	soft caramels, unwrapped (about 36)	270 g
3 tbsp	half-and-half (10%) cream	45 mL
1½ cups	crisp rice cereal	375 mL
1 cup	corn flakes cereal	250 mL
¾ cup	flaked coconut	175 mL
½ cup	dried cranberries	125 mL
⅓ cup	finely chopped walnuts	75 mL

1. In a small saucepan over low heat, cook caramels and cream, stirring with a wooden spoon until smoothly melted.
2. In a large bowl, combine rice cereal, corn flakes cereal, coconut, cranberries and walnuts. Add caramel mixture. With a wooden spoon, stir until all ingredients are coated. Shape mixture into 1-inch (2.5 cm) balls. Place on waxed paper. Let stand until set, about 1 hour.

No-Bake Strawberries

Here's a colorful cookie that kids can make.

**MAKES ABOUT
3 DOZEN
STRAWBERRIES**

- **Preparation: 20 minutes**
- **Chilling: 2 hours**
- **Standing: 2 hours**
- **Freezing: not recommended**

TIPS

Use fine or medium desiccated coconut. Shredded or flaked is too stringy to shape.

Use a tube of prepared green frosting that comes with a leaf icing tip.

- **Cookie sheet lined with waxed paper**

1	can (14 oz/396 g OR 300 mL) sweetened condensed milk	1
1	pkg (6 oz/170 g) strawberry gelatin powder, divided	1
1 tbsp	freshly squeezed lemon juice	15 mL
20 drops	red food coloring	20 drops
4½ cups	medium desiccated coconut (see Tips)	1.125 L
	Green frosting (see Tips)	

1. In a large bowl, using a wooden spoon, stir sweetened condensed milk, ⅔ cup (150 mL) of the gelatin powder, lemon juice and food coloring until blended. Add coconut, stirring until thoroughly blended. Cover and chill mixture until it is easy to shape, about 2 hours.

2. Shape tablespoonfuls (15 mL) into balls, slightly pointed at one end. Roll in remaining gelatin powder to coat. Put a dab of green frosting on the top to resemble leaves. Place on waxed paper. Let stand at room temperature until dry, about 2 hours. Store in airtight container in refrigerator.

No-Bake Chips 'n' Nut Treats

Potato chips make the special crunch in these candy-like balls.

**MAKES ABOUT
40 BALLS**

- **Preparation: 15 minutes**
- **Cooking: 8 minutes**
- **Chilling: 1 hour**
- **Freezing: not recommended**

- **Cookie sheet lined with waxed paper**

2 cups	semi-sweet chocolate chips	500 mL
2 cups	peanut butter chips	500 mL
2 cups	butterscotch chips	500 mL
1 cup	crushed regular potato chips	250 mL
1 cup	chopped peanuts	250 mL
¾ cup	miniature candy-coated chocolate pieces (such as M&M's)	175 mL

1. In a large saucepan over low heat, melt chocolate, peanut butter and butterscotch chips, stirring with a wooden spoon until smooth. Remove from heat. Add potato chips, peanuts and candy pieces. Mix well.

2. Drop by tablespoonfuls (15 mL) on waxed paper. Chill until firm, about 1 hour.

No-Bake Rocky Road Mounds

Kids know the ingredients for Rocky Road long before they are able to make the ice cream or the bars for which it is named, so it won't be hard to convince them to try this recipe.

MAKES ABOUT 5 DOZEN COOKIES

- Preparation: 15 minutes
- Cooking: 4 minutes
- Chilling: 1 hour
- Freezing: not recommended

- **Cookie sheet lined with waxed paper**

2 cups	semi-sweet chocolate chips	500 mL
1 cup	creamy peanut butter	250 mL
2 cups	coarsely chopped honey-roasted peanuts	500 mL
5½ cups	miniature white marshmallows	1.375 L

1. In a large saucepan over low heat, melt chocolate chips and peanut butter, stirring with a wooden spoon until smooth. Remove from heat. Stir in peanuts. Mix well. Add marshmallows and stir just until they are coated with chocolate.

2. Drop mixture by tablespoonfuls (15 mL) on waxed paper. Chill until firm, about 1 hour.

Variation
Use milk chocolate chips if you prefer a milder chocolate and stronger peanut butter taste.

Crunchy Sweet and Salty Clusters

This combination of sweet chocolate and butterscotch with salty nuts and pretzels is outstanding.

MAKES ABOUT 2 DOZEN COOKIES

- Preparation: 15 minutes
- Cooking: 4 minutes
- Chilling: 1 hour
- Freezing: not recommended

- **Cookie sheet lined with waxed paper**

1 cup	milk chocolate chips	250 mL
1 cup	butterscotch chips	250 mL
½ cup	chopped cashews	125 mL
½ cup	chopped pretzels	125 mL
½ cup	miniature candy-coated chocolate pieces	125 mL

1. In a large saucepan over low heat, melt chocolate and butterscotch chips, stirring with a wooden spoon until smooth. Remove from heat. Stir in cashews, pretzels and candy pieces, mixing until all ingredients are coated.

2. Drop mixture by tablespoonfuls (15 mL) on waxed paper. Chill until firm, about 1 hour.

Variation
Use your favorite nut. Peanuts also work well.

Chocolate Caramel Cereal Drops

If you plan to make these drops for a special occasion, I recommend making two batches. They won't last long.

MAKES ABOUT 2 DOZEN COOKIES

- **Preparation: 20 minutes**
- **Cooking: 8 minutes**
- **Standing: 1 hour**
- **Freezing: not recommended**

- **Cookie sheet lined with waxed paper**

4 oz	soft caramels, unwrapped (15)	125 g
2/3 cup	semi-sweet chocolate chips	150 mL
2 tbsp	water	25 mL
2 cups	corn flakes cereal, slightly crushed	500 mL
3/4 cup	peanuts	175 mL

1. In a medium saucepan over low heat, melt caramels, chocolate chips and water, stirring constantly with a wooden spoon, until smooth. Remove from heat. Stir in cereal and peanuts, mixing until all ingredients are coated.

2. Drop mixture by teaspoonfuls (5 mL) on waxed paper. Let stand until firm, about 1 hour.

Potato Chip Crisps

Potato chips will always be a favorite of kids young and old. Let your kids make these for Dad on Father's Day.

MAKES ABOUT 3½ DOZEN COOKIES

- **Preparation: 20 minutes**
- **Baking: 12 minutes**
- **Freezing: excellent**

TIPS

Use regular potato chips, not the flavored variety.

This is like a shortbread dough with lots of added crunch. Yes, there is no egg.

- **Preheat oven to 350°F (180°C)**
- **Cookie sheet, ungreased**

1 cup	butter, softened	250 mL
1/2 cup	packed brown sugar	125 mL
1 tsp	vanilla	5 mL
2 cups	all-purpose flour	500 mL
3/4 cup	crushed potato chips	175 mL
3/4 cup	chopped pecans	175 mL
1/2 cup	butterscotch chips	125 mL

1. In a large bowl, using a wooden spoon, beat butter, brown sugar and vanilla until light and creamy, about 3 minutes. Gradually add flour, stirring until smooth. Add potato chips, pecans and butterscotch chips, mixing until thoroughly blended.

2. Drop dough by tablespoonfuls (15 mL) about 2 inches (5 cm) apart on cookie sheet. Bake in preheated oven for 8 to 12 minutes or until golden around edges. Cool for 5 minutes on sheet, then transfer to a rack and cool completely.

Oatmeal Candy Cookies

◆

Although moms prefer that their kids not eat candy, it's easier to justify when it's combined in an oatmeal cookie.

MAKES ABOUT 3½ DOZEN COOKIES

- **Preparation: 20 minutes**
- **Baking: 13 minutes**
- **Freezing: excellent**

TIPS

The most common brands of candy-coated chocolate pieces are M&M's and Smarties. They are available in bulk stores and stores that carry candies and snacks.

When baking cookies, if you like the nutty flavor of whole wheat flour, you can substitute an equal quantity of it for all-purpose flour. When trying the substitution for the first time, I prefer to use half and half to see if I like the flavor.

- **Preheat oven to 350°F (180°C)**
- **Cookie sheet, greased or lined with parchment paper**

1 cup	all-purpose flour	250 mL
1½ tsp	baking powder	7 mL
½ tsp	baking soda	2 mL
¼ tsp	salt	1 mL
½ cup	butter, softened	125 mL
½ cup	granulated sugar	125 mL
½ cup	packed brown sugar	125 mL
1	egg	1
1 tsp	vanilla	5 mL
1 cup	quick-cooking rolled oats	250 mL
1 cup	candy-coated chocolate pieces	250 mL
½ cup	unsweetened flaked coconut	125 mL

1. On a sheet of waxed paper or in a bowl, combine flour, baking powder, baking soda and salt. Set aside.

2. In a large bowl, using an electric mixer on medium speed, beat butter, granulated and brown sugars, egg and vanilla until light and creamy, about 3 minutes. On low speed, gradually add flour mixture, beating until smooth. With a wooden spoon, stir in oats, candy pieces and coconut.

3. Drop dough by tablespoonfuls (15 mL) on prepared cookie sheet. Bake in preheated oven for 9 to 13 minutes or until golden. Cool for 5 minutes on sheet, then transfer to a rack and cool completely.

Variation

Replace the candy pieces with chopped chocolate-covered nuts or halved baking gumdrops, which are available at bulk stores. They are smaller than regular gumdrops and don't melt when heated.

Banana Granola Cookies

What could be better than wholesome granola in a soft cake-like banana cookie? Dress up these cookies with a banana frosting or leave them plain to pack for lunch or snacking. Packed in a school lunch box, they make a great treat.

MAKES ABOUT 4 DOZEN COOKIES

- **Preparation: 25 minutes**
- **Baking: 13 minutes**
- **Freezing: excellent**

TIP

If you don't have an electric mixer, most drop cookies can be mixed with a wooden spoon. It takes a little more work to get the mixture light and creamy. The cookies will have a more homemade look. Kids usually prefer using a spoon and don't mind the extra effort. Plus they get to lick the spoon.

- **Preheat oven to 375°F (190°C)**
- **Cookie sheet, greased or lined with parchment paper**

COOKIE

1 ½ cups	all-purpose flour	375 mL
½ tsp	baking soda	2 mL
¼ tsp	salt	1 mL
1 tsp	ground cinnamon	5 mL
½ cup	butter, softened	125 mL
1 cup	packed brown sugar	250 mL
1	egg	1
1 cup	mashed ripe banana (2 bananas)	250 mL
1 cup	granola cereal	250 mL
½ cup	unsweetened flaked coconut	125 mL
½ cup	raisins	125 mL
⅓ cup	sunflower seeds	75 mL

BANANA FROSTING, OPTIONAL

¼ cup	butter, softened	50 mL
¼ cup	mashed ripe banana (½ banana)	50 mL
2 cups	confectioner's (icing) sugar, sifted	500 mL
2 tsp	freshly squeezed lemon juice	10 mL

1. *Cookie:* On a sheet of waxed paper or in a bowl, combine flour, baking soda, salt and cinnamon. Set aside.

2. In a large bowl, using an electric mixer on medium speed or a wooden spoon, beat butter, brown sugar and egg until light and creamy, about 3 minutes. Beat in banana. Gradually add flour mixture, beating until blended. With a wooden spoon, stir in cereal, coconut, raisins and sunflower seeds, mixing until thoroughly blended.

3. Drop dough by tablespoonfuls (15 mL) about 2 inches (5 cm) apart on prepared cookie sheet. Bake in preheated oven for 9 to 13 minutes or until golden. Cool for 5 minutes on sheet, then transfer to a rack and cool completely.

4. *Banana Frosting, optional:* In a medium bowl, using an electric mixer on medium speed, beat butter and mashed banana until smooth. Gradually add confectioner's sugar and lemon juice, beating to a smooth, spreadable consistency. Spread frosting on top of cooled cookies.

Chocolate Marshmallow Sandwich Cookies

I had so much fun making these cookies, I can just imagine how much kids will enjoy the process.

MAKES ABOUT 2 DOZEN SANDWICH COOKIES

- **Preparation: 25 minutes**
- **Baking: 12 minutes**
- **Freezing: not recommended**

TIPS

Use colored marshmallows for fun.

Don't worry — the tops of these cookies will have a crackled look.

Marshmallows don't freeze well. For longer storage, freeze the cookies and assemble the sandwiches when you're ready to eat them.

- **Preheat oven to 350°F (180°C)**
- **Cookie sheet, ungreased**

2 cups	all-purpose flour	500 mL
½ cup	unsweetened cocoa powder, sifted	125 mL
2 tsp	baking soda	10 mL
⅔ cup	butter	150 mL
1½ cups	granulated sugar, divided	375 mL
1	egg	1
¼ cup	corn syrup	50 mL
⅓ cup	miniature chocolate chips	75 mL
24	large marshmallows	24

1. On a sheet of waxed paper or in a bowl, combine flour, cocoa and baking soda. Set aside.

2. In a large bowl, using an electric mixer on medium speed, beat butter, 1¼ cups (300 mL) of the sugar, egg and corn syrup until light and creamy, about 3 minutes. On low speed, gradually add flour mixture, beating until smooth. With a wooden spoon, stir in chocolate chips.

3. Shape dough into 1-inch (2.5 cm) balls. Roll in remaining ¼ cup (75 mL) sugar to coat well. Place about 2 inches (5 cm) apart on cookie sheet. Bake in preheated oven for 8 to 12 minutes or until set. Cool for 5 minutes on sheet, then transfer to a rack and cool completely.

4. *Assembly:* Place 1 marshmallow on the flat side of 1 cookie. Place on small paper plate. Microwave on high for 12 to 15 seconds or until marshmallow just starts to bulge and is hot. Immediately place another cookie, flat side down, on top of the marshmallow. Press gently so marshmallow spreads to outer edge of cookie.

Variation

Fill these cookies with a scoop of your favorite ice cream. Place in the freezer until you're ready to serve. For storage, wrap individually in plastic wrap.

Shortbread and Holiday Cookies

Shortbread originated in Scotland, where it was originally served during the Christmas season. "Short" means crumbly, which refers to its characteristic texture. Shortbread has three basic ingredients — butter, flour and sugar. However, the kinds of sugar and flour, as well as the method of mixing and baking, differ among recipes, resulting in an amazing range of tastes and textures.

Shortbread is easy to make. It can be mixed with an electric mixer or a wooden spoon, in a food processor or using a pastry blender. It can also be kneaded by hand. Most dough requires some kneading to become smooth since the batter doesn't contain liquid or eggs. Since shortbreads are easy to make, keep well and require no special ingredients, there's no reason not to enjoy them year-round.

Shortbread is a holiday favorite in the British Isles, but I've also included some time-honored recipes from around the world. These are also recipes for cookies that are colorful or filled with holiday ingredients, which make a much-appreciated gift. You'll even find some cookies that travel well.

Mom's Fancy Pressed Shortbread

These tiny, fragile, buttery cookies were my mother's specialty. Only she (not me) would have the patience to cut tiny pieces of red and green cherries to decorate her cookie wreaths. Use the holiday design you prefer in your cookie press — star, bell, tree, wreath or whatever you have — all work well.

MAKES ABOUT 10 DOZEN SMALL COOKIES

- **Preparation: 25 minutes**
- **Baking: 10 minutes**
- **Freezing: excellent**

TIPS

To color sugar, add a few drops of food coloring to granulated sugar. Mix well with the back of a spoon or a spatula until color is evenly distributed. Transfer to a saltshaker to sprinkle evenly over cookies.

There's no substitute for butter when making shortbread.

- **Preheat oven to 350°F (180°C)**
- **Cookie press fitted with holiday-design nozzle**
- **Cookie sheet, ungreased**

1 cup plus 2 tbsp	butter, softened	275 mL
½ cup	confectioner's (icing) sugar, sifted	125 mL
¼ tsp	salt	1 mL
2 cups	all-purpose flour	500 mL
	Colored sugar or candied cherries	

1. In a large bowl, using an electric mixer on medium speed, beat butter and confectioner's sugar until light and creamy, about 3 minutes. On low speed, gradually add salt and flour, beating until blended.

2. Pack dough into fitted cookie press and press about 1 inch (2.5 cm) apart on cookie sheet. Sprinkle with colored sugar and/or decorate with pieces of cherry, as desired. Bake in preheated oven for 5 to 10 minutes or until light golden around edges. Cool for 5 minutes on sheet, then transfer to a rack and cool completely.

Whipped Shortbread

This cookie has the same tender, melt-in-your-mouth texture and flavor as rolled shortbread, but with much less effort.

MAKES ABOUT 3 DOZEN COOKIES

- **Preparation: 15 minutes**
- **Baking: 25 minutes**
- **Freezing: excellent**

TIPS

If you don't have superfine sugar, whirl regular granulated sugar in a blender or food processor until fine.

Unsalted and salted butter are interchangeable. The difference is in the taste. The sweet, delicate flavor of unsalted butter really comes through in shortbread, where butter is the main ingredient.

- **Preheat oven to 300°F (150°C)**
- **Cookie sheet, ungreased**

1 ½ cups	all-purpose flour	375 mL
¼ cup	cornstarch	50 mL
1 cup	butter, softened	250 mL
½ cup	superfine granulated sugar (see Tips)	125 mL
1 tsp	vanilla	5 mL
	Candied cherries, halved, or pecan halves, optional	

1. On a sheet of waxed paper or in a bowl, combine flour and cornstarch. Set aside.

2. In a large bowl, using an electric mixer on medium speed, beat butter, sugar and vanilla until light and creamy, about 3 minutes. On low speed, gradually add flour mixture, beating until blended.

3. Drop dough by tablespoonfuls (15 mL) about 1 inch (2.5 cm) apart on cookie sheet. If desired, decorate top with a cherry half or pecan. Bake in preheated oven for 20 to 25 minutes or until light golden around edges. Cool for 5 minutes on sheet, then transfer to a rack and cool completely.

Oatmeal Pecan Shortbread

◆

Brown sugar gives this shortbread a nice caramel flavor and crisp texture.

MAKES ABOUT 4 DOZEN COOKIES

- **Preparation: 25 minutes**
- **Baking: 20 minutes**
- **Freezing: excellent**

TIPS

Use quick-cooking oats, not instant or old-fashioned large-flake oats, in this recipe.

Use an offset spatula to transfer cookies that are more fragile, such as these, to and from cookie sheets.

- **Preheat oven to 300°F (150°C)**
- **2-inch (5 cm) cookie cutters**
- **Cookie sheet, ungreased**

1 1/2 cups	all-purpose flour	375 mL
2/3 cup	quick-cooking rolled oats	150 mL
1/2 cup	packed brown sugar	125 mL
1/4 cup	finely chopped pecans	50 mL
1/2 tsp	ground cinnamon	2 mL
3/4 cup	butter, softened	175 mL

1. In a large bowl, combine flour, oats, brown sugar, pecans and cinnamon. Mix well. With a wooden spoon, blend in butter until mixture is crumbly. Using your hands, knead to form a soft, smooth dough. If necessary, cover and chill for 30 minutes for easy rolling.

2. Divide dough into halves. On floured surface, roll out 1 portion at a time to 1/4-inch (0.5 cm) thickness. Dip cutters in flour and cut into desired shapes. Place on cookie sheet about 1 inch (2.5 cm) apart. Bake in preheated oven for 15 to 20 minutes or until light golden. Cool for 5 minutes on sheet, then transfer to a rack and cool completely.

Variation

Divide dough into halves. Press each into a 5 1/2-inch (13.75 cm) round on cookie sheet. Mark into wedges and crimp the edges with a fork. Bake for 35 to 40 minutes.

Citrus Refrigerator Shortbread

A light sprinkling of granulated sugar before baking or confectioner's (icing) sugar after the cookies have cooled finishes these off nicely.

MAKES ABOUT 9 DOZEN COOKIES

- **Preparation: 25 minutes**
- **Chilling: 3 hours**
- **Baking: 15 minutes**
- **Freezing: excellent**

TIPS

If you don't have superfine sugar, whirl regular granulated sugar in a blender of food processor until fine.

You should get 1 tsp (5 mL) zest from a lime, 1 tbsp (15 mL) from a lemon and 4 tsp (20 mL) from an orange. Remove only the outer colored part. The white layer underneath, which is known as the pith, is bitter.

Use a sharp straight-edged knife to cut this dough.

- **Cookie sheet, ungreased**

1 ½ cups	all-purpose flour	375 mL
¾ cup	cornstarch	175 mL
¼ tsp	salt	1 mL
1 cup	butter, softened	250 mL
½ cup	superfine granulated sugar (see Tips)	125 mL
1 ½ tsp	grated lemon zest	7 mL
1 ½ tsp	grated lime zest	7 mL
1 ½ tsp	grated orange zest	7 mL
1 tbsp	freshly squeezed lemon, lime or orange juice	15 mL
	Granulated or confectioner's (icing) sugar, optional	

1. On a sheet of waxed paper or in a bowl, combine flour, cornstarch and salt. Set aside.

2. In a large bowl, using an electric mixer on medium speed, beat butter and sugar until light and creamy, about 3 minutes. Beat in lemon, lime and orange zests and juice until smooth. On low speed, gradually add flour mixture, beating until blended. Using your hands, knead to form a smooth dough. Divide dough into thirds. Shape each into a roll 9 inches (22.5 cm) long. Wrap and chill until firm, at least 3 hours.

3. Fifteen minutes before you're ready to bake, preheat oven to 350°F (180°C). Cut rolls into ¼-inch (0.5 cm) slices. Place about 1 inch (2.5 cm) apart on cookie sheet. Bake in preheated oven for 10 to 15 minutes or until golden around edges. Cool for 5 minutes on sheet, then transfer to a rack and cool completely.

Variation

Use 4½ tsp (22 mL) of only one kind of zest rather than a mixture.

Cherry Pistachio Shortbreads

These colorful cookies are particularly nice for the festive season. They also make a great treat year-round.

MAKES ABOUT 40 COOKIES

- **Preparation: 20 minutes**
- **Baking: 25 minutes**
- **Freezing: excellent**

TIPS

If you use unsalted butter for shortbread, add a pinch of salt along with the flour.

These cookies can also be shaped into 1-inch (2.5 cm) balls and flattened with a fork dipped in sugar. Same taste with a different look.

- **Preheat oven to 300°F (150°C)**
- **Cookie sheet, ungreased**

1 cup	butter, softened	250 mL
½ cup	confectioner's (icing) sugar, sifted	125 mL
1 tsp	vanilla	5 mL
1¾ cups	all-purpose flour	425 mL
¾ cup	coarsely chopped pistachios	175 mL
½ cup	chopped dried cherries	125 mL
2 tbsp	granulated sugar	25 mL

1. In a large bowl, using an electric mixer on medium speed, beat butter, confectioner's sugar and vanilla until light and creamy, about 3 minutes. With a wooden spoon, stir in flour, pistachios and cherries, mixing until thoroughly blended. Using your hands, knead to form a smooth dough.

2. Drop dough by tablespoonfuls (15 mL) about 1 inch (2.5 cm) apart on cookie sheet. Sprinkle tops evenly with granulated sugar. Bake in preheated oven for 20 to 25 minutes or until golden around edges. Cool for 5 minutes on sheet, then transfer to a rack and cool completely.

Variations

Replace cherries with dried cranberries. Try using cranberries flavored with cherry or orange for something different.

Replace pistachios with almonds or pecans.

Frosted Lemon Poppy Seed Shortbread Cookies

Poppy seeds give these cookies an interesting taste and appearance. The lemon frosting, which is a bit tart, adds a nice touch.

MAKES ABOUT 8 DOZEN COOKIES

- **Preparation: 35 minutes**
- **Chilling: 2 hours**
- **Baking: 15 minutes**
- **Freezing: excellent**

TIPS

Shortbreads are best stored at room temperature in a cool, dry place rather than in the refrigerator.

Store poppy seeds in the freezer so they don't develop a rancid flavor.

● **Cookie sheet, ungreased**

COOKIE

1¼ cups	all-purpose flour	300 mL
½ cup	cornstarch	125 mL
1 tbsp	poppy seeds	15 mL
¾ cup	butter, softened	175 mL
½ cup	confectioner's (icing) sugar, sifted	125 mL
1 tbsp	grated lemon zest	15 mL
1 tbsp	freshly squeezed lemon juice	15 mL

FROSTING

¾ cup	confectioner's (icing) sugar, sifted	175 mL
¼ cup	butter, softened	50 mL
1 tsp	grated lemon zest	5 mL
1 tsp	freshly squeezed lemon juice	5 mL

1. *Cookie:* On a sheet of waxed paper or in a bowl, combine flour, cornstarch and poppy seeds. Set aside.

2. In a large bowl, using an electric mixer on medium speed, beat butter, confectioner's sugar and lemon zest and juice until light and creamy, about 3 minutes. On low speed, gradually add flour mixture, beating until blended. Using your hands, knead to form a smooth dough. Divide dough into halves. Shape each into a roll 12 inches (30 cm) long. Wrap and chill until firm, at least 2 hours.

3. Fifteen minutes before you're ready to bake, preheat oven to 350°F (180°C). Cut rolls into ¼-inch (0.5 cm) slices. Place about 1 inch (2.5 cm) apart on cookie sheet. Bake in preheated oven for 11 to 15 minutes or until golden around edges. Cool for 5 minutes on sheet, then transfer to a rack and cool completely.

4. *Frosting:* In a small bowl, combine confectioner's sugar, butter and lemon zest and juice. Beat with an electric mixer on low speed or a wooden spoon until smooth. Spread over cooled cookies.

Variation

These cookies are also delicious without the frosting.

Nutty and Nice Shortbreads

I'm not sure which is better, the flavor of these cookies or their appearance. The sprinkling of sliced hazelnuts makes them particularly attractive. They are definitely a favorite at my house.

**MAKES ABOUT
4 DOZEN COOKIES**

- **Preparation: 25 minutes**
- **Baking: 20 minutes**
- **Freezing: excellent**

TIPS

You can buy thinly sliced unblanched hazelnuts, which look very attractive, in most grocery stores and bulk stores.

I recommend using parchment paper when baking these cookies because the egg white drips onto the cookie sheet and tends to stick.

- **Preheat oven to 325°F (160°C)**
- **2-inch (5 cm) round cookie cutter**
- **Cookie sheet, lined with parchment paper**

1 cup	butter, softened	250 mL
1/3 cup	granulated sugar	75 mL
2 tbsp	cornstarch	25 mL
1 tsp	vanilla	5 mL
2 cups	all-purpose flour	500 mL
1/3 cup	finely chopped walnuts	75 mL
1/3 cup	finely chopped pecans	75 mL
1/3 cup	finely chopped hazelnuts	75 mL
1	egg white, lightly beaten	1
1/2 cup	sliced unblanched hazelnuts	125 mL

1. In a large bowl, using an electric mixer on medium speed, beat butter, sugar, cornstarch and vanilla until light and creamy, about 3 minutes. With wooden spoon, stir in flour, walnuts, pecans and chopped hazelnuts, mixing until thoroughly blended. Using your hands, knead to form a smooth dough.

2. On floured surface, roll out dough to 1/4-inch (0.5 cm) thickness. Dip cutter in flour and cut into rounds. Place about 1 inch (2.5 cm) apart on prepared cookie sheet. Brush tops with beaten egg white. Sprinkle with sliced hazelnuts. Bake in preheated oven for 15 to 20 minutes or until golden around edges. Cool for 5 minutes on sheet, then transfer to a rack and cool completely.

Variation

For a glistening top, mix 1 tbsp (15 mL) granulated sugar with the sliced hazelnuts.

Bittersweet Cashew Rounds

Lots of chocolate and nuts make these hearty shortbreads hard to resist.

MAKES ABOUT 3½ DOZEN COOKIES

- **Preparation: 25 minutes**
- **Baking: 20 minutes**
- **Freezing: excellent**

TIPS

When you flatten the balls with a fork, it leaves interesting lines on top. The bottom of a glass leaves a flat surface. Try both ways for different looks.

A sprinkle of granulated sugar is always a nice finish on any shortbread cookie.

These cookies travel well, so they are a good choice for holiday care packages.

- **Preheat oven to 350°F (180°C)**
- **Cookie sheet, ungreased**

1¾ cups	all-purpose flour	425 mL
¼ cup	cornstarch	50 mL
1 cup	butter, softened	250 mL
½ cup	confectioner's (icing) sugar, sifted	125 mL
3	squares (1 oz/28 g each) bittersweet chocolate, chopped	3
½ cup	chopped cashews	125 mL

1. On a sheet of waxed paper or in a bowl, combine flour and cornstarch. Set aside.

2. In a large bowl, using an electric mixer on medium speed, beat butter and confectioner's sugar until light and creamy, about 3 minutes. On low speed, gradually add flour mixture, beating until blended. With a wooden spoon, stir in chocolate and cashews. Using your hands, knead to form a smooth dough.

3. Shape dough into 1-inch (2.5 cm) balls. Place about 2 inches (5 cm) apart on cookie sheet. Flatten slightly with a fork or the bottom of a glass dipped in granulated sugar. Bake in preheated oven or 15 to 20 minutes or until golden around edges. Cool for 5 minutes on sheet, then transfer to a rack and cool completely.

Variations

Substitute semi-sweet or milk chocolate for the bittersweet. Peanuts work well in place of the cashews.

Toffee Crunch Almond Shortbread

Pack some of these in a small, colorful cookie tin for a great holiday gift.

**MAKES ABOUT
5 DOZEN COOKIES**

- **Preparation: 25 minutes**
- **Baking: 30 minutes**
- **Freezing: excellent**

TIPS

I recommend using parchment paper when baking these cookies because the toffee is very sticky.

If you don't have superfine sugar, whirl regular granulated sugar in a blender or food processor until fine.

These shortbreads taste great with a bit of chocolate. You can drizzle melted chocolate over the tops, or dip half of the entire cookie in melted chocolate. If you choose to dip, you'll need about 8 oz (250 g) of chocolate.

Because shortbread recipes use no eggs, they can easily be halved or doubled. I usually make larger batches since the cookies keep well and disappear quickly.

- **Preheat oven to 300°F (150°C)**
- **Cookie sheet, lined with parchment paper**

3 cups	all-purpose flour	750 mL
1 cup	rice flour	250 mL
¼ tsp	salt	1 mL
2 cups	butter, softened	500 mL
1 cup	superfine granulated sugar (see Tips)	250 mL
1 cup	chopped unblanched almonds	250 mL
1 cup	toffee bits	250 mL

1. On a sheet of waxed paper or in a bowl, combine all-purpose and rice flours and salt. Set aside.

2. In a large bowl, using an electric mixer on medium speed, beat butter and sugar until light and creamy, about 3 minutes. On low speed, gradually add flour mixture, beating until blended. With a wooden spoon, stir in almonds and toffee bits. Using your hands, knead to form a smooth dough.

3. Shape dough into 1-inch (2.5 cm) balls. Place about 2 inches (5 cm) apart on prepared cookie sheet. Flatten to about ¼-inch (0.5 cm) thickness with the bottom of a glass dipped in granulated sugar or flour. Bake in preheated oven for 25 to 30 minutes or until lightly browned around edges. Cool for 5 minutes on sheet, then transfer to a rack and cool completely.

Mocha Java Shortbread Logs

A great choice for coffee-lovers. Enjoy them with an espresso coffee for a double dose of caffeine.

MAKES ABOUT 4 DOZEN COOKIES

- **Preparation: 25 minutes**
- **Baking: 20 minutes**
- **Freezing: excellent**

TIPS

These have a great coffee impact. For a milder flavor, decrease espresso to 1 tbsp (15 mL).

Roll warm cookies in confectioner's (icing) sugar.

- **Preheat oven to 350°F (180°C)**
- **Cookie sheet, ungreased**

2 cups	all-purpose flour	500 mL
2 tbsp	cornstarch	25 mL
2 tbsp	instant espresso coffee powder	25 mL
2	squares (1 oz/28 g each) semi-sweet chocolate, finely chopped	2
1 cup	butter, softened	250 mL
½ cup	granulated sugar	125 mL

1. On a sheet of waxed paper or in a bowl, combine flour, cornstarch, coffee powder and chocolate. Set aside.

2. In a large bowl, using an electric mixer on medium speed, beat butter and sugar until light and creamy, about 3 minutes. With a wooden spoon, stir in flour mixture, mixing until thoroughly blended. Using your hands, knead to form a smooth dough.

3. Shape into small logs, each about 2- by ½-inch (5 cm by 1 cm). Place about 1 inch (2.5 cm) apart on cookie sheet. Bake in preheated oven for 15 to 20 minutes or until lightly browned around edges. Cool for 5 minutes on sheet, then transfer to a rack and cool completely.

Variations

Drizzle the logs with melted chocolate or omit the chocolate in the recipe for a true coffee flavor.

For an interesting crunch, replace the instant espresso coffee powder with 3 tbsp (45 mL) finely crushed espresso or mocha java coffee beans.

Chocolate Ginger Shortbread

These look and taste great plain, but you can dress them up with a sprinkle of confectioner's (icing) sugar or a chocolate drizzle. Chocolate-lovers may want to dip the entire bottom in melted chocolate.

MAKES ABOUT 40 COOKIES

- **Preparation: 20 minutes**
- **Baking: 23 minutes**
- **Freezing: excellent**

TIPS

When creaming butter, it's important to have it at the right temperature. It should be a spreadable consistency. If it's too hard, it won't beat to a creamy texture; if it's too soft, the dough will be too soft to handle and your cookies won't hold their shape.

When wrapping dough for freezing or storage, wrap tightly in plastic wrap. If you plan to use it in the immediate future, waxed paper will do.

- **Preheat oven to 325°F (160°C)**
- **Cookie sheet, ungreased**

1 cup	butter, softened	250 mL
½ cup	granulated sugar	125 mL
2 cups	all-purpose flour	500 mL
¼ tsp	ground ginger	1 mL
½ cup	finely chopped crystallized ginger	125 mL
½ cup	chopped milk chocolate	125 mL

1. In a large bowl, using an electric mixer on medium speed, beat butter and sugar until light and creamy, about 3 minutes. With a wooden spoon, stir in flour, ground ginger, crystallized ginger and chocolate, mixing until thoroughly blended. Using your hands, knead to form a smooth dough.

2. Drop dough by tablespoonfuls (15 mL) about 2 inches (5 cm) apart on cookie sheet. Bake in preheated oven for 18 to 23 minutes or until lightly browned around edges. Cool for 5 minutes on sheet, then transfer to a rack and cool completely.

Variations

Omit ground ginger if you prefer a milder ginger flavor.

If you love dark chocolate, replace the milk chocolate with bittersweet.

Tropical Shortbread

These cookies are like a trip to the tropics without the flight.

MAKES ABOUT 6½ DOZEN COOKIES

- **Preparation: 25 minutes**
- **Chilling: 2 hours**
- **Baking: 15 minutes**
- **Freezing: excellent**

TIPS

Coconut extract is not as common as other extracts, such as vanilla. However, it has become one of my favorite ingredients for cookies that contain coconut. It adds a wonderful burst of coconut flavor.

Use a sharp serrated knife to cut this dough.

- **Cookie sheet, ungreased**

1 cup	butter, softened	250 mL
⅓ cup	granulated sugar	75 mL
1 tsp	coconut extract	5 mL
1¾ cups	all-purpose flour	425 mL
¼ tsp	salt	1 mL
1 cup	sweetened flaked coconut	250 mL
¾ cup	chopped macadamia nuts	175 mL
½ cup	chopped candied pineapple	125 mL

1. In a large bowl, using an electric mixer on medium speed, beat butter, sugar and coconut extract until light and creamy, about 3 minutes. On low speed, gradually add flour and salt, beating until blended. With a wooden spoon, stir in coconut, nuts and pineapple. Using your hands, knead to form a smooth dough. Divide dough into halves. Shape each into a roll 10 inches (25 cm) long. Wrap and chill until firm, at least 2 hours.

2. Fifteen minutes before you're ready to bake, preheat oven to 350°F (180°C). Cut rolls into ¼-inch (0.5 cm) slices. Place about 2 inches (5 cm) apart on cookie sheet. Bake in preheated oven for 10 to 15 minutes or until golden around edges. Cool for 5 minutes on sheet, then transfer to a rack and cool completely.

Variations

Replace macadamia nuts with almonds.

Omit candied pineapple or replace with candied cherries.

Slice-and-Bake Cherry Pecan Shortbread

Freeze a few of these rolls and get a head start on your holiday baking.

MAKES ABOUT 5 DOZEN COOKIES

- **Preparation: 25 minutes**
- **Chilling: 3 hours**
- **Baking: 25 minutes**
- **Freezing: excellent**

TIPS

These cookies are delicious two ways. You can bake them like most shortbreads, until they are lightly browned around the edges (20 minutes), which gives them a slightly softer texture than when they are baked until the tops, too, are lightly browned. The longer baking time (25 minutes) produces a crispier result, more like a tender sugar cookie.

Use a sharp serrated knife to cut this dough as it will easily cut through the nuts and cherries.

For make-ahead baking, you may want to double this recipe.

- **Cookie sheet, ungreased**

1¾ cups	all-purpose flour	425 mL
¼ cup	cornstarch	50 mL
Pinch	salt	Pinch
1 cup	butter, softened	250 mL
½ cup	confectioner's (icing) sugar, sifted	125 mL
1 tbsp	grated lemon zest	15 mL
½ cup	chopped red candied cherries	125 mL
½ cup	chopped green candied cherries	125 mL
½ cup	finely chopped pecans	125 mL

1. On a sheet of waxed paper or in a bowl, combine flour, cornstarch and salt. Set aside.

2. In a large bowl, using an electric mixer on medium speed, beat butter, confectioner's sugar and lemon zest until light and creamy, about 3 minutes. On low speed, gradually add flour mixture, beating until blended. With a wooden spoon, stir in red and green cherries and pecans. Using your hands, knead to form a smooth dough. Divide dough into halves. Shape each into a roll 8 inches (20 cm) long. Wrap and chill until firm, at least 3 hours.

3. Fifteen minutes before you're ready to bake, preheat oven to 300°F (150°C). Cut rolls into ¼-inch (0.5 cm) slices. Place about 2 inches (5 cm) apart on cookie sheet. Bake in preheated oven for 20 to 25 minutes or until lightly browned around edges. Cool for 5 minutes on sheet, then transfer to a rack and cool completely.

Variations

Omit green cherries and use twice the quantity of red cherries only.

Substitute walnuts for the pecans.

Replace the cherries with chopped mixed candied fruit.

Chocolate Caramel Shortbread

The best of both worlds — a melt-in-your-mouth shortbread cookie combined with a favorite crunchy toffee chocolate bar.

MAKES ABOUT 3 DOZEN COOKIES

- **Preparation: 25 minutes**
- **Baking: 25 minutes**
- **Freezing: excellent**

TIPS

A common brand of chocolate toffee bar is Toblerone Milk Chocolate with Almond Honey Nougat. Many store-brand bars are also available. For a stronger chocolate taste, buy the dark chocolate version. You should have about 1⅓ cups (325 mL) chopped chocolate bar.

Be sure to use parchment paper when baking these cookies, as the toffee is sticky.

- **Preheat oven to 325°F (160°C)**
- **Cookie sheet, lined with parchment paper**

1 cup	butter, softened	250 mL
½ cup	granulated sugar	125 mL
2 cups	all-purpose flour	500 mL
2 tbsp	cornstarch	25 mL
1	milk chocolate toffee bar (6 oz/175 g), coarsely chopped	1

1. In a large bowl, using an electric mixer on medium speed, beat butter and sugar until light and creamy, about 3 minutes. With a wooden spoon, stir in flour and cornstarch, mixing until thoroughly blended. Using your hands, knead to form a smooth dough.

2. Reserve 36 large pieces of the chocolate bar. Work remainder into dough, using your hands or a wooden spoon. Drop dough by tablespoonfuls (15 mL) about 1 inch (2.5 cm) apart on prepared cookie sheet. Press a reserved chunk of chocolate bar on top of each cookie. Bake in preheated oven for 20 to 25 minutes or until lightly browned around edges. Cool for 5 minutes on sheet, then transfer to a rack and cool completely.

Variation

Dust these cookies with confectioner's (icing) sugar before serving.

Halloween Pumpkin Cookies

◆

I'm always looking for new ways to use pumpkin at Halloween, and this combination with white chocolate and macadamia nuts is a real keeper. It will extend far beyond my Halloween cookie baking.

MAKES ABOUT 5 DOZEN COOKIES

- **Preparation: 25 minutes**
- **Baking: 15 minutes**
- **Freezing: excellent**

TIPS

Be sure to buy pure pumpkin. The pumpkin pie filling has sugar and spices already added to it.

Soft cookies like these should be stored in an airtight container at room temperature. They also freeze well.

When measuring brown sugar, press it firmly into a dry measuring cup. When turned out on a flat surface it should hold its shape.

- **Preheat oven to 350°F (180°C)**
- **Cookie sheet, greased or lined with parchment paper**

2 cups	all-purpose flour	500 mL
1 tsp	baking soda	5 mL
1/4 tsp	salt	1 mL
2 tsp	ground cinnamon	10 mL
1/4 tsp	ground nutmeg	1 mL
1/4 tsp	ground cloves	1 mL
1 cup	butter, softened	250 mL
1 cup	packed brown sugar	250 mL
1 cup	pumpkin purée (not pie filling)	250 mL
1	egg	1
2 cups	white chocolate chips	500 mL
1 cup	coarsely chopped macadamia nuts	250 mL
1/2 cup	pumpkin seeds	125 mL

1. On a sheet of waxed paper or in a bowl, combine flour, baking soda, salt, cinnamon, nutmeg and cloves. Set aside.

2. In a large bowl, using an electric mixer on medium speed, beat butter, brown sugar, pumpkin and egg until smooth, about 3 minutes. On low speed, gradually add flour mixture, beating until blended. With a wooden spoon, stir in white chocolate chips, macadamia nuts and pumpkin seeds.

3. Drop by tablespoonfuls (15 mL) about 2 inches (5 cm) apart on prepared cookie sheet. Bake in preheated oven for 11 to 15 minutes or until set. Cool for 5 minutes on sheet, then transfer to a rack and cool completely.

Variations

Replace pumpkin seeds with sunflower seeds or omit completely.

Replace macadamia nuts with almonds.

Shortbread Cutouts

Cut out these cookies into holiday shapes, such as trees or Santas, or turn them into personalized place cards for a special dinner or name tags for gifts.

**MAKES ABOUT
3 DOZEN COOKIES**

- **Preparation: 20 minutes**
- **Baking: 25 minutes**
- **Freezing: excellent**

TIPS

To use these as gift tags, make a hole in the end or the top of each cookie with a straw before baking. Re-cut the hole as soon as cookies come out of the oven. After decorating, put a thin ribbon or string through the hole. To decorate as place or name cards, use tubes of prepared icing or gel to write out the names. For decorating with candies, use icing as glue.

Icings and gels are available in many colors. They are ideal for writing on and decorating cookies and cakes. Kids can be very creative with these as tools.

- **Preheat oven to 300°F (150°C)**
- **Holiday or rectangular cookie cutters**
- **Cookie sheet, ungreased**

1 ½ cups	all-purpose flour	375 mL
¾ cup	cornstarch	175 mL
½ cup	superfine granulated sugar (see Tips, page 219)	125 mL
¼ tsp	salt	1 mL
1 cup	butter, softened	250 mL

DECORATIONS

Colored sugars, candies and frosting

1. In a large bowl, combine flour, cornstarch, sugar and salt. Add butter. With a wooden spoon, mix until blended, then, using your hands, knead to form a smooth dough.

2. Divide dough into halves. On a floured surface, roll out each to ¼-inch (0.5 cm) thickness. Dip cutters in flour and cut into desired shapes. Place about 1 inch (2.5 cm) apart on cookie sheet. If desired, sprinkle with colored sugar. Bake in preheated oven for 15 to 25 minutes or until golden around edges. (Time will depend on the size of the cookies.) Cool for 5 minutes on sheet, then transfer to a rack and cool completely.

Variation

Shape into 1-inch (2.5 cm) balls, flatten slightly and sprinkle with sugar.

Raspberry Almond Shortbread Wreaths

♦

These pretty cutout cookies make an attractive addition to your holiday cookie tray.

MAKES ABOUT 40 COOKIES

- **Preparation: 40 minutes**
- **Baking: 9 minutes**
- **Freezing: not recommended**

TIPS

Use different shapes for the center cutout. Stars and hearts are attractive.

Aspic or canapé cutters are great for cutting out the centers.

After you have removed the centers from the second batch of dough, piece them together and roll out again to make more cookies.

- **Preheat oven to 350°F (180°C)**
- **2-inch (5 cm) round cookie cutter**
- **¾-inch (2 cm) round cookie cutter (see Tips)**
- **Cookie sheet, ungreased**

1 cup	butter, softened	250 mL
⅔ cup	granulated sugar	150 mL
½ tsp	almond extract	2 mL
2 cups	all-purpose flour	500 mL
¾ cup	ground almonds	175 mL
½ cup	seedless raspberry jam	125 mL
	Confectioner's (icing) sugar	

1. In a large bowl, using an electric mixer on medium speed, beat butter, sugar and almond extract until light and creamy, about 3 minutes. On low speed, gradually add flour mixture, beating until smooth. With a wooden spoon, stir in almonds until blended, then, using your hands, knead to form a smooth dough.

2. Divide dough into halves. On a floured surface, roll out 1 portion to ⅛-inch (0.25 cm) thickness. Dip 2-inch (5 cm) cutter in flour and cut into rounds. Place about 1 inch (2.5 cm) apart on cookie sheet. Roll out remaining dough to ⅛-inch (0.25 cm) thickness and cut into 2-inch rounds, then, using the small cutter, cut the centers from this batch of cookies. Place about 1 inch (2.5 cm) apart on cookie sheet. Bake in preheated oven for 5 to 9 minutes or until lightly browned around edges. Cool for 5 minutes on sheet, then transfer to a rack and cool completely.

3. *Assembly:* Spread about ½ tsp (2 mL) jam over flat side of cookies without holes. Dust confectioner's sugar over top of the cookies with center holes. Place cookies, sugar side up, over jam.

Variations
Replace almonds with hazelnuts or pecans.
Replace raspberry jam with apricot.

Mincemeat Pillows

This tender cream cheese pastry is nice to work with and it tastes great, too. Prepared mincemeat makes an easy filling.

MAKES ABOUT 4 DOZEN SANDWICH COOKIES

- **Preparation: 35 minutes**
- **Baking: 18 minutes**
- **Freezing: excellent (filled)**

TIP

Coarse sugar is available in bulk stores and cake supply stores. You can also use regular granulated sugar, turbinado sugar or Demerara sugar.

- **Preheat oven to 375°F (190°C)**
- **3-inch (7.5 cm) round cookie cutter**
- **Cookie sheet, greased or lined with parchment paper**

PASTRY

1 cup	butter, softened	250 mL
1	pkg (8 oz/250 g) cream cheese, softened	1
¼ cup	granulated sugar	50 mL
2 cups	all-purpose flour	500 mL
½ tsp	ground cinnamon	2 mL

FILLING

1½ cups	prepared mincemeat	375 mL
2 tsp	ground cinnamon	10 mL

GLAZE

1	egg, beaten	1
¼ cup	coarse sugar	50 mL

1. *Pastry:* In a large bowl, using an electric mixer on medium speed, beat butter and cream cheese until smooth. On low speed, gradually add sugar, flour and cinnamon, beating until blended. On a floured surface, roll out dough to ⅛-inch (0.25 cm) thickness. Dip cutter in flour and cut into rounds.

2. *Filling:* In a small bowl, combine mincemeat and cinnamon. Mix well. Place about 1 tsp (5 mL) mincemeat in center of each cookie. Fold to form a half-moon. With a floured fork, seal edges together. Place about 1 inch (2.5 cm) apart on prepared cookie sheet.

3. *Glaze:* Brush top of cookies with beaten egg. Sprinkle sugar over top. Bake in preheated oven for 13 to 18 minutes or until golden around the edges. Cool for 5 minutes on sheet, then transfer to a rack and cool completely.

Variation

Replace mincemeat with an equal quantity of whole-berry cranberry sauce or a thick red jam.

White Chocolate Cranberry Drops

Sweet, creamy white chocolate blends beautifully with tart cranberries in a rich shortbread dough. These are so easy to make, there's no excuse for not baking.

MAKES ABOUT 4 DOZEN COOKIES

- **Preparation: 25 minutes**
- **Baking: 18 minutes**
- **Freezing: excellent**

TIPS

If you don't have superfine sugar, whirl regular granulated sugar in a food processor or blender until fine.

I recommend using parchment paper when baking these cookies, as the white chocolate is likely to stick.

- **Preheat oven to 350°F (180°C)**
- **Cookie sheet, lined with parchment paper**

2 cups	all-purpose flour	500 mL
¼ cup	cornstarch	50 mL
1 cup	butter, softened	250 mL
½ cup	superfine granulated sugar (see Tips)	125 mL
1 tsp	vanilla	5 mL
1 cup	chopped dried cranberries	250 mL
¾ cup	white chocolate chips	175 mL

1. On a sheet of waxed paper or in a bowl, combine flour and cornstarch. Set aside.

2. In a large bowl, using an electric mixer on medium speed, beat butter, sugar and vanilla until light and creamy, about 3 minutes. On low speed, gradually add flour mixture, beating until blended. Using your hands, knead to form a smooth dough. Add cranberries and white chocolate chips. Knead well.

3. Drop dough by tablespoonfuls (15 mL) about 2 inches (5 cm) apart on prepared cookie sheet. Bake in preheated oven for 13 to 18 minutes or until lightly browned around edges. Cool for 5 minutes on sheet, then transfer to a rack and cool completely.

Variations

Add a drizzle of white chocolate over tops of cookies.

Replace white chocolate chips with semi-sweet chocolate chips.

Replace cranberries with dried cherries or dried blueberries.

Candy Cane Twists

Kids will enjoy making these cookies and leaving them for Santa as much as Santa will enjoy receiving them.

MAKES ABOUT 4 DOZEN COOKIES

- **Preparation: 25 minutes**
- **Baking: 11 minutes**
- **Freezing: excellent**

TIP

If you like peppermint, increase the extract to ¾ tsp (3 mL).

- **Preheat oven to 375°F (190°C)**
- **Cookie sheet, ungreased**

2½ cups	all-purpose flour	625 mL
1 tsp	baking powder	5 mL
1 cup	butter, softened	250 mL
¾ cup	granulated sugar	175 mL
1	egg	1
½ tsp	peppermint extract	2 mL
½ tsp	red food coloring	2 mL
¼ cup	crushed red and white peppermints or candy canes, optional	50 mL

1. On a sheet of waxed paper or in a bowl, combine flour and baking powder. Set aside.

2. In a large bowl, using an electric mixer on medium speed, beat butter, sugar, egg and peppermint extract until light and creamy, about 3 minutes. On low speed, gradually add flour mixture, beating until blended. Divide dough into halves. Add food coloring to 1 portion and, using your hands, knead until thoroughly mixed in. If using, knead crushed candies into other portion.

3. For each candy cane, roll 1 tsp (5 mL) of each kind of dough into a rope 5 inches (12.5 cm) long. Place 2 ropes side by side and twist together, then gently roll to meld. Place about 2 inches (5 cm) apart on cookie sheet. Curve one end to form handle of cane. Bake in preheated oven for 7 to 11 minutes or until light golden around edges. Cool for 5 minutes on sheet, then transfer to a rack and cool completely.

Variation
Use green food coloring, mints or candy canes that have green stripes on them.

Cherry Almond Coconut Macaroons

These colorful, candy-like cookies are always a hit with coconut fans. These are a particularly easy-to-make version of macaroons.

MAKES ABOUT 5 DOZEN COOKIES

- **Preparation: 20 minutes**
- **Baking: 15 minutes**
- **Freezing: excellent**

TIP

Use sweetened coconut if you prefer. Both work well — it's simply a matter of taste.

- **Preheat oven to 350°F (180°C)**
- **Cookie sheet, greased or lined with parchment paper**

5½ cups	unsweetened flaked coconut	1.375 L
1	can (14 oz/396 g OR 300 mL) sweetened condensed milk	1
½ tsp	almond extract	2 mL
½ tsp	coconut extract	2 mL
1 cup	chopped red candied cherries	250 mL
¾ cup	slivered almonds	175 mL

1. In a large bowl, combine coconut, sweetened condensed milk and almond and coconut extracts. Using a wooden spoon, mix well until all ingredients are thoroughly moistened. Stir in cherries and almonds.

2. Drop mixture by tablespoonfuls (15 mL) about 2 inches (5 cm) apart on prepared cookie sheet. Bake in preheated oven for 10 to 15 minutes or until light golden. Cool for 10 minutes on sheet, then transfer to a rack and cool completely.

Variations

Decorate the tops with a cherry half before baking.

Replace cherries with regular or miniature chocolate chips. Semi-sweet, milk or white chocolate chips would work well in this recipe.

Omit cherries. Increase almonds to 1 cup (250 mL).

Holiday Haystacks

This creamy, crunchy confection demonstrates that cookies don't need to be difficult to make to taste superb.

MAKES ABOUT 3 DOZEN COOKIES

- **Preparation: 15 minutes**
- **Cooking: 4 minutes**
- **Chilling: 1 hour**
- **Freezing: not recommended**

- **Cookie sheet, lined with waxed paper**

12	squares (1 oz/28 g each) white chocolate, chopped	12
1 cup	sliced almonds, toasted (see tip, page 108)	250 mL
1 cup	sweetened flaked coconut, toasted	250 mL
1 cup	quartered red candied cherries	250 mL

1. In a saucepan over low heat, melt white chocolate, stirring until smooth. Remove from heat. Stir in almonds, coconut and cherries. Mix until evenly coated with chocolate.
2. Drop mixture by tablespoonfuls (15 mL) on waxed paper. Chill until firm, about 1 hour. Store in a cool dry place in an airtight container with waxed paper between layers.

Almond Pine Nut Drops

If you enjoy marzipan, you'll love these Italian specialties, which are served during the holidays.

MAKES ABOUT 3 DOZEN COOKIES

- **Preparation: 15 minutes**
- **Baking: 18 minutes**
- **Freezing: excellent**

TIP

Store these in an airtight container in layers separated with waxed paper. Store at room temperature for up to 5 days or freeze for up to 6 months.

- **Preheat oven to 350°F (180°C)**
- **Cookie sheet, lined with parchment paper**

12 oz	almond paste, broken into small pieces	375 g
¾ cup	superfine granulated sugar (see Tips, page 219)	175 mL
½ cup	confectioner's (icing) sugar, sifted	125 mL
2	egg whites	2
1¼ cups	pine nuts, coarsely chopped	300 mL

1. In a large bowl, using an electric mixer on low speed, beat almond paste, granulated sugar, confectioner's sugar and egg whites until blended, then increase speed to medium and beat for 2 minutes. With a wooden spoon, stir in pine nuts.
2. Drop mixture by tablespoonfuls (15 mL) about 2 inches (5 cm) apart on prepared cookie sheet. Bake in preheated oven for 13 to 18 minutes or until lightly browned. Cool completely on sheet.

Variation

Replace half or all of the pine nuts with chopped blanched almonds.

Cranberry Walnut Icebox Cookies

Fresh or frozen cranberries, which are so much a part of the holiday season, have a wonderful tart flavor. They work well in these cookies, giving them not only great taste but a terrific appearance as well.

MAKES ABOUT 7 DOZEN COOKIES

- **Preparation: 25 minutes**
- **Chilling: 4 hours**
- **Baking: 15 minutes**
- **Freezing: excellent**

TIPS

Fresh cranberries work best in these cookies, but if you're using frozen ones, chop them frozen and add them to the batter in that state. If they have thawed, pat them dry with paper towels and mix them into the dough after you have mixed in the walnuts, to prevent the dough from turning pink.

Check the expiry date on your baking powder to ensure it is fresh. Nothing is more disappointing than making cookies and ending up with poor results because your baking powder did not work. Your cookies will be tough and won't rise during baking.

- **Cookie sheet, greased or lined with parchment paper**

3½ cups	all-purpose flour	875 mL
1 tsp	baking powder	5 mL
¼ tsp	baking soda	1 mL
¼ tsp	salt	1 mL
1¼ cups	butter, softened	300 mL
1 cup	packed brown sugar	250 mL
⅔ cup	granulated sugar	150 mL
2	eggs	2
1 tbsp	orange zest	15 mL
1 cup	chopped walnuts	250 mL
2 cups	chopped cranberries	500 mL

1. On a sheet of waxed paper or in a bowl, combine flour, baking powder, baking soda and salt. Set aside.

2. In a large bowl, using an electric mixer on medium speed, beat butter and brown and granulated sugars until light and creamy, about 3 minutes. Add eggs, one at a time, beating well after each addition. Beat in orange zest. On low speed, gradually add flour mixture, beating until blended. With a wooden spoon, carefully stir in walnuts and cranberries. Divide dough into thirds. Shape each into a roll 7 inches (17.5 cm) long. Wrap and chill until firm, at least 4 hours.

3. Fifteen minutes before you're ready to bake, preheat oven to 375°F (190°C). Cut rolls into ¼-inch (0.5 cm) slices. Place about 2 inches (5 cm) apart on prepared cookie sheet. Bake in preheated oven for 11 to 15 minutes or until lightly browned around edges. Cool for 5 minutes on sheet, then transfer to a rack and cool completely.

Variations

Replace walnuts with pecans.

Replace orange zest with lemon or with ½ tsp (2 mL) almond extract or 1 tsp (5 mL) vanilla.

Danish Hazelnut Spice Cookies

These cookies are similar in flavor to gingerbread, with the addition of crunchy hazelnuts. They can be rolled and cut out with cookie cutters (see Tips) or shaped into rolls and chilled, ready to bake when you need them.

MAKES ABOUT 9 DOZEN COOKIES

- **Preparation: 25 minutes**
- **Chilling: 4 hours**
- **Baking: 14 minutes**
- **Freezing: excellent**

TIPS

To make cutout cookies, divide dough into halves and, on a floured surface, roll each to ¼-inch (0.5 cm) thickness. Using a cookie cutter dipped in flour, cut out desired shapes. Bake as above.

These rolls can be frozen for up to 3 months. Thaw before slicing. (See page 10 for instructions on freezing and thawing dough.)

Because the recipe uses no eggs, it can easily be halved.

- **Cookie sheet, greased or lined with parchment paper**

2¾ cups	all-purpose flour	675 mL
1 cup	finely chopped hazelnuts	250 mL
1 tsp	baking soda	5 mL
¼ tsp	salt	1 mL
1 tbsp	ground cinnamon	15 mL
2 tsp	ground ginger	10 mL
1 tsp	ground cloves	5 mL
½ tsp	ground nutmeg	2 mL
1 cup	butter, softened	250 mL
1 cup	packed brown sugar	250 mL
½ cup	corn syrup	125 mL

1. On a sheet of waxed paper or in a bowl, combine flour, hazelnuts, baking soda, salt, cinnamon, ginger, cloves and nutmeg. Set aside.

2. In a large bowl, using an electric mixer on medium speed, beat butter, brown sugar and corn syrup until smooth. Gradually add flour mixture, beating until blended then, using your hands, knead to form a smooth dough. Divide dough into halves. Shape each into a roll 14 inches (35 cm) long. Wrap and chill until firm, at least 4 hours.

3. Fifteen minutes before you're ready to bake, preheat oven to 375°F (190°C). Cut rolls into ¼-inch (0.5 cm) slices. Place about 1 inch (2.5 cm) apart on prepared cookie sheet. Bake in preheated oven for 10 to 14 minutes or until golden. Cool for 5 minutes on sheet, then transfer to a rack and cool completely.

Variation
Replace hazelnuts with unblanched almonds or Brazil nuts.

Apricot Pecan Rugelach

These cookies, which are Jewish in origin, are a traditional favorite during the holiday season.

MAKES ABOUT 4 DOZEN COOKIES

- **Preparation: 40 minutes**
- **Chilling: 2½ hours**
- **Baking: 29 minutes**
- **Freezing: excellent**

TIPS

The flavor of these cookies depends on the jam. Choose a thick, tart jam with a nice fruit flavor. Be sure to chop any large pieces of fruit before combining with the lemon juice, and mix well.

The cream cheese should be soft for mixing. If it's too hard, place on a piece of waxed paper and soften in a microwave oven on high power for about 10 seconds.

I recommend using parchment paper as the jam tends to stick.

• **Cookie sheet, lined with parchment paper**

DOUGH

8 oz	cream cheese, softened	250 g
1 cup	butter, softened	250 mL
3 tbsp	granulated sugar	45 mL
2 cups	all-purpose flour	500 mL

FILLING

1 cup	apricot jam (see Tips)	250 mL
1 tsp	freshly squeezed lemon juice	5 mL
1 cup	finely chopped pecans	250 mL
1 tsp	ground cinnamon	5 mL

TOPPING

1	egg	1
2 tbsp	coarse or regular granulated sugar	25 mL

1. *Dough:* In a large bowl, using an electric mixer on medium speed, beat cream cheese, butter and sugar until smooth. On low speed, gradually add flour, beating until dough becomes too stiff for the mixer, then finish mixing with a wooden spoon. Divide dough into quarters. Wrap and chill for 2 hours.

2. *Filling:* In a small bowl, combine jam and lemon juice. Set aside.

3. On lightly floured surface, roll out dough, 1 portion at a time, into an 11-inch (27.5 cm) circle. Using a small offset spatula, carefully spread with ¼ of the jam mixture. Sprinkle ¼ of the pecans and cinnamon over jam. Using a long, sharp knife, cut circle into 12 pie-shaped wedges. Starting from the wide end, tightly roll up each wedge to form a crescent. Place crescents on prepared cookie sheet about 2 inches (5 cm) apart. Repeat with remaining dough and filling. Chill for 30 minutes. Fifteen minutes before you are ready to bake, preheat oven to 350°F (180°C).

4. *Topping:* Beat egg lightly. Brush over surface of chilled cookies. Sprinkle sugar evenly over tops. Bake in preheated oven for 25 to 29 minutes or until golden. Cool for 15 minutes on sheet, then transfer to a rack and cool completely.

Variations

Replace pecans with almonds or hazelnuts.

Replace apricot jam with raspberry.

Honey Fruit Drops

These cookies taste like a light fruitcake in bite-size form. The honey gives them great flavor and a soft, moist texture.

MAKES ABOUT 4 DOZEN COOKIES

- **Preparation: 25 minutes**
- **Baking: 15 minutes**
- **Freezing: excellent**

TIP

Honey keeps cookies soft and moist during storage. Because they don't dry out, they are great to have on hand during the holidays.

- **Preheat oven to 350°F (180°C)**
- **Cookie sheet, greased or lined with parchment paper**

2 cups	all-purpose flour	500 mL
½ tsp	baking powder	2 mL
½ tsp	baking soda	2 mL
¼ tsp	salt	1 mL
½ cup	butter, softened	125 mL
½ cup	granulated sugar	125 mL
½ cup	liquid honey	125 mL
1	egg	1
1 tsp	lemon extract	5 mL
¾ cup	chopped pecans	175 mL
½ cup	chopped candied cherries	125 mL
½ cup	chopped candied pineapple	125 mL
½ cup	chopped dried cranberries	125 mL
½ cup	chopped dates	125 mL
½ cup	chopped dried apricots	125 mL

1. On a sheet of waxed paper or in a bowl, combine flour, baking powder, baking soda and salt. Set aside.

2. In a large bowl, using an electric mixer on medium speed, beat butter, sugar, honey, egg and lemon extract until smooth, about 3 minutes. On low speed, gradually add flour mixture, beating until blended. With a wooden spoon, stir in pecans, cherries, pineapple, cranberries, dates and apricots.

3. Drop dough by tablespoonfuls (15 mL) about 2 inches (5 cm) apart on prepared cookie sheet. Bake in preheated oven for 10 to 15 minutes or until golden. Cool for 5 minutes on sheet, then transfer to a rack and cool completely.

Variations

Vary the fruits to suit your taste, keeping the amounts the same as in the original recipe. Use candied peel, raisins, figs or dried cherries.

Replace lemon extract with an equal quantity of ground cinnamon or vanilla.

Cranberry Walnut Wheels

These attractive spirals take a little extra time to prepare, but the rolls can be made ahead and baked at a later date. The cranberries add special holiday appeal.

MAKES ABOUT 4 DOZEN COOKIES

- **Preparation: 35 minutes**
- **Chilling: 4½ hours**
- **Baking: 16 minutes**
- **Freezing: excellent**

TIPS

If you're using frozen cranberries in the filling, thaw them and pat dry with paper towels before blending.

When you need both the zest and juice from citrus fruit, you need to use fresh fruit. If you only need the juice, refrigerated or bottled juice works fine, although the taste of freshly squeezed juice is always preferable.

Make the bottom sheet of waxed paper long enough so you have a substantial overhang to help you roll up the dough.

Use a sharp serrated knife to cut this dough.

- **Cookie sheet, greased or lined with parchment paper**

DOUGH

1½ cups	all-purpose flour	375 mL
¼ tsp	baking powder	1 mL
¼ tsp	salt	1 mL
½ cup	butter, softened	125 mL
¾ cup	granulated sugar	175 mL
1	egg	1
1 tsp	vanilla	5 mL

FILLING

½ cup	cranberries, thawed if frozen (see Tips)	125 mL
½ cup	walnuts	125 mL
¼ cup	packed brown sugar	50 mL
1 tbsp	grated lemon zest	15 mL
2 tsp	freshly squeezed lemon juice	10 mL

1. *Dough:* On a sheet of waxed paper or in a bowl, combine flour, baking powder and salt. Set aside.

2. In a large bowl, using an electric mixer on medium speed, beat butter, sugar, egg and vanilla until light and creamy, about 3 minutes. On low speed, gradually add flour mixture, beating until blended. Using your hands, knead to form a smooth dough.

3. Between 2 sheets of waxed paper, roll out dough into 12-inch (30 cm) square. Slide onto cookie sheet. Chill until starting to firm up, about 30 minutes.

4. *Filling:* In a food processor, combine cranberries, walnuts, brown sugar and lemon zest and juice. Process until finely chopped. Remove top sheet of waxed paper from dough and spread evenly with filling, leaving ½-inch (1 cm) border on 2 opposite edges. Starting with one of those edges and using the bottom sheet of waxed paper to help you, roll up the dough jelly-roll fashion. Press to firm up roll and seal edge. Wrap in waxed paper and chill until firm, at least 4 hours.

5. Fifteen minutes before you're ready to bake, preheat oven to 375°F (190°C). Cut roll into ¼-inch (0.5 cm) slices. Place about 2 inches (5 cm) apart on prepared cookie sheet. Bake in preheated oven for 12 to 16 minutes or until golden around edges. Cool for 5 minutes on sheet, then transfer to a rack and cool completely.

Gingerbread People

The holidays wouldn't be complete without making at least one batch of these traditional favorites for the kids to decorate.

MAKES ABOUT 3 DOZEN COOKIES

- **Preparation: 25 minutes**
- **Chilling: 1 hour**
- **Baking: 20 minutes**
- **Standing: 1 hour**
- **Freezing: excellent (not decorated)**

TIPS

Don't limit gingerbread making to the holiday season. Let the cutters you use and how you decorate determine the theme. Pumpkins, bunnies, hearts, dogs, teddy bears and so on, all work well with the dough.

The baking time will depend upon the size of the cookies.

Royal Icing can also be made with meringue powder in place of the egg white. Just follow the package directions. It can be purchased in bulk stores and cake decorating supply stores.

- **Gingerbread people cookie cutters**
- **Cookie sheet, greased or lined with parchment paper**

COOKIE

2¼ cups	all-purpose flour	550 mL
¾ tsp	baking soda	3 mL
¼ tsp	salt	1 mL
1¼ tsp	ground ginger	6 mL
1 tsp	ground cinnamon	5 mL
½ tsp	ground cloves	2 mL
½ cup	butter, softened	125 mL
⅔ cup	packed brown sugar	150 mL
1	egg	1
¼ cup	molasses	50 mL

ROYAL ICING

1	egg white	1
Pinch	cream of tartar	Pinch
Approx 1½ cups	confectioner's (icing) sugar, sifted	375 mL

DECORATIONS

Colorful candies, raisins and sprinkles

1. *Cookie:* Combine flour, baking soda, salt and spices. Set aside.

2. In a large bowl, using an electric mixer on medium speed, beat butter, brown sugar, egg and molasses until smooth. On low speed, gradually add flour mixture, beating until blended, then knead to form a smooth dough. Wrap and chill dough 1 hour.

3. Fifteen minutes before you're ready to bake, preheat oven to 350°F (180°C). Divide dough into halves. On a floured board, roll out each to ¼-inch (0.5 cm) thickness. Using cookie cutters dipped in flour, cut out cookies. Place about 2 inches (5 cm) apart on prepared cookie sheet. Bake in preheated oven for 15 to 20 minutes or until set. Cool for 5 minutes on sheet, then transfer to a rack and cool completely.

4. *Royal Icing:* In a bowl, beat egg white and cream of tartar until frothy. Gradually add confectioner's sugar, beating until stiff, shiny peaks form. Using a pastry bag fitted with a plain tube, pipe icing onto cookies to create faces and other features. Add candies, etc. to make buttons and eyes. Use the icing as a glue. Let stand until icing dries, about 1 hour.

Green Cherry Christmas Trees

These three-dimensional trees make great centerpieces for your festive holiday dinner table.

MAKES 6 TREES

- **Preparation: 45 minutes**
- **Baking: 20 minutes**
- **Freezing: not recommended**

TIPS

Edible glitter is great sprinkled on the melted chocolate while it is still wet.

Colored sugar also looks wonderful.

Omit the candied cherries. They add a nice flavor, but make the dough a bit more difficult to cut out.

Omit the food coloring and sprinkle plain cookies with green sugar sprinkles.

◆

- **Preheat oven to 325°F (160°C)**
- **5 progressively larger star-shaped cookie cutters**
- **Cookie sheet, ungreased**

1 cup	butter, softened	250 mL
½ cup	granulated sugar	125 mL
2¼ cups	all-purpose flour	550 mL
	Green food coloring	
½ cup	finely chopped green candied cherries	125 mL
6	squares (1 oz/28 g each) white chocolate, chopped	6
1 tsp	vegetable oil	5 mL

DECORATIONS

Colored sprinkles or candies

1. In a large bowl, using a wooden spoon, beat butter and sugar until smooth and creamy, about 3 minutes. Gradually add flour, mixing until blended, then, using your hands, knead to form a smooth dough. Add enough green coloring to make a green dough and knead until evenly colored. Knead in cherries.

2. Divide dough into sixths. On floured surface, roll out each portion to ¼-inch (0.5 cm) thickness. Using 5 progressively larger star-shaped cookie cutters, dipped in flour, cut out cookies. Use a 1-inch (2.5 cm) cutter for the top and 4 more that gradually increase in size from 2½ inches (6 cm) to 4 inches (10 cm). Repeat with 5 remaining portions of dough. Place cookies about 1 inch (2.5 cm) apart on cookie sheet. Keep similar sizes on the same sheet for even baking. Bake in preheated oven for 15 to 20 minutes or until set. Cool for 5 minutes on sheet, then transfer to a rack and cool completely.

3. In a small saucepan on low heat, melt chocolate and oil, stirring until smooth.

4. *Assembly:* On a work surface, place a 4-inch (10 cm) star. Stack 4 stars in order of size, largest to smallest, on top, spreading a little melted chocolate between each layer and allowing it to drip down over the sides of the stars. Place a dollop of melted chocolate on top star and stand the smallest star on edge on top. Drizzle trees with melted chocolate and sprinkle with colored sprinkles or candies.

Library and Archives Canada Cataloguing in Publication

Snider, Jill, 1947–
    Cookies : more than 200 recipes / Jill Snider.

Includes index.
ISBN 978-0-7788-0168-9

1. Cookies. I. Title.

TX772.S63 2007   641.8'654   C2007-902862-4

Index